THE NEW PSYCHOMETRICS

Psychological testing is increasingly used in selection and appraisal. *The New Psychometrics* shows that although the results are useful, their scientific basis is weak. Paul Kline reveals that many psychological factors are little more than statistical descriptions of particular sets of data and have little or no real significance. However, truly scientific forms of measurement could be developed using measurement theory, to create a new psychometrics.

Paul Kline uses his long and extensive knowledge of psychological measurement to argue that the new psychometrics could be used as the basis for a truly scientific discipline of psychology. This would transform the basis of psychology and change it from a social science to a pure science. This book should be read by all those interested in psychometrics and everyone interested in the theoretical underpinnings of psychology.

Paul Kline, Emeritus Professor of Psychometrics at the University of Exeter, sadly died before this edition of his work was complete. He was a leading authority in the field and author of many books, including *An Easy Guide to Factor Analysis* (1994), *Personality: The Psychometric View* (1993), *The Handbook of Psychological Testing* (1992) and *Intelligence: The Psychometric View* (1990).

THE NEW PSYCHOMETRICS

Science, psychology and measurement

Paul Kline

London and Philadelphia

First published 1998
by Routledge
11 New Fetter Lane, London EC4P 4EE

Simultaneously published in the USA and Canada
by Routledge
29 West 35th Street, New York, NY 10001

First published in paperback 2000

Routledge is an imprint of the Taylor & Francis Group

Typeset in Baskerville by
J&L Composition Ltd, Filey, North Yorkshire
Printed and bound in Great Britain by
Biddles Ltd, Guildford and King's Lynn

British Library Cataloguing in Publication Data
A catalogue record for this book is available
from the British Library

Library of Congress Cataloging in Publication Data

Kline, Paul
The New Psychometrics: Science, Psychology and Measurement/Paul
Kline.
p.   cm
Includes bibliographical references and indexes.
1. Psychometrics.   2. Psychological tests.   I. Title.
BF39.K57   1998   98–13276
50'.15195–dc21   CIP

ISBN 0–415–22821–2 (pbk)
ISBN 0–415–18751–6 (hbk)

To Ray Cattell and to the memory of Hans Eysenck, who died in November 1997 as this book was being completed.

CONTENTS

CONTENTS

ILLUSTRATIONS

Figures

Tables

Boxes

PREFACE

The inspiration for this book came from refereeing a paper by Joel Michell which forced me to examine afresh the assumptions on which psychometrics is currently based. This paper tied in with reservations which I have held for some time concerning the limitations of personality questionnaires as scientific measurement. The result of this consideration of the problems of measurement raised by Michell is this book – *The New Psychometrics* – in which, I hope, I develop some new approaches to psychological measurement which will lead to a genuinely scientific psychology.

ACKNOWLEDGEMENT

I want here to express my thanks to Dr Paul Barrett, Chief Scientist at Carstairs Hospital, for his enthusiasm and help in writing this book.

ABBREVIATIONS

AEP	average evoked potential
BER	brainstem evoked response
BIP	basic period of information processing
CAB	Comprehensive Ability Battery
CAT	Children's Apperception Test
dR analysis	factor analysis of differences between scores
DT	decision time
DZ	dizygotic
ECT	elementary cognitive task
EEG	electroencephalogram; electroencephalography
EPI	Eysenck Personality Inventory
EPQ	Eysenck Personality Questionnaire
EPQ-R	Eysenck Personality Questionnaire (revised)
ERP	event-related potential
FAST	Frequency Accrual Speed Test
GCSE	General Certificate of Secondary Education
GMR	glucose metabolic rate
HIT	Holtzman Inkblot Test
HTP	House–Tree–Person test
IT	inspection time
MAB	Multidimensional Aptitude Battery
MAT	Motivation Analysis Test
MMPI	Minnesota Multiphasic Personality Inventory
MZ	monozygotic
NEO, NEO-PI	personality scales devised by Costa and McCrae (N = neuroticism, E = extraversion, O = openness)
OAB	Objective Analytic Battery
ORT	Object-Relations Technique
PET	positron emission tomography
PGR	psychogalvanic response
PRF	Personality Research Form
RMS	root mean square

RT	reaction time
SCL	skin conductance level
SCR	skin conductance response
SEM	standard error of measurement
16PF	16 Personality Factor test
TAT	Thematic Apperception Test
VIM	Vocational Interest Measure
WAIS	Wechsler Adult Intelligence Scale
WISC	Wechsler Intelligence Scale for Children
WPPSI-R	Wechsler Pre-school and Primary Intelligence Scale – Revised

Part 1

SCIENTIFIC METHOD, SCIENTIFIC MEASUREMENT AND PSYCHOMETRICS

1

SCIENTIFIC METHOD, REALISM, TRUTH AND PSYCHOLOGY

In this first chapter I shall argue that the scientific method, which is put forward as the only way ahead for psychology, will not necessarily lead to success. There are a number of reasons for this. In the first place, the fact that the scientific method has worked so well in the natural sciences does not mean that it works well in psychology, whose subject matter is different from that of the natural sciences. An examination of the scientific method reveals that, even in the sciences where it has been successful, it is not without problems. Thus the Popperian notion of refutability (Popper, 1959) has the difficulty that the meaning of refutable is not clear. Furthermore, the method itself has a number of philosophical problems. Thus it relies considerably on inferential logic, but there is no necessity that inferential logic, in contrast to deductive reasoning, as used in mathematics, will arrive at the truth. This introduces further difficulties. The notion that science, by means of the scientific method, aims to discover the truth about the external world implies a realist view that there is a world out there that can be discovered. In addition, to be at all coherent the scientific endeavour assumes a correspondence theory of truth. Both these philosophical viewpoints – realism and the correspondence theory – have been seriously challenged in philosophy. Careful examination of these philosophical points reveals that both realism and the correspondence theory are tenable so that the scientific method, *per se*, cannot be dismissed as naïve. However, the justification for its use in science has no other basis than its success in that field, which has been greater than for any other known procedure, rather than that it must inevitably arrive at the truth. In psychology, where, so far, it has not been as successful, it is clear that the nature of the subject may be a cause of the difficulty, since psychological variables are far more difficult to measure than those in the natural sciences, and some subjective aspects of psychology may well resist measurement of any kind.

The success of the natural sciences in obtaining knowledge and understanding of the world has led psychologists to argue that the scientific method is the road to developing a successful psychology. This is most clearly stated by Eysenck in the concluding chapter of a book about his work. He writes:

My belief is that psychology is a science in the same sense that physics or chemistry or astronomy are sciences. I believe that psychology should follow the same path as other sciences, namely the construction of theories, the deduction of consequences from these theories and the testing of these deductions. . . . In other words I believe that we must follow the hypothetico-deductive method of all the other sciences if we are to prosper.

(Eysenck, 1986: 397)

As a matter of fact there is something odd in this quotation. The triple reiteration of 'I believe' is in ill accord with what is generally understood by the scientific method, which is noted for the rigour of its thinking and contrasted as a basis of knowledge with the belief systems of religions and quasi-scientific cults. However, it is necessary to examine the scientific method since it is by no means self-evident that, just because a method works well in one sphere of knowledge, it is necessarily applicable to another. This is particularly pertinent to psychology since it is obvious that its subject matter differs greatly from that of the natural sciences.

The scientific method

One of the problems in attempting to define the scientific method is that it has become the province of philosophers. There is, indeed, a recognised branch of philosophy known as the philosophy of science. Needless to say, this has complicated the field without adding clarity. Furthermore, in elucidating the matter one is well aware of the claim made by Swift, that there is scarcely a matter of any importance on which philosophers have not been entirely wrong.

Despite these difficulties it is obvious that the scientific method should be a province of philosophy since it presupposes a view of the world which may not be tenable, and a superficial support of the scientific method, without understanding, can lead to a narrowing of vision which allows only somewhat trivial experiments. Often there is an emphasis on method at the expense of substance. As Bannister (1970) aptly put it, some psychologists are desperate to join the science club. There is an even greater problem which is particularly relevant to this book. This concerns the fact that some psychologists are content to assume that quantification, *per se*, implies that the scientific method has been followed, regardless of the nature of such quantification. Since psychometrics deals with psychological measurement it is a field where this particular error is highly important, and, as we shall see, many well-regarded areas of psychometrics have foundered on this difficulty.

The work of Popper

I shall begin with a discussion of the work of Karl Popper who has been highly influential in this field, particularly among psychologists. His is effectively an operational definition of the scientific method (Popper, 1959). To Popper the essence of the method lies in falsification. Hypotheses cannot be proven, only refuted. Thus the whole edifice of science is provisional. One counter-example is all that is needed to refute a hypothesis. This is what makes the scientist different from the believer in religion. Scientists, the theory goes, are open minded, ready to modify their theories in the light of new evidence. The latter cling grimly to their beliefs regardless of the facts. This is another form of the old Platonic distinction between belief and knowledge.

For the working research psychologist this is a highly useful system. For example, I attempted to apply the method to Freudian theory, which is regarded by most scientific psychologists as hopelessly unscientific, a view derived from Eysenck (1953). I combed Freud for testable hypotheses and then searched the psychological literature for relevant experimental evidence. The results reported in Kline (1981) indicate that a number of hypotheses were not refuted, although, as Eysenck has argued, many were. In fact this Popperian approach to science is the one taught in many university departments of psychology in the UK and the USA. As Scruton (1994) has pointed out, one of the attractive features of Popper's theory is that it appears to discriminate between science and pseudo-science. In the former the theories are clearly stated, with the aim of refutation in mind. In the latter they are deliberately vague with the aim of making such refutation impossible. It is this aspect of Freudian theory which both Popper and Eysenck have found particularly objectionable.

Problems with the Popperian position

Nevertheless, there are some difficulties with the Popperian position which need to be clarified. The first concerns the meaning of testable. This is crucial, since a theory or hypothesis is said to be unscientific if it is stated in such a way that it cannot be tested. After considerable and detailed analysis Gruenbaum (1984) was forced to conclude that the only meaning of untestable was that Popper was unable to devise a method of testing. There is a further point, not dissimilar to an infinite regress, namely that this aspect of Popper's theory, that good science demands refutability, is itself difficult to test. However, there are other, perhaps more substantial, points. The first of these involves the differences between inductive and deductive inference. In deductive reasoning, the reasoning of mathematics and logic, we argue from the general to the particular. If the premises are true the conclusions cannot be false. In induction, however, we reason from the particular to the general. Induction leads us to conclusions which are not entailed by the premises. Thus conclusions could be false even when the premises are true. With inductive reasoning, therefore, other evidence of the truth of conclusions is required than the truth of the premises.

Inductive reasoning

Scruton (1994) makes two further important points about such inductive reasoning, which is, of course, employed in many scientific experiments. Inductive inference often proceeds from the particular to the general by the postulation of laws. From the law a deductive inference is then made. Scruton has a good example in the rising of the sun. From observation one can induce the law that the sun rises in the morning and deduce that it will do so tomorrow. However, the law embraces an infinity of instances and goes well beyond the evidence. Its validity must, therefore, be in doubt. There is a further argument which Scruton refers to as Hume's law. This is the claim that if one thing follows or precedes another then the connection between them can only be contingent since the world could come to an end at time t before the second event occurred. This is a severe blow to inductive reasoning since no matter how many times A may have preceded B, no general law can be made. Anything before time t will always be compatible with events after t.

Popper's emphasis on falsification is an attempt to overcome this difficulty with induction. Rather than induction, scientific thinking, the story goes, is a matter of hypothesis and refutation. As has been pointed out, scientific hypotheses are held provisionally until they are refuted. The fact that, despite our best efforts, they have not been refuted is the evidence for their truth. However, as Scruton (1994) argues, this will not do, on two counts. In the first place, the fact that the method has worked in the past and yielded what are regarded as true hypotheses (although 'true', it is to be noted, means only 'as yet not refuted') does not mean, on the arguments of Hume, that it will work in the future. Indeed, the fact that it is thought to do so is itself an example of induction. Furthermore, despite obeisance to the notion of their provisionality, scientific laws are accepted as true, although because they are based on inductive reasoning they cannot attain that epistemic status.

The problems of induction and the circularity which appears to be involved in any rigorous defence of it as a method of reaching truth are beyond the scope of this first chapter, and a more complete discussion is given by O'Hear (1989). As is pointed out there, a pragmatic approach can be adopted in which the argument supporting induction is that it works and that it is useful for those who employ it. This is implicitly the belief of the working scientist. Of course this does not evade the original problem because it requires induction to recognise that the method yields truth. On the other hand, the pragmatic position can, in principle, support methods that yield false beliefs if such beliefs are valuable. An obvious example might be the belief from the observation of a small number of judges that judges are wise and just. Such beliefs, if widely spread, regardless of their truth or falsity, greatly improve the administration of a justice system. The pragmatic justification of induction will not stand scrutiny, although the argument that inductive inference appears to work and is the best we can do, is not unreasonable.

There is a further difficulty with induction which Scruton (1994) discusses, one which deserves a brief consideration because it has relevance to some of the methods used in psychology and psychometrics. This is Hempel's paradox (Hempel, 1945). The claim that all oranges are orange is a general law which by the principles of induction is confirmed by specific instances. The obvious instance is an orange orange. However, there are other kinds of confirming instance including the claim that all non-orange things are non-oranges. However, if this so there is an infinity of confirmations that oranges are orange: black ties, white swans and so on. This example illustrates the difficulty of formulating the principles of induction, of recognising an instance, which is essential since laws are confirmed by their instances. The paradox lies in the fact that, despite the logical equivalence, the observation of a white swan and an orange orange are not equivalent as confirmations of the law that oranges are orange. Thus there are severe logical problems in the notion of inductive reasoning.

I have raised these problems of inductive reasoning and falsification simply because it is generally assumed by practising psychological researchers that the scientific method, as described by Popper, necessarily leads to truth and that by following it they are bound, as Eysenck (1986) desires, to construct a natural science. Hempel's paradox of confirmation is actually relevant to the notion of construct validity in psychometrics. This will be discussed in detail in Chapter 2 but it is pertinent to note here that the validity of a test, say a personality test, is often said to be confirmed because it correlates zero with an intelligence test; that is, we have shown that a non-personality test is not a personality test. These problems are particularly important in psychology because its subject matter is different from and not so clearly defined as that in the natural sciences. However, this topic will be discussed on pp. 23–4.

Of course, as has been noted, the scientific method makes use of deductive logic. Indeed, it is referred to as the hypothetico-deductive method. Thus not only is induction employed on the basis of observations of the particular instances, but also the general laws are put to the test of refutation by deducing instances which can then be observed to see whether they are confirmed or not. The scientific method proceeds most fruitfully through an interaction of these two processes, induction and deduction. If the general laws are falsified, then they have to be rejected or modified in the light of the evidence. In fact, in the natural sciences, it is the impressive accuracy of the deductions, as evinced in their engineering applications and in medicine, which is such convincing evidence that the basic laws are indeed true. Some philosophers have attempted to argue that the notion of truth is so problematic that the idea of science tracking it down is false and that scientific hypotheses about the natural world are no more true than any other set of hypotheses, for example hypotheses drawn from mysticism or religion. This relativistic position, which is the one favoured in social psychology, I find absurd, but it needs to be refuted and it is to this problem, the problem of truth and an external reality, to which I shall now turn. If there is no external reality and all accounts are relative then the programme of science is doomed.

Truth and reality

The programme of science is doomed because the aim, of the natural sciences at least, is to seek out the truth about the natural world, and science does this by means of the scientific method. Yet if there is no external reality, independent of the human mind, the scientific objective is impossible. The scientific account is different from other accounts only in that it was produced through the procedures of the scientific method.

The work of Searle: brute and institutionalised facts

Searle (1995) has a cogent discussion of this issue and I shall summarise some of his arguments which are particularly relevant to the utility of the scientific method in psychology and psychometrics. First, a useful distinction can be made between what Searle (1995) refers to as brute and institutionalised facts. Brute facts are those which are totally independent of human opinion. Obvious examples are the facts that elephants have four legs and pigs cannot, by their own exertions, fly. Institutionalised facts are dependent on human institutions for their existence. Examples of these are money or chess. That my heptagonal silver piece of metal is a fifty-pence coin depends on the agreement of government and people that this is so. Similarly, that a chequered board and black or white pieces of wood is a chess set is purely a matter of agreement. This distinction is important because, as Searle points out, some respectable philosophers, and many others, argue that all reality is a human creation and that there is nothing beyond the human mind and that, as a consequence of this, statements are not true merely because they correspond to the facts – a view which, as has been said, is fatal to the sciences. Implicit in these statements are two philosophical viewpoints which must be scrutinised, namely realism – claims that the real world does exist – and the correspondence theory of truth. Each of these topics is highly complex but I shall try to deal with the most pertinent points as briefly as possible.

Realism

Realism can be defined as the view that the world exists independently of any human representation. If *Homo sapiens* had never developed, Loch Ness would be still as deep as it is. When I am dead it will remain the same. This is the common-sense view of the man on the Clapham omnibus, who by some Oxonian snobbery is deemed to be ignorant of philosophy. As Searle points out, realism is not a viewpoint which attempts to state how the world is, merely that there is an external world. He derives some interesting and important implications from this. For example, if it were the case that reality were causally dependent on consciousness, such that when the last conscious agent dies all physical reality disappears, this would not be fatal to the realist position. This is because the causal dependence of matter on consciousness is no different from any other causal dependence. Even the proof that the only things that exist are states of disembodied consciousness does not destroy the realist position since realism *per se* makes no statement of how the world is, merely that it is independent of human representation.

If realism is denied, then science as the pursuit of truth, the understanding of the external world, makes no sense. What are the arguments against realism and can they be sustained?

Arguments against realism and their refutations

Searle has some devastating criticisms of arguments against realism. Thus one claim by Maturana and Varela (1980) is that there is no objective reality because nervous systems, which are autopoietic, construct their own reality. There are two obvious objections to this argument. First, the fact that our knowledge of reality is constructed by human brains does not entail that this reality is itself thus constructed. It is, Searle asserts (and it is difficult to disagree), fallacious, a non-sequitur, to argue that a neurological, causal explanation of knowledge implies the non-existence of the external world. There is, of course, a second and perhaps more obvious point, namely the human brains which are supposed to have constructed reality. There is here an infinite regress, unless these brains are the god in the machine or the first mover.

CONCEPTUAL RELATIVITY

However, some more powerful arguments against realism are discussed by Searle, and these must also be scrutinised. The first is derived from the notion of conceptual relativity, which states that all representations of reality are made relative to some arbitrary set of concepts. Searle cites an example from Putnam. Thus, in normal mathematics, three small circles x, y, z on a white space can be counted as three objects. However, according to Polish logic there are seven: x, y, z, x+y, x+z, y+z and x+y+z. Thus relative to one world there are seven objects, relative to the other world there are three. The notion of an external reality, in this argument, allows for inconsistent descriptions of an allegedly independent reality. Thus we make reality; the mind and the world construct the mind and the world.

However, this contradiction is more apparent than real. The only difference lies in the description because different systems for counting have been used; depending on the description, both are correct. As a matter of fact this is no different from a simple scaling problem in which the same distance can be given as *x* miles and *y* kilometres. Of course, in psychometrics the scaling difficulties in tests allow of many problems of this kind, and it would appear quite absurd to deny the reality of an individual's intelligence simply because two tests gave different scores. Indeed, the person's intelligence would have to be thought of as unchanged whether that individual were given no tests or twenty tests none of which agreed. These inconsistencies refer to the descriptors, not the real world itself.

There is a further point. To use the fact of conceptual relativity (or differing but equivalent descriptions) against realism in fact is incoherent since it presupposes that there is a reality to be described. Indeed, Searle argues that all these examples illustrate a use-mention fallacy: the fact that a description can only be made relative to a set of linguistic categories does not entail that what is described can exist only relative to those categories. Even though the definition of an object may be arbitrary, say a monkey or dog, whether something in the world satisfies those definitions is not relative.

At this point an issue raised by J.S. Mill (1943) is highly relevant. He argued that the world contains what he referred to as kinds. These are not constructions of the human mind; they exist in the word. Their members are bound together by what they have in common (genes in the case of natural flora and fauna, for example), and they belong together regardless of how we describe them. Kinds, it can be seen, are highly similar to Searle's brute facts.

The objects of scientific investigation, according to this argument, are kinds, a category into which all the fundamental objects of the universe fall. As Scruton (1994) points out, while kinds are not created by our classifications many concepts are, and these correspond to Searle's institutional facts.

Associated with this distinction is that between real and nominal essences. For example, we can discriminate a (male) lion by its nominal essences, its huge mane and its loud roar, but its real essence lies in its unique genome. The real essence has to be discovered through scientific research. Lions must have their leonine genome or they are not lions, but a lion is still a lion even if its mane is shaved and its vocal cords excised. This distinction is of great interest and significance for science since it suggests that science is concerned with the real essences of natural kinds, the things which form the basis of the world, rather than observation, the description of appearances. This, of course, is reminiscent of the Platonic view of the forms, which should be the objects of investigation by mathematics rather than the everyday objects which in part instantiate them.

All these arguments about conceptual relativity, as is obvious from what has been written, do not counter the notion of the reality of the external world. They have been unable to write off the fact that there is something out there. If there is, it is the aim of science to elucidate its nature and the aim of a scientific psychology to investigate the real essence of human beings. With such a view the correspondence theory of truth makes good sense, as will be discussed later in this chapter. However, conceptual relativity is not the only argument against realism.

REALITY AND EXPERIENCE

Searle (1995) examines and rejects two others. First he considers the verificationist argument. This essentially makes the point, which Berkeley made famous, that the only things we really know are our experiences. For example, I know that at this moment I am typing at my computer keyboard. However, what I know is only my experience of this: the tactile experience of the keys under my two fingers, the auditory experience of the clacking of the keys and so on. And this is true of everything. All our knowledge of the world comes from experiences. Thus knowledge is either the content of one's experiences or something beyond, but the problem here is that validation of anything beyond itself depends on experience. Thus reality is constructed from experience. There can be nothing else.

There are many arguments against this metaphysical antirealism and these have been neatly summarised by Butchvarov (1995). The main one rests on the patently absurd and ultimately incoherent views that must follow from its adoption. If we accept the argument, then there are no real objects, and that includes minds and their states, concepts, words, properties and relations, experiences, since it is impossible to believe in the reality of things of which no concept can be formed. Furthermore, notions of knowledge and truth are changed and problematic in meaning. Actually, it may be the case, as Butchvarov argues, that the whole argument is a tautology: we (can) know reality only as we (can) know it; and tautologies can form no basis for a thesis. Searle makes some more detailed criticisms of these arguments. For example, the fact that one has a visual experience when one sees the computer keyboard does not mean that the object of perception was that experience. Of course it is true that perceptions may be wrong: I may be hallucinating, I might be dreaming, deceived by a demon. However, all this supposes that there is a real stimulus about which I am mistaken. In any case, as has been argued, the reality of experience itself in this approach is dubious.

PERCEPTIONS AND PERCEPTUAL SCHEMES

Searle examines a final argument against realism. This makes the point that all our perceptions are within some conceptual scheme. There is no such thing as the naïve perception of a stimulus: our actual perception is modified by our past experiences and by knowledge, which is itself derived from experience. The only reality that we can access is that which is internal to our system of representations. Any other external reality is unknowable and thus nonsensical. Searle faults this argument on the grounds that even if it is impossible to step outside cognitive states and systems in order to survey their relationship with the reality which they represent, it does not follow that no cognition is ever of a reality that exists independently of cognition. With the argument put thus, it seems difficult to disagree with Searle.

For example, if different conceptual schemes are used there is an apparent superficial conflict of description. If I describe a small red-breasted bird as a robin or a symbol of Christmas or as *Erithacus rubecula melophilus*, the same reality is represented by all three descriptions but under different aspects. Since there are many aspects, conceptual systems and viewpoints under which anything can be represented, it follows that there is bound to be considerable difficulty in obtaining a perfect fit between representation and reality. Thus we can represent reality only from a point of view but objective reality has no point of view. It is interesting to note here that there might be a possible exception to this formulation, when science seeks out the real essences of kinds.

So far I think it can be said that I have been able to show that the standard arguments against realism do not hold water. As I have argued, it is essential if we are going to construct a genuinely scientific psychology that we show that a notion of external reality is tenable since the procedures of science, in any sphere, are aimed at reaching an accurate description of that reality. Having rejected these arguments against realism, Searle examines some of the arguments in its favour. However, before I come to scrutinise theories of truth, particularly the correspondence theory, which is the second philosophical notion underpinning the scientific endeavour, and one usually taken by working scientists as given, these arguments require some discussion.

Convergence of scientific findings

One of the supports for the notion of external reality, 'something out there', is the fact that in the sciences, or more strictly in the natural sciences, there is a convergence of results. Investigators working in different laboratories, in different countries and, often, using different methods come up with same results. Despite the provisional nature of scientific hypotheses, as has been fully discussed, there is general agreement that the earth revolves round the sun, that the heart pumps blood around the body. Other views which still exist are considered to be alternative, and such is human gullibility that, in the medical field, people will spend considerable sums to have their chakras and kundalinis dealt with, despite the lack of evidence for their existence. However, as Searle points out, these arguments are strictly irrelevant. The very fact that we can say that a set of observations converges implies that there is a reality to which it can converge. Similarly the counter-argument that a set of observations fails to converge, as regrettably is often the case in psychometrics, carries the same implication. It cannot make the case for or against external reality.

Intelligibility of human communication

This argument is developed further by Searle (1995). Just as the very notion of convergence in scientific theorising implies external reality so also does the intelligibility of much human discourse and communication. It is a necessary condition for the understanding of thought and language. It cannot be given up, as can some other beliefs, such as, for example, that a rainbow is the goddess Iris. What the thesis of external realism states is that there is a way that things are which is independent of all representations of how things are. According to Searle, this view identifies 'a space of possibilities'. For example, the sentence 'I have no gloves in my pocket' does not imply the existence of either gloves or pockets. I could say 'I have no unicorns in my groll', and this example makes the argument easy to see. However, the first sentence makes sense only in the context that gloves and pockets do exist, that there is a space of possibilities for gloves and pockets. This example illustrates the problem with the second sentence. There is a space of possibilities for unicorns, although they are considered to be mythical, but there is none, as far as I know, for groll, which is consequently unintelligible. Thus Searle concludes that external realism sets out a space of possibilities for statements.

Indeed, Searle goes well beyond this first claim. He argues that external realism is a background supposition without which a very large class of utterances cannot be normally understood. Normal understanding is exemplified thus. N.F. Simpson, the playwright, had a character claim that he had some black blood. He then produced a bottle. This was amusing, inasmuch as it was, because it contradicted our normal understanding of the external world, where the claim of having blood refers to the biological fact of its running in our veins. Indeed, in all ordinary speech there are a huge number of presuppositions, derived from notions of an external reality, which make normal understanding possible.

The point is that a public language demands that the same utterances are understood in the same way by different individuals. This is the meaning of 'public'. However, such understanding requires that these utterances refer to an external reality, which is publicly accessible and objective. If I say that 'Loch Ness is deep yellow and covered in concrete' this is perfectly intelligible, even if it turns out not to be the case. Indeed, if it turned out that there were no Loch Ness, this would still be intelligible, since we understand the sentence because it depends on the existence of an external reality. The understanding of the sentence does not depend on the truth condition, that there is a Loch Ness, but on the condition that there is an external world independent of our representations. This is, Searle argues, necessary for normal intelligibility. If external reality is denied, then intelligible communication is impossible. Berkeley, the great idealist and antirealist, recognised this problem but countered it by the claim that God allowed successful communication; but such a *deus ex machina* argument is not any longer satisfactory.

These are the arguments which can be used to support the notion of an external world against the claims of the idealist antirealists and they appear to be convincing. Thus far scientific psychologists can feel that there is some philosophical underpinning for their work.

Reality is not socially constructed

As Searle (1995) points out, however, there is another common antirealist argument. This is the claim that all reality is socially constructed. This is a particularly important argument for psychometrics since it has been argued by many social psychologists that psychometric variables such as intelligence and extraversion are nothing more than social constructs. Researchers of this kind who call themselves social scientists are necessarily engaged in an activity – I cannot call it intellectual activity – which is very different from that of the natural sciences. Hampson (1997:

75) could not be more explicit, in discussing Potter and Wetherell (1987): 'The social world does not exist independent of our constructions of it. There is nothing out there against which to validate our constructions. Therefore an objective, scientific approach to social psychology is impossible.' Hampson herself, to be fair, does not adopt this extreme position but regards external reality as the basis of personality perception even though the process of personality perception, she believes, is a constructivistic one – an argument which cannot be impugned.

Searle demonstrates, however, that the social construction argument cannot bear scrutiny. First, as we have seen, there is no difficulty with the notion that some constructs are socially constructed. These were referred to as institutionalised facts; money and marriage are easy and uncontroversial examples. Such facts as money, unlike brute facts, do not exist independently of their representations. One counter-argument is clear. That there is a socially constructed reality actually implies a reality independent of social construction. There have to be raw materials to construct money, or even language: sounds and paper or metal. Furthermore, these raw materials cannot be socially constructed except out of some yet more basic materials. In other words, Searle argues, the ontological subjectivity of the socially constructed world requires an objective reality for its construction.

Perhaps it might be pointed out here that in addition to the confusion in the social psychologists mentioned above concerning the fact that the existence of institutional facts does not mean that there is no external reality, there is another severe problem. It is sometimes argued that concepts such as intelligence or extraversion cannot be the subject of science because they are abstract rather than concrete. This, however, is nonsensical. The concept of 'mammal' has been highly valuable in zoology, although it is an abstract category, of which only the exemplars are concrete. 'Gravity' is another such notion. These brilliant social scientists would no doubt argue that gravity is a construction with no external reality, although it should be noted that such theorists on the way to their many conferences are careful to travel by the safest aeroplanes.

Realism is acceptable

In brief, so far in this chapter I have argued that it is not satisfactory for psychologists to assume that their work is scientific and therefore yielding results which are bound to be true simply because they are following the scientific method. There are several reasons why that is the case, of which an important one is the difficulty with induction. Inductive reasoning does not necessarily lead to truth, and psychologists need to be aware of this problem. In addition, the scientific programme assumes that science seeks to reach the truth. But the concept of truth, in this sense, presupposes an external reality. Again it is necessary to counter the arguments against the notion of reality and the claims that all reality is simply a construction. This has been done, and the concepts of primary qualities – essences, brute facts or kinds – contrasted with secondary qualities –

nominal essences and institutionalised facts. Certainly some aspects of the world are socially constructed, but such construction implies an objective reality. None of these points infirms the notion of reality or thus destroys the programme of scientific investigation. However, the establishment of the philosophical propriety of external reality is only the first step in the argument. The second concerns the nature of truth. Even if there is such a reality, how can we know that our descriptions of it are true?

The correspondence theory of truth

As has been indicated throughout this chapter, the programme of science and the scientific method imply both some kind of external reality and the notion of truth, which involves describing that reality as it actually is. This is usually known as the correspondence theory of truth, although there are other theories, and the acceptance of external reality does not of itself imply the correspondence theory.

The correspondence theory of truth is intuitively acceptable. It states that a statement is true if and only if it corresponds to the facts. On this account the statement that I am sitting typing on my word-processor is true. However, this definition requires, as Searle (1995) argues, some expansion. It all depends on what is meant by 'corresponds' and by 'the facts'.

One point needs to be made clear. There are many things, other than statements, which can be true. Thus beliefs, thoughts, propositions and sentences can also be true. Fortunately, as Scruton (1994) points out, the arguments apply similarly to all these terms since propositions entail what is stated, believed and said in statements, beliefs and sentences.

The disquotation criterion

Searle first examines the 'disquotation' criterion of truth, which is sometimes held to run against the correspondence theory. This states that any account of truth has to meet the following condition: for any sentence s, s is true if and only if p, where for 's' we put a specification of a sentence by quotation and for 'p' we put the sentence itself. For example, 'Ravens are black' is true if and only if ravens are black. There are minor variants of this disquotation criterion to deal with different languages, minor differences between sentences, statements and propositions and indexical statements such as 'I am ill'. As Searle shows, these can be easily dealt with: 'I am ill' said by a speaker S at time t is true if and only if S is ill at time t.

The disquotation criterion appears to reduce the correspondence theory of truth to triviality since it states, essentially, that what makes the sentence on the left side true is simply repetition of the sentence. However, Searle argues that there are two important ideas in this criterion. The first is that sentences are made true by satisfying a condition which stands outside the sentence. The second point concerns the fact that for many cases the truth condition is specified just by repeating the sentence.

All those conditions on the right-hand side of T sentences, as they are named, which make sentences true, if they are true, require a name or term to describe them, and Searle argues that the following terms are used: 'fact', 'situation', 'state of affairs'. 'Corresponds' is similarly the general term to name the various ways in which sentences are made true in virtue of these facts, situations and states of affairs. Furthermore, this explication of facts and corresponds in the disquotational criterion implies the correspondence theory of truth because if the left side of a T sentence really is true it must correspond to the fact stated on the right side. From this analysis of the disquotational criterion Searle restates the correspondence theory: for any s, s is true if and only if s corresponds to the fact that p.

Strawson (1964) raised some severe problems with the correspondence theory of truth, as clarified in the disquotational form, which are well discussed by Searle (1995). Perhaps the most salient of these arguments is the problem arising from the theory where it attempts to state that truth lies in the match of elements of the statement and elements of the fact. This is because once the statement and fact have been identified, there is nothing more to do to make the comparison. The only way of identifying a fact is to make a true statement. Thus, according to the argument, the true statement and the fact are not independent entities. Facts are what true statements state. Facts are not, therefore, extra-linguistic but the notions of truth and statement are built into them since the specification of a fact depends on a true statement. From this it does not follow, of course, that facts are simply true statements. An example will clarify this point. It makes causal sense to say that the fact that my computer is playing up has led to errors, but the true statement that my computer is playing up has led to errors seems nonsense.

This relationship, not identity, between fact and true statement which is revealed in the disquotation formulation of the correspondence theory has made the notion of 'true' appear to be redundant. To say 'it's true that my computer is playing up' seems to add nothing to the statement, if true, 'my computer is playing up'. This has led to the redundancy theory of truth, that the word 'true' is literally inane, or, if this is extreme (since occasionally as a shorthand to avoid infinite sets of disquotations, 'true' is required), then such arguments claim that there is no property or relation denoted by 'true'.

In other words, as Searle argues, to continue to make use of the correspondence theory of truth two objections have to be answered. The first is that there really are non-linguistic facts in the world to which true statements can correspond (refuting the disquotational criterion) and the second is that the relationship between fact and true statement is one of correspondence (Strawson's objection).

Searle's attempt to justify the use of the correspondence theory of truth and to show that it is essentially no different from the disquotation formulation turns upon his analysis of the general meaning of 'true' as trustworthy and reliable. On this analysis the disquotation criterion is consistent with our intuition that truth, true statements and propositions imply accuracy, reliability and trustworthiness. Truth, Searle argues, is a term of assessment which implies trustworthiness, and disquotation is a criterion for such trust. So much for truth. Now the meaning of fact is subjected to a similar analysis.

The meaning of fact

Fact, then, refers to what it is that makes statements trustworthy, the character-istics which make them reliable. What makes it true, if it is true, that my computer is playing up is simply that my computer is playing up. And this is the case for every true statement, and the term for what makes statements true is 'fact'. Thus to specify a fact we require a true statement; that is, facts cannot be named but have to be stated.

This analysis of the disquotation criterion, which cannot be impugned, is essential because it enables Searle to demonstrate that it fits rather than runs counter to the correspondence theory of truth. His argument, much abbreviated, is now set out. It does not follow from the fact that facts can only be stated, not named, that facts are linguistic, with the notion of statement implicit. This is absolutely not the case, since the term 'fact' refers to what makes a statement true and stands outside the statement. Facts, in Searle's analysis, are conditions: 'specifically, they are the conditions in the world that satisfy the truth conditions expressed by the statements'. For example, if the statement that 'my computer is playing up' is true, there will be a condition in the world that satisfies the truth condition of the statement, and this condition is, of course, the fact that my computer is playing up. This definition of fact as what is sufficient to make a statement true enables us to deal with negative facts, such as that there are no dinosaurs in my room, although such a concept appears to have been a problem in philosophy. Thus it can be concluded that because of the connection between fact and true statement, which was demonstrated above, facts have to be stated and there is no inconsistency between the correspondence criterion and the disquota-tional criterion. Fact is what makes a statement true and disquotation gives the form of what makes each statement true, by repeating the statement.

The first step in the argument has been completed. It can be seen that there is no contradiction between the disquotation criterion and the correspondence theory of truth.

The meaning of correspondence

The second task still remains: to give some meaning to the notion of correspon-dence, one of the original objections of Strawson. Again I shall summarise, as briefly as possible, the arguments adduced by Searle. Just as a term was necessary to describe those features of the world which rendered statements true – 'facts' – so a term is required which can describe how true statements can accurately represent the state of the world, and that phrase is 'correspond to the facts'. This phrase embraces a number of ways in which things can be represented. It is possible for statements to be only approximately true; that is, approximately correspond to the facts.

This reanalysis of the terms of the correspondence theory indicates not only that there is no conflict between the theory and the disquotation criterion but that there is no real problem with the notion of correspondence. As Searle argues, the problems arose because facts were taken to be objects, and if this is the case, the meaning of 'corresponds' requires some precise isomorphism, which cannot of course be specified, and the meaningfulness of negative and hypothetical facts becomes dubious.

However, as I have now shown, objections to both the correspondence theory and the disquotational criterion are founded on linguistic misconceptions concerning the meaning of 'correspond' and 'fact'. This is especially important in relation to the disquotation criterion, which has been taken up, in redundancy theory, to demonstrate that there is no meaning to 'true'. The only common property of true statements is that they satisfy the disquotation criterion, which, as we have seen, involves repeating the statement. By any standards, this is an unsatisfactory conclusion and a false one, since facts are not statements but the conditions in the world which render statements true or false. Facts are not *per se* linguistic.

Conclusions

This section on the correspondence theory of truth is long and I want to summarise the argument up to this point. This is necessary, essential even, because it is evident that the correspondence theory of truth underpins the scientific method. Science makes observations and tries to fit them to nature. It is essential, therefore, to ensure that the theory is tenable and that a scientific psychology is possible, especially since some psychologists have attempted to deny the objectivity of the field at all, thus making the subject subjective. Finally, it is not sufficient to admit that there are difficulties with the notion of truth but to plough on regardless, hoping that, in the end, some scientific truth will emerge.

It seems to me that Searle (1995) has managed to demonstrate that the standard philosophical objections to the correspondence theory of truth are unfounded. He has shown that facts are not *per se* statements but rather state the conditions in the world which would render any particular statement true or false. That my computer is playing up is the condition which renders true the statement that my computer is playing up. Statements and facts are not the same since, as has been shown, the statements can be causal and facts cannot. Furthermore, different statements can refer to the same fact, as, for example, 'my computer is playing up' and 'my Apricot is playing up'. With this definition and the consequent understanding that the fact and the statement are different, the term 'correspond' becomes meaningful since it indicates that the statement represents more or less accurately or falsely some condition in the world. This description indicates immediately the significance of the correspondence theory for scientific psychology. For in this subject we make statements or hypotheses about the world and judge them for truth by our observations of the world.

The argument of Davidson

There is a final argument, first advanced by Davidson (1984), against the correspondence theory of truth, which Searle also demolishes in considerable detail. This takes the assumption of correspondence theory: if a statement (e.g. 'that snow is white') corresponds to the fact described by the expression 'the fact that p' (e.g. that snow is white), then, Davidson argues, it corresponds to 'the fact that q' provided that the sentences p and q are logically equivalent or that p differs from q only in that a singular term has been replaced by a coextensive singular term (e.g. snow is white and a hedgehog has prickles). Logical equivalence is defined thus: if and only if two statements have the same truth value in every model, they are logically equivalent (e.g. 'coal is black' is logically equivalent to 'snow is white'). By the insertion and substitution of logically equivalent statements and coextensive singular terms in this way it is possible to arrive at the following: the statement that snow is white corresponds to the fact that coal is black. This is because by such substitutions it is possible to show that for any two true statements the first corresponds to the fact stated by the second. Indeed, it follows, if this so, that any true statement corresponds to any and all true facts and thus the theory is refuted.

This is, of course, absurd, but this is the point of Davidson's argument that the correspondence theory leads to absurdity. However, when examined in detail there appear to be considerable problems with the arguments, mainly about the propriety of the substitutions. With the notion of facts that is proposed by Searle, it is by no means obvious that such substitutions are permissible. For example, that snow is white does not necessarily (without good argument, which is not presented) correspond to the fact that snow is white and hedgehogs are prickly. This latter statement has simply nothing to do with the fact that snow is white. These substitutions provide false bases for the steps of the arguments so that the conclusions cannot be valid.

Some other theories of truth

Although, as we have seen, the objections to the correspondence theory of truth are not overwhelming, they have been sufficient to persuade philosophers of other theories. However, I do not intend to discuss these here other than to mention that these also have severe problems and that they are not so useful from the viewpoint of science as the correspondence theory.

Scruton (1994) argues that in the coherence theory, truth lies in the relationships between propositions. Thus a false view of the world is incoherent, while in a true description the parts fit and hang together. Thus science, in this view, is the development of a coherent account of the world. However, this is manifestly not satisfactory. In the first place it is possible to have a coherent account which is untrue. The Ptolemaic system of astronomy or even psychoanalytic theory fall into this category. Indeed, this definition of truth would have to embrace hermeneutic theories, which most scientists would like to distinguish from science. A further objection is also raised by Scruton, namely that if a set of coherent propositions were negated, the new set would be coherent but false, given that the first set were regarded as true.

Another theory which some philosophers have maintained, particularly those in the USA, is the pragmatic theory of truth. This states that truthfulness implies utility. Thus a criterion of a true proposition is that it is useful; truth is what it is good for us to believe. Rorty (e.g. 1991), who is a recent advocate of the pragmatic position and a proponent of the relativistic notion of truth, has argued that science and truth are nothing more, or less, than what is agreed upon by the scientific community until something better comes up, 'better' being defined as more useful or more agreeable. This theory, too, has obvious objections. It was certainly useful in pre-war Germany to hold to fascistic beliefs, just as now, in the UK, in the social sciences it is useful to propound what is politically correct. By the standards of Rorty political correctness is the truth. Furthermore, as studies of the history of medicine show, there have been many highly useful practices derived from theories which are manifestly false.

Even these brief descriptions of these theories of truth are sufficient to make it clear that they have no advantages over the correspondence theory. Indeed, they appear to have even more severe problems. I think it is safe to conclude that the correspondence theory of truth can remain as a sound philosophical basis for scientific investigation.

Summary: conclusions and implications for psychology and psychometrics

In this chapter I have examined the philosophical basis of certain key features of the scientific method. I have done this because, in this book, I want to construct a genuinely scientific theory of human behaviour based in psychometrics. It was necessary because in psychology, generally, there is an obeisance to science (testing hypotheses, measuring variables and writing up reports in scientific jargon) which creates an illusion of science. However, it is by no means obvious that this methodology is suited to the subject matter of psychology or in what the essence of the scientific method lies. In the natural sciences – well established and yielding great insight into their fields, and many having been applied with great success – it is sufficient, perhaps, to follow the well-tried procedures of the scientific method. In psychology, where such success has not been achieved, to proceed without careful consideration, as if the scientific method is bound to be successful, is not justified or justifiable.

In our examination of the scientific method in general and as advocated by

Popper, i.e. the holding of hypotheses until they are refuted, a number of difficulties were exposed.

- The meaning of testable. To say that a hypothesis is untestable may mean little more than that it defies the inventiveness of the investigator.
- The problem of inductive reasoning. Inductive reasoning cannot demonstrate truth, in contradistinction to deductive reasoning. This is a serious problem for a science based on observation.
- The meaning of truth and the nature of external reality. Since the aim of science is to seek out the truth about the natural world, this is doomed if it is evident that there is no reality independent of the human mind. If the natural world is simply another construct then there is nothing special about science. It is, indeed, another hypothesis about the world no different from the ramblings of lunatics and the effusions of poets (if these are to be discriminated).

This last point is a massive philosophical problem on which there is and probably can be no complete agreement. There are two separate issues. The first concerns the nature of external reality and the second the nature of truth. The two are independent in that it could be meaningful to postulate an external reality yet impossible to know it.

External reality

Searle (1995), I argued, has made a number of important and pertinent points.

- Distinction between brute and institutionalised facts. Brute facts are independent of human opinion. Institutionalised facts are not; they depend on human institutions for their existence. This is an important distinction in countering the claim that all reality is a human creation. Brute facts are similar to Mill's kinds, and are the objects of science.
- The argument that, because our knowledge of reality is constructed by the brain, reality itself is thus constructed, is false.
- That there can be different descriptions of reality, conceptual relativity, does not mean that reality itself is thus constructed. Resulting inconsistencies refer to the limitations of the descriptions and say nothing about external reality.
- The fact that descriptions are held to be incoherent itself implies an external reality.
- That all we know are our experiences, the case made by Berkeley, cannot stand scrutiny.
- The notion of convergence in scientific theorising implies an external reality.
- Intelligibility and understanding in discourse and thought imply an external reality, which states that there is a way things are, independent of human

representation. Berkeley countered this difficulty with the claim that God, in His wisdom, rendered communication intelligible.

From these arguments it was concluded that it is not philosophical nonsense to maintain the reality of the external world which can be regarded as the object of scientific investigation. Claims by social scientists that there is no reality, that reality is a social construct, are unfounded and confused.

However, even if it is meaningful to talk of an external reality, how is it possible to know that our descriptions of it are true? Science itself aims to describe this real world, and this aim implies that we seek to refine our descriptions by inference and deduction until we have reached the truth. The heart does pump blood and is not the seat of the emotions. This implies the correspondence theory of truth: a proposition is true if and only if it corresponds to the facts. This apparently unexceptionable account has been subject to huge philosophical attack, and Searle mounts a powerful defence of which the main points are set out.

- The difficulty with the correspondence theory lies in two places: the meaning of correspondence and the meaning of facts. It is this dual problem which has caused this intuitively attractive notion to be abandoned.
- The disquotation criterion, which is sometimes held to disconfirm the correspondence theory, in fact can be shown to confirm it. Thus the truth of the left-hand side of the sentence is confirmed by something outside it (the right-hand side of the sentence), as exemplified by 'Ravens are black', which is true if and only if ravens are black.
- One objection to the disquotational criterion states that the only way to identify a fact is to make a true statement; thus the two concepts are not independent. However, facts and statements are not the same: facts can be causal, statements cannot.
- True statements imply accuracy, trust and reliability. Truth implies trustworthiness, and disquotation is a criterion for such trust.
- Facts refer to what it is which makes statements trustworthy. What makes it true that my computer is playing up is simply that my computer is playing up. Thus facts cannot be named but have to be stated. To specify a fact we require a true statement.
- Facts are not simply linguistic entities. They stand outside the statement and refer to what makes it true, if it is true. Facts are the conditions in the world which satisfy the truth condition of statements.
- Thus there is no contradiction between the disquotation criterion and the correspondence theory of truth.
- The meaning of 'correspond to the facts' is to indicate how true statements can accurately reflect the state of the world, and this can be done with varying degrees of precision.
- The argument of Davidson (1984), that the correspondence theory allows any true statement to correspond to any true fact, is also shown to be false.

On this basis it can be argued that it is philosophically tenable to hold to the correspondence theory of truth. Thus the scientific endeavour which seeks to build up a picture of the external world by searching for the truth is not invalidated. Since, too, it has been shown that it is philosophically tenable to hold to the notion of an external world and quite false to conceive of it as a construction of the mind – although some aspects of the world, institutionalised facts, are of this kind – again the use of the scientific method in psychology can be supported.

It is important that it be shown, as I believe I have shown, that the scientific method is philosophically reputable, if we are to use it in psychology where as yet it has not been as successful as in the natural sciences. Here the success has been so great that practitioners might well feel that even if there are philosophical problems, these are irrelevant.

Differences between psychology and the natural sciences

The natural sciences have progressed through the testing of clear hypotheses against precise observations and measurement. If we take biology as an example, superbly accurate observation of the brain down to the molecular level has led to an improved understanding of the function and nature of the neuron. However, the neuron is an object in the real world, as are its constituent chemicals, and slowly pharmacology is uncovering the chemistry of neural function as it studies its biochemistry. Part of this accurate observation requires precise measurement and measurement is usually regarded as a *sine qua non* of the natural sciences.

We have seen how some social psychologists have tried to argue that in social psychology at least, there are no brute facts. Their subject of study is a subjective world which they contrast to the objective world of science. If this were true – that psychology is the study of institutionalised facts, human constructs which are necessarily subjective – the programme for a scientific psychology might well be hopeless. However, this is clearly not the case. Let us take intelligence and anxiety as an example. These are obviously not things which can be observed and measured as one might a brain. Clearly they reflect some kind of brain function. Yet they are not simply subjective notions. Organisms demonstrate intelligence or anxiety regardless of human classification. Suppose that a troop of early human beings, with no notion of intelligence or brute facts, were faced with a severe problem: their path homewards was blocked by a huge stone. If they could not move it they were doomed. Already they could hear the baying of wolves. Some of the troop, we can imagine, are panicking, weeping and shouting. Others are stolid and chew a few nuts or grasses. Perhaps a few contemplating the boulder see that with a large branch it might be levered clear, and look round for materials. Those people are showing both anxiety and intelligence. These are aspects of human behaviour which exist regardless of their names. This example demonstrates that the subject matter of psychology is not entirely subjective. Intelligence and anxiety, although abstract, are, in principle, capable of objective study.

However, this example also shows that there is a genuine distinction between the subject matter of psychology and that of the natural sciences. Although I have tried to show that anxiety might be conceptualised as a brute fact, there is another, subjective aspect to it. Feelings of anxiety and other emotions are private and subjective, and not obviously suited to public observation, a necessity for the scientific method. Indeed, the whole problem of human consciousness, which it is quite reasonable to expect psychology to deal with – the world of the mind, feelings, thoughts, emotions and, if we are to believe dynamic psychologists, unconscious mental processes – also leads to appalling problems of observation and measurement. Thus there may be aspects of psychology which are beyond measurement and which, therefore, can never become scientific.

It is clear from this that the whole problem of psychological measurement becomes crucial. Velocity, given good measures of time and length, can easily be measured. Yet the measurement of intelligence and anxiety and other psychological variables presents no such obvious solutions. It could well be the case that no psychological variables are capable of measurement, or that some are and others not.

A scientific psychology depends on good measurement. The subject matter of psychometrics is the measurement of psychological traits and characteristics, and it is the problems of scientific psychological measurement in psychometrics to which we must turn in the next chapter.

2

SCIENTIFIC MEASUREMENT IN PSYCHOMETRICS AND MEASUREMENT IN THE NATURAL SCIENCES

Need for precise measurement

In Chapter 1 I pointed out that Eysenck (1986) had argued that psychology, if it is to progress, must follow the scientific hypothetico-deductive method of the natural sciences. Part, an intrinsic part, of the scientific method involves quantification and measurement. Cattell (1981), like Eysenck a student of Burt and a leading member of the London school of psychology, has demonstrated with great clarity the necessity of precise measurement in psychology. Scientific psychology, he argues, seeks to understand personality and ability as an astronomer the spectrum of an ancient star or a biologist the biochemistry of mammalian functions. Yet psychologists have been slow to realise that to carry this out, to formulate general laws and principles, precise measurement is essential. That, indeed, is what Cattell has attempted to do in a long career, still continuing after sixty years of research. His tests of personality, intelligence and motivation are still in use. Yet although these are among the best tests of their kind ever to be developed, there is still disagreement even among putative experts as to whether they measure what they claim to measure, and this is particularly true of his personality and motivation tests. Indeed, to measure human motivation is a task of great difficulty and there are no motivation tests which are universally or even generally agreed to be accurate measures.

The reasons for this reside in the nature of motivational variables. But these are typical of psychological variables generally and it is necessary to examine the nature of psychological variables and measurement in general in order to understand better the severe problems of psychological measurement.

Psychological variables and problems of measurement

The statement of Cattell referred to above is particularly illuminating. Thus there is no problem concerning the observation of a star. That a star is present in a particular area of the sky is a verifiable, public datum. Given adequate vision, there would be no disagreement among sane observers. Similarly, its exact position could be located with great accuracy and virtually 100 per cent agreement by trained users of a good telescope. Likewise, its spectrum could be analysed in a spectrometer with no disagreement. This measurement is accurate and of high reliability, both between observers and if the measurement is done on different occasions. This notion of reliable measurement, without variation regardless of when the measurement is made or who makes the measurement, provided only that the individual is sane, in possession of his or her faculties and trained to use the instrument, is an essential for all scientific measures. In psychometrics and psychological measurement this is known as test reliability, and is a concept which will be constantly under discussion in this book.

Accuracy was also mentioned. Accuracy is not identical to reliability. A measure cannot be accurate if it is unreliable, but it can be reliable yet inaccurate. It is possible, in principle, to conceive of an instrument which always gives reliable measures but which is inaccurate. Of course, if the error were always the same, it could be easily corrected, but if it differed for different measurements, it would render the instrument of little value. The simplest example of just such an inaccurate but reliable measure would be a 12-inch ruler of which each of the twelve inch divisions was wrong but by a differing amount. However, this example also raises another point: how is it possible to assess the accuracy of measurement? To say that a measure is accurate presupposes that there is some other, independent method of measuring the variable. In general accuracy is held to be a matter of concordance between different measures. Originally there were benchmark measures which were agreed to be as perfectly accurate as possible. The metre rule and the prototype kilogram kept at Sèvres were well-known examples. Now, however, units of measurement are defined in terms of some fundamental property of matter, which is more convenient than having to make comparisons with a unit at Sèvres and, of course, more accurate. For example, a metre is defined by the length travelled by light in a vacuum in a given number of seconds and the kelvin (the unit for measuring temperature) as a given proportion of the triple point of water, although mass is still compared with the kilogram at Sèvres. There is a key concept in measurement here: the unit. All these scientific measures depend on units of measurement. Those which have been discussed – the metre and the kelvin, for example – are known as base units. However, derived units can be constructed from base units. Speed is an obvious example, being measured in terms of metres per second.

For psychological tests, accuracy is far more difficult to assess because of the difficulty of establishing units of measurement. As we shall see, this is a profound difference between psychological tests and measures in the natural sciences. Instead, psychological test scores have a standard error of measurement derived from the notion of a true score. The more reliable a test is, the lower its standard error and the more closely it approximates to the true score. Clearly, here all depends on how true this true score really is. All this is discussed in detail later in this chapter. Suffice it say here that this concept of the true score may allow accurate and reliable measurement but it does not, *per se*, ensure that the test measures what it claims to measure; that is, that the test is valid. This has to be demonstrated. Actually, as Ellis (1966) points out, there were similar arguments as to whether thermometers did measure temperature or not, it being only assumed that the expansion of mercury reflected increasing temperature.

Validity and accuracy in measurement

I want to return to the examples of scientific measurement given by Cattell (1981). The variables which he mentioned (the spectrum of a star's light, the biochemistry of the blood) and the examples I have used (distance and time) are fundamental brute facts of external reality. Regardless of my presence or that of any other individuals, the distance between Everest and Snowdon remains the same; the light of that star, emitted before any human beings were conceived, remains the same; and time passes.

These brute facts are clearly in the public domain. If we attempt to measure them, there is no doubt what we are measuring. If we set a ruler alongside a house to measure its length, there is no dispute about what we are measuring. The notion of validity for a ruler, as a measure of length, is redundant. The only doubt concerns its accuracy, and in general the accuracy of rulers for all but enormous or very short lengths is satisfactory for practical purposes. The same is true of time. Modern quartz watches can now equal or exceed the accuracy of the finest hand-made mechanical chronometers, and only over very long periods of time, such as the number of seconds between now, as I write (April 1997), and the new millennium, will any small inaccuracies be revealed. Again if I buy a watch, of whatever variety, there is no question of its validity. This seems true of most of the measures used in the natural sciences. No one questions the validity of barometers, thermometers, voltmeters, ammeters, spectrometers, Geiger counters, light or sound meters. This is because the variables which they measure are in the public domain and because they utilise clear units of measurement. In the case of electricity they are part of a complex theory which can predict the measurements concerned, and it would become obvious if the instruments were inaccurate or not measuring the variables they claimed to measure. In short, the notion of validity is essentially redundant for measurement in the natural sciences.

I shall now list the variables measured by some well-known psychological tests: verbal ability, numerical ability, speed of closure, memory span, aesthetic judgement, aiming, mechanical aptitude, form perception, clerical perception, manual dexterity, timbre, warmth, dominance, boldness, radicalism, conformity, suspiciousness, self-discipline, agitation, depression, anxiety, openness, empathy, hoarding, masculinity, ascendance, exhibitionism. This is simply a random sample taken from my *Handbook of Psychological Testing* (Kline, 1995), which discusses a hundred or so well-known tests, among many other aspects of psychological testing. These are enough to make the necessary contrast with the variables in the natural sciences.

It is quite clear that none of these is in the public domain. Although it can be argued, as I demonstrated in Chapter 1, that problem solving in human beings is a brute fact, it does not follow from this that the measurement of intelligence, a construct held by some psychologists to account for problem solving, is thus in the public domain and hence, in principle, simple to measure. In the case of intelligence, all we can do is see how quickly individuals can solve problems of varying degrees of difficulty. Indeed, it is from the analysis of the results of such problem solving that the modern concept of intelligence has been derived, as will be fully discussed later in this book. However, it is obvious from this that tests of intelligence, consisting of the scores on a number of problems, are very different from measures of length. Clearly there could be, and is, disagreement on what an intelligence test measures. It might be verbal reasoning or spatial reasoning or mathematical reasoning, depending on the particular items. Again, such a test might be measuring little more than previous experience in problem solving, and it is a matter of judgement and argument as to what intelligence test do measure (see, for example, Jensen, 1980, or Kamin, 1974). It is not my intention here to argue the case for or against intelligence tests. This issue will be fully examined in Chapter 6. My intention here is simply to demonstrate that it is by no means certain what intelligence test do measure. Hence evidence for their validity is essential.

I deliberately began this discussion with intelligence tests because of all psychological variables, intelligence is probably the easiest to measure, and there is some agreement, especially among those who work in this field, as to the validity of tests that purport to measure it. The other variables, especially personality variables, are far more difficult to measure. Take a variable such as dominance. It is by no means clear what items might measure dominance or how it might be shown that any group of items did in fact measure that variable. Actually, the very definition of dominance might be hard to agree upon. Thus studies of the validity of a putative measure of dominance are essential, and to demonstrate perfect validity is virtually impossible since it is by no means clear what this might mean.

In the field of intelligence testing there are two benchmark tests, those of Wechsler (1944, although the test has been regularly updated) and the Stanford–Binet (Terman and Merrill, 1960). Most intelligence tests are deliberately designed to correlate highly with these two tests, and there is a reasonable degree of agreement in the assessment of IQ, the intelligence quotient, among the best intelligence tests. However, agreement is on average within a band of about 5 points. There is nothing like the agreement or accuracy to be expected of the instruments of the natural sciences. With tests of other psychological variables, accuracy, as measured by agreement between different measures, is far lower. If a psychologist uses a test, that test must be named in any report of results because the scores from another purported measure would be different.

From this it is argued that the nature of psychological variables means that their measurement is inevitably somewhat different from that of the variables in the natural sciences. It is not self-evident what psychological tests do measure, hence the need for the concept of validity. Certainly, even from this initial discussion it is clear that psychological measurement must lack the precision of that in the natural sciences. How these problems can be overcome, if they can, will be now examined.

As might be expected, enormous efforts have been made by psychometrists in an attempt to overcome the difficulties of measuring psychological variables, ever since such psychological testing began (around the turn of the century). In these hundred years psychometrics has developed theory and practices which are generally accepted as leading to scientific measurement. Good psychological tests are characterised, in psychometrics, by high reliability, high validity and good discriminatory power. In addition, good psychological tests have representative norms to allow them to be interpreted. These characteristics will be described and scrutinised, as will the methods of test construction, in order that their adequacy as scientific measures can be evaluated.

The characteristics of good psychometric tests

Before reliability and other characteristics of good tests can be discussed it is necessary to define more accurately what is meant by a psychometric test. Up to this point I have used the term to refer to psychological tests of all kinds. However, strictly a psychometric test is a psychological test which is made up from a collection of items. In the case of an ability test, an item is a problem which has to be solved, or, in the case of measures of personality, attitude or motivation, it is a statement or question, typically answered by 'Yes' or 'No' or by stating one's position on a continuum from 'strongly agree' to 'strongly disagree'. There are other kinds of psychological test, such as projective tests, or objective tests where subjects have to complete some task, such as slow line drawing, but these do not usually possess the characteristics of high-quality psychometric tests which I am about to describe. This is because these characteristics are built into them at the stage of test construction, as will be described.

Reliability

In our general discussion of measurement I have already referred to reliability. In psychometric testing the term is used in two ways with different meanings, and both are of considerable importance.

A. *Test–retest reliability* (r_{tt}). This is an essential attribute for any good measure, whether psychometric or not. A test should yield the same score for each subject when he or she takes the test on another occasion, given that their status on the variable has not changed. This reliability is easily measured by giving the test to the same subjects on two occasions, separated by a time-span so that they cannot remember their previous responses, and computing the correlation. The higher it is, the higher the reliability. A reliability coefficient of 0.7 is usually regarded as a minimum for tests which are to be used with individuals. This is because of the relationship between test–retest reliability and the standard error of measurement which is discussed below. It is obvious, however, that the lower the reliability, the less any particular score can be trusted since it is likely to be different if we were to test again. It is equally obvious that unreliable scores are not likely to be useful in a precise, quantified science.

B. *Internal consistency.* If a test measures a particular variable, say intelligence, then it is obvious that each item in the test should also measure that variable. If each item measures the same variable the test must be internally consistent. To this extent internal consistency, known as reliability, is an essential for a good test. If a test were not internally consistent it could only be because some of the items were not measuring the same variable as the rest of the items. This could not be a good thing, it goes without saying.

There are several important implications for psychometric testing in this simple notion of internal consistency.

1   Internal consistency matters: good psychometric tests are required to be internally consistent because this ensures that they are univariate, measuring only one variable. If we consider a barometer and a thermometer we take it as given that they measure, respectively, pressure and temperature. We should be annoyed if we discovered that the measurement of either was modified to even a small extent by measurement of the other variable; if the single reading reflected the two variables, in some unknown mix.

In many psychometric tests this is precisely what happens. The test is not univariate but measures more than one variable. An example will clarify the issue and indicate clearly why this is an undesirable state of affairs in scientific measurement. One of the best-known intelligence tests, the Wechsler Adult Intelligence Scale (WAIS) (Wechsler, 1958), measures two factors, as indicated by factor analysis: fluid intelligence and crystallised intelligence (Woliver and Saeks, 1986). This means that apparently identical scores may have different psychological meaning. Thus IQs of 130, for example, can be differentially constructed from the two factors, and are of different psychological significance. This is *per se* bad measurement. As it happens, the WAIS is still an effective measure in practice, simply because the common concept of intelligence, as will be fully discussed in Chapter 6, comprises a mixture of these factors. It does mean, however, that for more theoretical research into human abilities the WAIS has some problems. Ideally we need separate measures of these two factors.

2   A test can be too internally consistent. On intuitive common-sense arguments it can be seen that the set of items in a test must be internally consistent; that is, they must correlate among themselves to some extent if they are measuring the same variable. However, this raises the question of to what extent.

Most textbooks in psychometrics argue that the internal consistency reliability of a test should be as high as possible (Cronbach, 1984; Nunnally and Bernstein, 1994). This is because what is regarded as the best measure of internal consistency, Cronbach's alpha (Cronbach, 1951), measures the average correlation between the set of test items and any other set measuring the same variable. This, ideally, should be unity, a perfect correlation, and inasmuch as alpha departs from unity, so then the test must be contaminated by error. For more on test error see below, but the argument is clear at this point. If two tests purportedly measuring the same variable do not agree, then error must be present. Almost all reputable test constructors and psychometrists accept this argument.

However, there is one dissenting voice, that of Cattell (1957), and the argument needs to be heard. If we think of the total test score as the criterion score, each item can be thought of a predictor for that criterion. We can thus see the problem of this prediction in terms of multiple regression. In multiple regression the best prediction is made by variables which do not correlate with each other. If variables correlate highly with each other, each adds little to the overall correlation. On this model we would like best for a test items which correlate each with the criterion and zero among themselves. Items which correlate highly with each other add little to the multiple correlation and are therefore redundant. On this criterion high alphas can detract from validity. This is particularly true, on this argument, if the variable measured by the test is broad, such as anxiety or extraversion. Indeed, Cattell has claimed that some techniques of test construction lead to tests measuring variables which are so specific that they are of little or no psychological interest. These are called bloated specifics (Cattell and Kline, 1977), and I have argued previously that such variables have contributed greatly to the detriment of much social psychology (Kline, 1995). On these arguments, therefore, we would allow the internal consistency of a test, especially in the sphere of personality or motivation, to fall as low as 0.7, even though, in terms of the theory of coefficient alpha, this means that only half the variance of the test may be regarded as reliable, the rest being error.

3   I have mentioned in the previous paragraphs several times the notion of error. This is highly important in psychometric testing and many of the major textbooks in psychometrics have large sections on error, its theory and how to eliminate its effects, since clearly error detracts from the validity of test scores. I shall deal first with the important notion of the standard error of measurement (SEM), although its explanation is bound up closely to what is referred to as the classical theory of test error, classic status, in this case, being conferred by about 50 years of discussion.

The score that a subject obtains on a test is known as the fallible or obtained score. An obtained score is held to comprise two sources of variance: true score and error.

Definition of 'true score'

The true score is the score a subject would obtain if he or she were to complete all the items in the relevant universe of items. This, of course, is a notional concept. It is assumed that any set of items in a test is a random sample of the items from this universe. Inasmuch as it is not a random sample it contains error, hence the assumption that an obtained score consists of true score plus error variance.

Error in the sense used here is by definition uncorrelated with anything; it is random, to be distinguished from the systematic error in a bad test, for example if all the items were not equally familiar to males and females, thus introducing a sex bias in the results. Since error is random it follow that repeated testing of the same subject will produce a distribution of scores for a particular subject, the mean of the distribution being the best estimate of that subject's true score. It is assumed that this distribution of scores would be normal. Of course, it is not usually possible to retest the same subject on many occasions, so such a distribution cannot normally be obtained. In any case, even if it could, it would not be useful, since continual testing with the same test brings in its own form of distortion: subjects remember their responses or grow so bored with the procedure that they complete it in an absurd manner, and so on.

If, on repeated measurement, a subject obtained the same score every time, and this was true for all subjects, the test would be error free. The test–retest reliability would be 1 and the variance of the distribution of scores for each individual would be 0. There would be no error in the scores. From this it can be seen that, although we do not normally have a distribution of scores for an individual, we do have the test–retest reliability of the test itself, which is obtained from giving the test twice to the same subjects, and which therefore can yield an estimate of this distribution of scores, or the standard error of measurement.

$$\text{SEM} = \text{SD}_t / \sqrt{(1 - r_{tt})} \tag{2.1}$$

where SD_t is the standard deviation of the test and r_{tt} is the test–retest reliability.

Meaning and importance of the standard error of measurement

From equation (2.1) it can be seen that the SEM increases as reliability falls. An unreliable test yields a high SEM. In practice this means that where decisions have to be made about individuals, only highly reliable tests can be used. The SEM assumes that the distribution of obtained scores is normal. This means that, on the basis of the areas under the normal curve, we can say that approximately 68 per cent of obtained scores would fall between the actual score plus or minus 1 SEM. Ninety-five per cent of obtained scores would fall between the obtained score plus or minus 2 SEMs and 99.9 per cent would be embraced by 3 SEMs. This can be clarified by an example. Take a test with an SEM of 2 and suppose that a subject obtained a score of 8 on the test. Then it follows that 68 per cent of that subject's scores would fall between 10 and 6 and 95 per cent would fall between 12 and 4. Thus we could be confident in this case, following the usual statistical conventions, only that the subject's score on the test was between 12 and 4. This is an enormous margin of error. It means that in job selection, for example, another individual would have to score at least 13 before we could be convinced that he or she was a higher scorer.

It is sufficient to note at this juncture that test–retest reliability and internal consistency reliability, although they are different in meaning, as we have seen, are, in fact, related. Both give estimates of error in the test, error being defined as departure from the true score. Internal consistency reliability, measured by alpha, does this on the basis of the intercorrelations of the items while the test–retest reliability depends on differences in scores on retesting. Classical test theory demonstrates clearly the relationship between these two indices of reliability. However, such a demonstration is not necessary for the purposes of the argument in this section of the chapter and readers are referred to Kline (1995) or Nunnally and Bernstein (1994).

Before we leave the topic of reliability, it is worth pointing out that reliability increases with the length of a test: the more items, the more reliable the test, unless there are so many that subjects become bored or fatigued, or, in the case of children, the length of the test exceeds their attention span. (This varies with age, but it is important in the testing of children that tests are not too long.) The Spearman–Brown prophecy formula (equation (2.2)) shows how reliability increases with the number of items. In fact, 10 items can yield a reliable test but such a small number of items is unlikely to cover a broad spectrum of either problem solving or personality and attitude. For these reasons longer tests are preferable.

$$\text{Test reliability} = k(r)/1 + (k-1)r \tag{2.2}$$

where k is the number of items and r the average intercorrelation of items.

Finally, another type of reliability should be mentioned: parallel form reliability. As the name suggests, this is reliability as measured by the correlation between two different versions of the same test. Many tests have such parallel forms because it makes retesting, should it be required, more convenient – or it would, if the two versions of the test were perfectly correlated. In fact, this is rarely the case, so it makes comparison difficult. For them to be useful as parallel forms the reliability should be greater than 0.9. In principle this reliability is little different from that measured by the alpha coefficient, which estimates the correlation of a set of test items with another set drawn from the same universe.

Conclusions concerning reliability

I have not attempted to discuss reliability or to examine its theoretical basis in every detail. Rather I have selected the points essential for understanding the concept, which is central to psychometric testing. (As I have indicated, reliability is a characteristic of good psychometric tests.) I have done this so that later in this chapter we shall be able to compare psychometric measurement with measurement in the natural sciences, which, because their subject matter is probably more amenable to quantification, is somewhat different.

A summary of the main points is set out below.

- A test score consists of true score variance plus error.
- The true score is the score a subject would obtain on the universe of relevant items.
- Perfect reliability indicates that there is no error variance.
- The standard error of measurement increases as reliability falls.
- Thus reliability is generally seen as necessary, if not sufficient, for valid tests.

This last point is most important. It is possible to have highly reliable tests which yet are not valid. The views of Cattell have been mentioned. He argued that high reliability could yield tests so narrow that they measured nothing of psychological interest, variables which he called bloated specifics. This raises the whole problem of validity and what it means to say that a test is valid, and I shall now turn to this topic, validity, certainly the most important of the characteristics of good psychometric tests.

Validity

As was discussed earlier in this chapter, the very notion of validity is strange. With most instruments of measurement, what they measure is not called into question. Normally the only problematic issue concerns their accuracy. However, perhaps for obvious reasons, this is not the case with psychometric tests.

A test is said to be valid if it measures what it purports to measure. This is the standard textbook definition (e.g. Cronbach, 1984). The only modification of this definition of which I am aware is that of Vernon (1963), who pointed out that a test is valid for some purpose. This is a useful gloss, although, in my view, a truly scientific psychometric test would be valid *per se*; that is, for all purposes to which the test legitimately might be put. Vernon's definition raises a further interesting point which needs to be noted. While the reliability of a test can be easily measured, for example by the alpha coefficient, the measurement of validity is not simply the matter of calculating some statistical index. Consideration of the concept of validity as what a test measures indicates immediately why this is so. Unless there were some clear unequivocal criterion which a test was supposed to measure there could be no single index. Suffice it to say that there are no such criteria for psychometric tests or psychological variables: intelligence, extraversion, depression – these examples make it obvious that this must be the case.

As a consequence of this, the validity of a test has to be demonstrated. There are various different types of validity and ultimately whether or not a test is valid is a matter of opinion in the light of the evidence about its validity. It is usual to consider the validity of a psychometric test as falling into different categories, and these will now be discussed.

Face validity

Face validity refers to the appearance of a test. It is said to be face valid if it looks as though it measures what it claims to measure. In the case of tests of intelligence and ability, an experienced psychometrist may be able to assess what the test measures. For example, a test which involves algebra and mathematical problems is likely to be measuring mathematical reasoning. However, even with ability tests there can be confusion. Vernon reports that, in the army, selection for cooks involved cookery tests demanding information on methods and recipes. This looked like a test of cooking but analysis revealed that, effectively, it was a test of reading ability (Vernon and Parry, 1949).

In the field of personality, motivation and attitude testing, however, face validity generally bears little relation to true validity. This is because the items in these tests do not sample the test variable in the way that tests of ability do. Thus an intelligence test item is an actual problem which requires intelligence to solve. A typical personality test item is not of this kind. Thus a sample extraversion item might be: 'Do you enjoy going out with a large group of people?' to which the subject responds by ticking the appropriate 'Yes' or 'No'. This is the crucial difference between ability and other tests. This item is not an example of group behaviour. It requires the subject to be cooperative, truthful and insightful. Cooperative because the subject must agree to sit down and take the test seriously and think carefully about his or her responses; and truthful because there is an assumption, particularly in attitude measures and those used in social and health psychology, that the items reflect the actual behaviour of the subject. In selection, for example, it is common to lie, and this is a difficulty in the use of face-valid tests. Finally, insight is required. Individuals who never went out, and felt terror with more than two people might genuinely consider themselves as enjoying being in a group.

Guilford (1959) argued that face validity in personality tests was actually bad for true validity since it caused subjects to distort their results according to how they liked to appear on the variable. What was required, in his view, was items which the subject could not guess. This reduced deliberate distortion. In any case it can be concluded that face validity has no necessary connection with true validity.

Concurrent validity

The concurrent validity of a test is demonstrated by correlation with another similar test taken at the same time. There are obvious difficulties here since this presupposes that there is a good test of the variable, the criterion test, against which the other test can be validated. This is rarely the case, although there are benchmark tests for intelligence, the Wechsler scales and the Stanford–Binet test (Wechsler, 1958; Terman and Merrill, 1960), and perhaps for extraversion and anxiety, the old Eysenck Personality Questionnaire (EPQ) (Eysenck and Eysenck, 1975).

Even if it were agreed that these tests were suitable as criteria for establishing concurrent validity, the question remains as to how high the correlation has to be. Since a test cannot correlate with anything more than itself, the reliability sets a limit to this correlation, and since most tests do not exceed a reliability of 0.9, this has to be the upper limit of what can be expected. Normally if a test correlates more than 0.7 with the criterion test, this is regarded as good evidence for concurrent validity. However, since squaring a correlation coefficient indicates how much variance there is in common between the two sets of scores, it is evident that 0.7 is not, in reality, powerful evidence. More than half the variance is not shared.

There is a further difficulty. Sometimes a test constructor may, in writing a new test, paraphrase or actually use the same items as another test of the variable which he or she is trying to measure. If the new test is correlated with the test from which items were extracted or modified, there is almost certainly likely to be a substantial correlation. This is unsurprising and leads to the rapid agreement and ossification of how to test a variable. This appears to have occurred with measures of self-esteem (Kline, 1995). If there is doubt, anyway, as to what the original test, the master copy, measured, this whole procedure is dubious in the extreme. Although relatively high correlation coefficients may be obtained, it is unlikely to lead to good scientific measurement.

Where, as is usually the case, no good test of the variable exists, concurrent validity studies become matters of opinion. Tests can be validated against others which are somewhat similar and correlations of about 0.3 can be expected. Such studies become, then, part of construct validity, which is scrutinised on pp. 37–8.

Predictive validity

Predictive validity refers to the ability of a test to predict a relevant criterion. For example, Terman and Oden (1959) administered an intelligence test to gifted children and their controls at the age of 5 years. These children were followed up and it was shown that the intelligence test scores were good predictors of, *inter alia*, academic success, books and articles published, companies directed, patents granted and income. All this could be regarded as impressive evidence for the predictive validity of the test – in fact, the Stanford–Binet. If a test can predict, then this is good evidence of its validity unless the correlations have some other explanation.

However, there are two difficulties with the notion of predictive validity. The first concerns the fact that for many tests it is difficult to set up a criterion for predictive validity. Intelligence is by far the easiest example, but neuroticism is another possibility. Here subjects could be tested, and there should be a correlation between scores and the need for psychological and psychiatric treatment. In fact, this has been done for the EPQ (Eysenck and Eysenck, 1975), and there is evidence for the predictive validity of the N scale of this test. However, predictive validity studies for tests of extraversion, or openness – variables claimed by Costa and McCrae (1997) as two of the five most salient personality factors – are hard to conceptualise.

Even if, as is the case with intelligence and anxiety, studies can be carried out, there is still the question of what results constitute evidence of validity. While it is obvious that correlations of zero with academic success or unity would be unequivocal for a test of intelligence, in real life nothing is so clear-cut. Many investigators simply use statistical significance as the criterion. However, this is an easy way to mislead oneself. For example, with large samples a correlation of 0.18 would be statistically significant. However, such a correlation implies that the test can explain 3.2 per cent of the variance in the criterion. This is not impressive, since it means that more than 96 per cent remains unexplained – almost evidence of invalidity. Even what is often regarded as a good result – a correlation of 0.3 – leaves 90 per cent of the criterion variance unexplained.

There are really two different arguments in this interpretation of correlations. From a theoretical point of view the explanation of only 10 per cent of variance is not impressive. Even for the practitioner it does not permit accurate prediction. However, the argument runs, 10 per cent is better than zero, and if other variables can be used in the practical prediction of neurosis or job success some useful outcome may emerge.

In summary, therefore, it can be seen that where predictive validity is high, as it is with intelligence tests, it can be used as powerful evidence to support the validity of a test. However, often it is not possible to set up such a criterion, and even where it is, results are rarely unequivocal.

Construct validity

I hope it is clear from these discussions of validity that there are considerable problems in demonstrating the validity of a psychometric test. The fact is that it is not easy to assess what a test measures. Cronbach and Meehl (1955) introduced, accordingly, the concept of construct validity. They accept all these problems and difficulties in establishing the validity of a test. In their view the test variable should be regarded as a construct, and thus validity is demonstrated if one can show that the results obtained with the test fit the construct. Thus for construct validity a whole pattern and mosaic of test results is presented. Then there is the admittedly subjective task of deciding whether these results fit the construct or not.

Usually a set of hypotheses is set out, derived from the psychological characteristics of the variable measured by the test. Thus in the case of an intelligence test the following hypotheses would be put to the test:

- The test should correlate at least 0.8 with other intelligence tests.
- The test should correlate around 0.5 with other tests of ability.

- The test should have very low or zero correlations with most personality tests.
- The test should correlate about 0.3 with measures of authoritarian personality.
- There should be positive correlations with academic success.
- These correlations should be greater for some subjects (physics, Greek) than for others (dance studies, sociology).
- There should be correlations of around 0.3 with job success.
- Scores should be higher for the occupants of some jobs than for others.
- Scores should show a heritability of around 0.7.

All these hypotheses can be derived from the research on intelligence (e.g. Saklofske and Zeidner, 1995) and will be fully scrutinised in Chapter 6. Note that construct validity includes all the forms of validity which we have so far discussed. It is obvious that if all these hypotheses were clearly confirmed it would be good supporting evidence that the test was an intelligence test, or measured intelligence as it was conceived in research into human abilities. However, if the results were not so clear-cut and if it were not so easy to establish clear hypotheses about results, as is usually the case in the field of personality and motivation, then construct validity would become equivocal and subjective.

Content validity

In the field of abilities, content validity is sometimes claimed for tests. An obvious example could be found in music or medicine, and some medical exams are of this kind. Thus an item might be used which requires the candidate to list eight symptoms of tuberculosis. The examiners require students to know these symptoms, and thus this item has content validity, as would a test constructed from such items. If the candidates respond to these items correctly, they know what they are required to know. The test is, *per se*, valid. However, it is usually only in the ability field and especially concerning attainments, which can be clearly defined, that content validity is useful or applicable.

Conclusion concerning validity of psychometric tests

From this discussion of the main ways in which psychological tests are validated, it is clear that validity is ultimately a matter of judgement. Only in cases where there are clear and replicable results of which the psychological significance is a matter of no disagreement can a test be said to be completely valid. The best intelligence tests approach this criterion, yet even with these there are some psychologists who would dispute that what they measure is closely aligned with what is generally thought of as intelligence (e.g. Gardner, 1983).

Discriminatory power

Test constructors are keen to make their tests as discriminating as possible. This is measured by Ferguson's delta (Ferguson, 1949). If all subjects obtain the same score on a test its discriminatory power is zero. Since the point of psychometric testing is to understand individual differences, such a test is valueless. The maximum discriminatory power that a test could have is achieved if the same number of subjects score each possible score; that is, a horizontal distribution of scores is obtained. This is, needless to say, as unlikely as its opposite. Nevertheless, a good test will show a large scatter of scores, and when it does so, delta approaches 1. Since the maximum discrimination a dichotomously scored item can make is to have a 50 per cent response rate, test constructors aim to include a good proportion of such items in their tests, thus making the test highly discriminating. Discriminatory power – the ability to differentiate among those taking the test – is one of the advantages of psychometric testing compared with rating scales. It is relatively easy to rate subjects into three categories, with the middle category the largest, but to go beyond this is difficult, and nine categories is about the maximum possible (Vernon, 1963). For these reasons discriminatory power is regarded as an important characteristic of good tests.

Summary: the characteristics of good psychometric tests

From our discussion so far it will be useful for the subsequent arguments of this chapter briefly to summarise the qualities which are possessed by good psychometric tests:

- high reliability, test–retest consistency and internal consistency: 0.7 is a minimum figure;
- low standard error of measurement;
- good evidence of validity, especially construct validity; and
- high discriminatory power.

Psychometrists argue (e.g. Cattell, 1981) that with high-quality psychometric tests of this kind it is possible to construct a genuinely scientific quantified psychology, similar to the natural sciences in its rigorous quantification. However, some distinguished scientists, of whom Medawar (1984) is perhaps the best known, have claimed that psychometric testing is pseudo-science (although it must be borne in mind that Medawar's knowledge in the field is not confirmed by publications of any kind). For this reason, in the final section of this chapter I want to scrutinise the truth of claims such as these by comparing psychometric measurement with that in the natural sciences, which, as we have seen early in this chapter, appears to differ from it in certain ways.

Before I do this, however, I shall discuss the standardisation of psychometric tests. This is not an intrinsic characteristic of tests but, as shall be seen, standardisation is necessary to make sense of them. It is discussed here because it is highly relevant to any comparison with the quantification of the natural sciences.

Norms and the standardisation of psychometric tests

The difficulty with psychometric tests is that scores, *per se*, have no meaning. Thus if I score 23 on the N scale of the EPQ the significance of the score, whether it is high, low or average, is impossible to determine. For this reason, for every psychometric test norms have to be established; that is, the test has to be standardised. Norms are defined as the scores of a particular group which may then be used for comparison. It should be obvious that norms, if they are to be of any value, should be based on large and representative samples. Depending on the purposes of a test, norms may be set up for the general population or for special groups. For example, if a test is designed for clinical psychology, it makes sense to have norms for the relevant clinical or psychiatric groups, perhaps obsessionals or anxiety neurotics. If the test is an ability test for children, norms should be established for 6-month age-groups, or there will be serious inaccuracy.

How standardisation is to be carried out, the numbers required for reliable norms, the methods to ensure a representative sample, the form the norms should take are not relevant to the arguments of this chapter. Details may be found in Kline (1995) or Nunnally and Bernstein, (1994). Some points should be noted:

- Normalisation is essentially a scaling procedure: raw scores on the test are converted to the normalised scores.
- The scaling depends on the scores of the normative groups.
- Intelligence tests are usually given norms which are normally distributed with a mean of 100 and a standard deviation of 15. From the area under the normal curve it can be seen that approximately 68 per cent of scores fall between 85 and 115 and 95 per cent between 85 and 130.
- Often tests are given standardised scores with the same agreed mean, standard deviation and distribution (normal). This ensures that there can be meaningful comparison between different tests because identical scores are equivalent, representing the same point in the distribution. This, of course, is not the case with raw scores or with standard scores with different means and standard deviations. A well-known example of this can be found in the intelligence tests of the Mensa society. Their selection score is 140. However, their test has a mean of 100 and a standard deviation of 20. Thus 140 on their test is equivalent to 130 on most intelligence tests.

Conclusions concerning standardisation

Enough has been said to show that the interpretation of psychometric tests depends upon the establishment of norms. On their own, scores are impossible to interpret. This is because, from the nature of their construction and perhaps from the nature of psychological variables, there is no true zero. This is certainly an important difference from at least some of the measures in the natural sciences, and it is to a consideration of these which we now turn.

Measurement in the natural sciences

Earlier in this chapter I pointed out some obvious differences between psychological measurement and measures of length and weight. In both these latter cases it is clear what is being measured and there are well-known units of measurement in the scales. However, these are somewhat intuitive differences, and the nature of scientific measurement needs to be accurately characterised in order that it may be compared with that of psychometric tests.

Fortunately this task has been greatly eased by work directly precisely at this problem by Michell (e.g. 1990, 1994a and particularly 1997). His arguments go to the philosophical and mathematical basis of measurement and are complex but I shall summarise them here as clearly as possible. It should be pointed out that there is a body of previous work on measurement theory which makes similar points to those of Michell, for example that of Luce and colleagues (Krantz *et al.*, 1971) and the work of Coombs (e.g. Coombs *et al.*, 1970). I have summarised the recent paper by Michell (1997) because it succinctly makes the critical points, which tie in also with the analysis of the scientific method in Chapter 1. In the conclusion of this chapter, I shall link them together to form a critique of psychometrics as a scientific endeavour which will allow us to evaluate what has been achieved in its various branches and to provide a basis for further research and development.

I shall summarise the main points of Michell's arguments under a number of heads, to aid clarity.

- The scientific enterprise of which measurement is an essential part, if it is to be rational, requires the realist position, that there is a world out there, as has been argued in Chapter 1.
- Some attributes, quantities, e.g. length, are measurable; that is, they have a quantitative structure. Magnitudes (specific instances of a quantity) are measurable because, on account of this structure, they stand in ratios to one another, ratios which can be expressed as real numbers.
- Holder (1901), cited by Michell (1997), argued, on the basis of seven axioms, that if an attribute has a quantitative structure, in principle it is measurable. He demonstrated that for any two magnitudes x and y, the ratio of x to y is a positive real number and is the measure of x in units of y. Thus scientific measurement requires that we discover the additive structure of the attribute in order that we can calculate the ratios between the magnitudes.
- Thus to quote Michell (1997), 'Scientific measurement is properly defined as the estimation or discovery of the relation of some magnitude of a quantitative unit to a unit of the same attribute.' Given the quantitative structure

of an attribute it is a mathematical theorem that magnitudes of a quantity stand in numerical relations one to another. Measurement is the discovery or estimation of these relations. This is the logic of quantitative science, according to the arguments of Michell, and it is difficult to refute their logic.

- The claim that an attribute is quantitative is a hypothesis. There is no logical necessity that an attribute should be quantitative; the hypothesis that it is so is empirical. It requires evidence to make the case. Thus there are two tasks for any quantitative science: to demonstrate that the attribute is quantitative and to devise procedures to measure the magnitudes. Failure in the first task means that subsequent measurement tasks are simply speculative and cannot be called scientific. This has been called the representational problem, since it is necessary that the measurement system be shown to represent some relationship in the real world (Coombs *et al.*, 1970).

Measurement in psychology

Michell, having defined the nature of scientific measurement, then proceeds to examine, from this standpoint, measurement in psychology, which I have described in some detail. He claims that psychological measurement is quite different from the scientific on a number of grounds which I shall summarise below and which, in the light of my description of psychometric testing, can be seen to be largely true. But before I discuss these differences I want to make one further point which leads to considerable confusion but which is actually somewhat trivial. In the example of length, the evidence that the attribute is additive is physically obvious, direct: one can lay inch rods end on end and so on, for any but enormous or minute lengths. However, for many well-accepted scientific variables, e.g. density, the evidence that they are quantitative is indirect. Nevertheless, it must be noted, there is evidence.

- As we have seen, psychometrics, as a subject, is concerned with the measurement of psychological traits in the field of ability, personality and motivation. Psychometrics assumes, therefore, that these traits are measurable and have a quantitative structure, although no evidence is usually present that this is the case. Thus one of the tasks of quantitative science is simply ignored or assumed as obviously true. For example, Thorndike (1919) claimed that if something exists it exists in some quantity and can thus be measured.
- Given that psychological attributes are quantitative in structure, Michell (1997), who surveyed a large number of psychology textbooks, argues that the definition of measurement used in psychology is unlike that in the natural sciences. Essentially psychologists follow Stevens (1946) and define measurement as the assignment of numerals to objects or events (e.g. behaviour, attributes, responses) according to a rule. However, as Ellis (1966) points out, this definition is clearly flawed. It is possible to assign

objects a number by a rule – for example, taking the numbers of all the houses I have ever lived in and adding 1 to them – without this being measurement. As Michell stresses, this psychological definition is quite different from the scientific: the discovery or estimation of the ratio of magnitudes of a quantity.

Furthermore, as Michell points out, these same texts rarely discuss the fact that before measurement it is essential that the attribute to be measured is shown to be quantitative in structure. It is Stevens' definition, taught to most psychologists, which has led to the belief that all that is involved in measurement and scientific measurement is the invention of some procedure to assign numbers.

Michell (1997) then tries to demonstrate, through a study of the development of quantitative psychology, both psychophysics and psychometrics, how this dichotomy between psychological and scientific measurement came about. An important influence was the need and desire to show that psychology was a scientific discipline and one that could be applied.

Spearman (1904), for example, wrote a paper on intelligence which has become the basis of psychometrics. He showed how in the field of human abilities factor analysis could be used as a method of simplification. His methods, developed, of course, are still central to psychometrics and we shall examine them carefully in the next chapter. However, as Michell, points out, Spearman did not question the assumption that abilities were quantitative variables. His great contribution lay in the analysis of the data obtained from measurement. He believed that his factor analysis of abilities would prove fruitful in applied psychology. (Despite the unfounded nature of this assumption, his belief was correct. In occupational selection the intelligence test is still a powerful tool (Furnham, 1995), probably the most powerful (Schmidt and Hunter, 1998). But this is another point.)

Thorndike (1919), another of the pioneers in psychometrics, knew that measurement in psychology was different from that in physics because the former was relative and was not a ratio scale involving units of measurement. However, he claimed that relative measurement could be no less precise than scientific ratio scales, and this hopeful assertion quickly became the dogma of psychology. As Michell (1997) shows from a study of journal articles from the end of the First to the end of the Second World War, psychological measurement assumed that the assignment of numbers to a variable by a rule, usually counting responses, constituted scientific measurement, with no questions asked about additivity or the quantitative structure of the variables. Psychometricians regarded themselves as applied scientists predicting, by the use of tests, academic success, clinical outcomes and occupational success. However, as Michell argues, even if these tests could predict, their use was not the application of science since it did not involve the application of a body of knowledge to solve a problem. The fact is that empirical work, *per se*, is not applied science. At best it provides hypotheses for further study.

Psychometrists up to this time had used their tests in applied settings and in the development of theory with no little success. Thus it had been shown that g was a good predictor of academic and occupational success and that in addition it had a considerable genetic determination. Thus the scientific shortcomings of the tests were simply not called into question until the Ferguson Committee (1940) claimed that the scales used in psychophysics were not scientific in the sense we have described. This brought a reply from the great Harvard psychophysicist Stevens (1946, 1951) which, Michell argues, appeared to demonstrate that psychophysical measurement was scientific. His arguments were also absorbed into psychometrics so that the objections which have been raised in this section were never again considered. These arguments of Stevens will now be examined.

Stevens' defence of psychological measurement

Here for the sake of brevity I shall merely summarise the points.

- Stevens utilised representational theories of measurement which postulate that measurement is the numerical representation of empirical relationships. In this way measurement no longer had to be additive. Stevens (1951) claimed that measurement essentially implied isomorphism between objects and events and the properties of numerical systems. As Michell (1997) argues, this was the basis of Stevens' measurement scales (nominal, ordinal, interval and ratio), which have entered into every text on psychology and measurement.
- However, as Michell points out, there is now a further problem. If measurement represents an empirical relational structure and this is viewed realistically as independent of the observer, then it is necessary to demonstrate, before measurement, that such a structure exists. This is a severe problem and has rarely been done.
- Stevens, Michell argues, avoided this difficulty: he constructed an operational interpretation of representational theory. Thus according to Bridgman (1927) the meaning of a concept is identical with the operations used to identify it, a form of logical positivism. If the meaning of a concept arises from the operations by which it is identified, it follows that the empirical relations which are represented numerically in measurement must be defined by their identifying operations.
- However, there is an unfortunate incoherence in this line of argument. It is normal to distinguish between an operation and a relation, for example the relation that A is longer than B and the operation of measuring A and B. Usually one would say that measuring A as longer than B depended upon A's being longer than B. However, Stevens' operational definition would force one to argue that the measurement and its results are all that is meant in saying that A is longer than B. Thus by such operational arguments any measurement can be taken as defining the relation and representing it.

Hence it can be argued, as Stevens did, that measurement is the assignment of numerals to objects or events according to rules. However, this operationalist approach to representation denies the realism of the external world and, as has been discussed in Chapter 1, science without a realist view makes no sense. If the subject matter of science consists of the operations used to study it, then, as Michell points out, there is no it to study. Scientists simply study their operations. Science is no longer trying to determine the truth about the external world.

Summary and conclusions

The argument raised by Michell can be briefly summarised. Scientific measurement of any attribute entails, first, that the attribute is shown to possess a quantitative structure. If this is the case, then scientific measures of the attribute must be addititive and be ratio scales with a known unit of measurement. Psychological tests are not of this kind. Few are ratio scales, and they are simply assumed to be interval scales, although the units of measurement are not stated. This is because in psychology measurement is defined, on the basis of Stevens' arguments, as the assignment of numbers to objects by a rule, a definition which in its deployment of operationalism denies the reality of the external world and is not coherent with the scientific endeavour.

Some comments about the arguments of Michell (1997) are necessary. The fundamental and extensive measurement typified in the measurement of length is not the only kind of fundamental measurement possible. As Krantz *et al.* (1971) argue, sometimes the attributes we wish to measure have a different kind of internal structure with no obvious extensive concatenation. Density is an example of just such an attribute. Objects of different densities when combined do not yield one object of a density which is the sum of their densities. However, density is measured in terms of a relationship between two other fundamental measures: mass and volume. Such measurement is referred to as derived measurement.

In addition to derived measurement there is additive conjoint measurement, developed by Luce and Tukey (1964) especially for the social sciences, where, as we have seen, fundamental measurement is difficult. This provides a method for the demonstration of quantitative structure where physical concatenation is impossible. This is obviously important, since if scales can be developed to fit this model, then we have scientific measures and evidence of the quantitative nature of the relevant variables. Furthermore, there is a special method of psychological test construction – Rasch scaling (Rasch, 1960) – which is of this type, and this will be examined in Chapter 4, together with the more general implications of conjoint measurement for psychology. Clearly, additive conjoint measurement must be described.

Additive conjoint measurement

Luce and Tukey (1964) provide the full, logical and mathematical rationale for conjoint additive measurement. However, this is, for the non-mathematician, a difficult paper and for my description I am indebted to Michell (1990).

As mentioned, conjoint measurement makes possible the establishment of quantitative structure from the ordinal relationships upon a variable, relationships which psychology can establish. To clarify this abstract definition I shall illustrate conjoint measurement from a paper by Stankov and Cregan (1993), who attempted to establish the quantitative properties of a measure of intelligence. In this paper, the intelligence test was a letter series in which subjects had to complete a series of letters. The simplest example of conjoint measurement is that where P (the variable) $= f(A, X)$, where A and X are independent and f is some mathematical function. In our example A was working memory placekeepers, a factor known to affect letter series performance. This refers to how many letters one has to hold in short-term memory to work out the series: the more it is necessary to hold, the harder the series. The X variable was motivation. This was changed by asking subjects to complete the series at their own pace and then 50 per cent and 75 per cent more quickly. Thus performance in letter series was a function of two independent variables, motivation and working memory placekeepers.

DEMONSTRATION OF QUANTITATIVE STRUCTURE

The letter series test is quantitative if certain conditions are fulfilled. In this paper there were three conditions for working memory placekeepers and three for motivation. If these are designated W1,2,3 (in order of complexity) and M1,2,3 (in order of speed, i.e. difficulty), we can create a nine-cell matrix: W1,2,3 on the horizontal axis and M1,2,3 on the vertical. In each cell the means of the scores for each condition are inserted. Then the variable letter series completion is quantitative if the following conditions are met.

Single cancellation   The single cancellation condition is established if the cells in all rows and in all columns are ordered in exactly the same way. This is sometimes referred to as independence.

Double Cancellation

　If M2W1 is equal to or greater than M1W2
　and M3W2 is equal to or greater than M2W3
　then M3W1 is equal to or greater than M1W3.

In any three-by-three matrix there are six such independent double cancellation tests and all must be met.

If these two conditions of single and double cancellation are met in the case of three-by-three matrices, as here, then this is sufficient to show that the variable, series completion, is additive. Although the satisfaction of the single and double cancellation conditions is sufficient to demonstrate additive structure in three-by-three matrices, for more complex matrices other conditions have to be met.

Solvability   Solvability means that any value of the quantitative variable must be able to be derived from the function of the two variables, in this instance motivation and working memory placekeepers.

Archimedean condition   The Archemedian condition states that no value of a quantitative variable must be infinitely larger than any other value.

It is pointed out by Michell (1990) that these last two conditions are not directly testable, unlike single and double cancellation. However, if higher-order cancellation conditions are fulfilled then it can be inferred that these conditions are also met. In this way, by meeting the conditions of conjoint additive measurement it can be shown that a variable is quantitative and that the measure possesses additivity. Finally, it should be mentioned that Michell (1990) demonstrates that fundamental, extensive measurement is a special case of conjoint additive measurement.

Conclusions concerning the work of Michell

I think it has to be accepted that psychometric tests, even the best, are not the same as the measures used in the natural sciences. They are not ratio scales and they do not have units of measurement. I think also that Stevens' operational definitions of variables can be antithetical to the realistic view implied by science but are not necessarily so, as will be argued later in the chapter. So where does this leave psychometrics and psychology as a science?

This book is concerned with psychometrics as the basis for a scientific psychology. Since it has continued beyond this point it is obvious that I do not believe these arguments to be fatal, as I shall now demonstrate. As regards psychophysics I shall ignore that aspect of the argument as not relevant.

To make my points I shall use intelligence and intelligence testing as my examples all through this concluding section, but it has to be emphasised that these same arguments apply to any good psychometric test.

1   Psychometric tests are not truly scientific. Even if this is accepted, the fact remains that intelligence testing has considerable predictive power in applied psychology. This fact alone deserves further study and requires explanation. Indeed, all the facts suggest that what intelligence tests measure is close to what is conceived of as intelligence. Thus what is now required – and this applies to all spheres of psychometric testing – is that better tests, i.e. tests more like those in the natural sciences, be developed. Whether

conjoint measurement is a satisfactory alternative to fundamental measurement is discussed in Chapter 4.

2   There has been no prior investigation of the quantitative structure of intelligence. This is a genuine flaw in the scientific process. However, given that without measurement this is hard to do, it is reasonable to assume that the attribute is quantitative, on the grounds that measurement represents empirical relationships in the real world, unless this obviously becomes untenable. Indeed, as Jensen (1980) has argued, this is to some extent the case. Thus he has attempted to justify intelligence tests on the grounds that their scores are normally distributed, as is to be expected on theoretical grounds. In fact this particular argument does not seem strong since the distribution of test scores depends upon the selection of items, but in principle, at least, here is an attempt to investigate the quantitative nature (rather than the structure) of the variable. In any case it is a reasonable scientific procedure to assume quantitative structure until the assumption becomes untenable (see Cattell, 1957). The place of conjoint measurement in this endeavour will be examined in Chapter 10.

3   There are problems concerning the mathematics of non-ratio scales. Although it is true that the power of the natural sciences has sprung from the mathematical properties of their quantitative measurements, as psychometrists have demonstrated (e.g. Nunnally and Bernstein, 1994), powerful multivariate analytic procedures can be used without contravening their assumptions. Thus what results have been obtained are worthy of consideration.

4   There is a pragmatic argument. In Chapter 1 it was shown that it is not easy to justify the scientific method except by the argument that it works well. Problems of induction and the notion of truth still engulf it. The same pragmatic approach can be applied to psychometrics. Despite the measurement problems, there are too many solid, replicable findings which make good psychological sense for them to be dismissed as worthless. It would be like ignoring the findings of earlier astronomers because their instruments were imperfect.

Final conclusion from Chapters 1 and 2

In this second chapter it has been shown that the best psychological tests are internally consistent and reliable over time. They can discriminate well among subjects, compared with rating scales, and can be valid in that they correlate with other similar tests, give reasonable predictions. In terms of construct validity, they generally perform as one might expect them to if they were valid. Almost always they require norms because they are not ratio scales with true zeros. Most good psychometric tests are constructed according to the classical theory of test error. Thus they measure true and error variance and, the more reliable they are, the less error variance contaminates their scores. Test constructors also aim to make their scales univariate, measuring only one variable, as far as is possible, and the best psychometric tests again possess this important characteristic.

Superficially it is obvious that such scales differ from some scientific measures, of the simplest kind, such as measures of length and weight, in that these unquestionably measure what they measure and can be shown to be accurate because they agree with other purported measures of those variables. However, a careful study of what precisely is entailed in scientific measurement, as described by Holder (1901), indicates that these measures possess additivity and are ratio scales with a clear unit of measurement and a true zero. Other scientific measures, but indirect ones, such as those of density, also can be shown to possess these characteristics and it is these which allow the elegant mathematical procedures which have led to such progress in the natural sciences.

However, there is a further characteristic of measurement in the natural sciences which finds no counterpart in psychometrics or psychological measurement and it is this defect which, perhaps, differentiates them most sharply. In the scientific model it is required that the variable under consideration be shown to be quantitative in structure. That a variable is thus quantitative is a hypothesis in itself, and there is no a priori, logical necessity that variables should be quantitative. Scientific measurement, it was argued by Michell (1990, 1997), is defined as the estimation or discovery of a ratio of some magnitude of a quantitative attribute to a unit of the same attribute, a definition implicit in the structure that quantitative attributes are held to possess.

This contrasts with the definition of measurement in psychology, one most fully developed by Stevens in an attempt to answer criticisms of the unscientific nature of psychological measurement, especially that it was not necessarily additive. In psychology, measurement is, according to Stevens, the assignment of numbers to an object or process according to a rule. This stems from his argument that measurement was the numerical representation of empirical relations in the real world, and from this Stevens asserted that scales need not be additive or ratio scales; interval scales were satisfactory. These relations, however, did not have to be shown to be numerical because, by his operational account of representational theory, measurement and representation could not be separated. However, as Michell points out, this is incoherent in that it denies external reality, which is, as was shown in Chapter 1, a necessity for the scientific endeavour. Without it the only subject of measurement is measurement itself.

It has to be concluded that Michell (1997) is correct and psychometric measurement is not the same as measurement in the quantitative sciences. However, this does not mean that psychometrics should be dismissed as worthless. On the contrary, the best scales have been shown to be effective in prediction and to have a considerable genetic determination. It is the task of psychometrics, therefore, to use these findings as a basis for further research, to discover more precisely what they do measure and to attempt to provide measurements, psychometric tests, which could be classified as scientific in the sense used in this chapter. Conjoint additive measurement was suggested by Michell (1990) as an answer to these problems. Its effectiveness will be discussed in Chapter 4.

However, there is remarkable similarity to our conclusions to our first chapter. There it was shown that while many psychologists are keen to make psychology a science like any other of the established natural sciences there are, in fact, problems with the scientific method: problems of induction, and problems with the notion of an external reality, which is central to science. If realism is denied there is no point in science, and even if it is accepted, there are problems as to whether it is knowable, the intuitive notion of the correspondence theory of truth having come under fire. In that chapter we showed that it is not philosophically implausible to adopt the scientific method, entailing realism and the correspondence theory of truth, although there was no a priori necessity that science would end up with the truth, as some psychologists seem to assume. Indeed, one of the best supports for the scientific method comes from its achievements in the natural sciences. However, this does not mean that it would necessarily work in psychology, especially since psychology's subject matter and consequent problems of measurement are so different.

Thus in Chapter 1 we saw that the scientific method is not bound to produce the truth, even in the natural sciences, let alone psychology, but that there is no sound argument against its use in psychology. It is the best, though not a perfect, method. In Chapter 2 I showed that even the best psychometric measurement falls short of scientific quantification. It fails to demonstrate that the attributes it measures are quantitative, and the tests themselves are quite different from scientific measures, having no additivity, not being ratio scales, with no units of measurements or true zeros. However, again it was argued that all is not lost. The best tests clearly measure some important psychological variables, despite their scientific imperfections. The task of psychometrics is to explicate what these are and to improve the quality of measurement until it equals that of the natural sciences. What can be concluded from these first two chapters is this: the use of the scientific method and psychometric quantification is no guarantee that we will get at the truth. Rather it is necessary to realise that the scientific method is the best we know and that it is important to develop theories so that we can use deductive logic which is impeccable, and improve our measurement techniques. As it stands, psychometrics is not yet the equal of the best in physics.

3

FACTOR ANALYSIS AND PSYCHOMETRIC MEASUREMENT

In Chapter 2 I showed that even the best psychometric tests, which have good evidence for reliability and validity, such as intelligence tests, and which perform well in applied settings, fall far short of the precision of the measures used in the natural sciences. I argued that psychometric tests would have to be considerably improved before any true psychological science based upon measurement could be developed. I also argued that the best tests, although imperfect, had yielded data which should not be abandoned.

In this chapter I shall examine and scrutinise the principles and methods of factor analysis. This is because factor analysis is the statistical method used for the construction of many of the best psychometric tests, although there are other methods of test construction. Furthermore, factor analysis is the statistical method which was developed for psychometrics and which distinguishes this field of psychology from most others. It has been used to establish psychometric theories of personality and ability, as well as to establish the relevant tests, and it is further used in the psychometric application of these tests in clinical, educational and occupational psychology.

However, there is a further, perhaps more important, reason for a careful scrutiny of factor analysis. As Cattell (1978) has demonstrated, many factor analyses are technically flawed, flaws which render their results of little scientific value. Indeed, Cattell has argued that this is the main cause of the striking failures of factor analysts to agree among themselves concerning the number and nature of factors, especially in the field of personality. To understand and evaluate critically the findings of psychometrics, it is essential to understand the principles of factor analysis and the limitations of its methods.

Factor analysis and quantified attributes

There were two objections raised by Michell (1997) to current psychological measurement: that the tests themselves were flawed and that it was simply assumed that the attributes to be measured were quantitative. This second point is particularly relevant to the technique of factor analysis and it will be examined before I describe factor analytic methods.

In a critique of the article by Michell, Laming (1997), with the traditional Cantabrian opposition to factor analysis, has described the factor analysis of psychometric tests of intelligence as a nonsense. It assumes that the normalised scores are normally distributed, an assumption which Laming regards as deceitful. However, as Cattell (e.g. 1978) has argued, it is perfectly reasonable, in terms of scientific methods, to proceed as if intelligence and personality scores were normally distributed until forced to abandon the hypothesis. The fact that resulting factors appear to be meaningful and allow predictions and have high heritabilities all suggests that the assumptions of normality are not unfounded. Furthermore, since there are good reasons to expect that intelligence and personality factors would be normally distributed because they are conceived as polygenic in the sense of being determined by a combination of genes and environmental factors, the claims of Laming as to the nonsensical and deceitful nature of factor analysis are fanciful. He has attacked and destroyed an old, Bartlettian straw schema. The only argument in support of his case would be the one that the scores on intelligence tests are normally distributed. This, of course, is simply a function of the test items, but no reputable psychometrist makes any such argument. Thus, in conclusion, while it is true that factor analysts do assume normal distributions of the variables, they do so explicitly and on reasonable grounds, holding the hypothesis provisionally, until refuted, exactly as with all hypotheses in science.

Factor analysis

There is some argument as to who was the true originator of factor analysis. However, beyond all dispute is the fact that Spearman (1904) first used the technique in the analysis of human abilities and intelligence, in a paper which has already been referred to. This was truly a landmark publication, in that it demonstrated the power of the statistical method, which in almost a hundred years has been extensively developed but is still employed in the analysis of psychometric test scores and the development of psychometric tests. Factor analysis is essential to the understanding of psychometrics, yet it is sad to say that even now the majority of psychologists have not mastered even the basics of the method. As Cattell (1981) claimed, too many psychologists are refugees from the hard sciences. This would be bad enough, but the advent of powerful computers and efficient, relatively user-friendly software has meant that it is a simple matter to factor analyse huge sets of data without any understanding of the technique whatever. As an examiner of higher degrees and a referee for journal articles I regularly see factor analyses which are so flawed by technical error that they are worthless, and results misinterpreted through failure to understand the method. Here I shall keep the mathematics to the absolutely necessary minimum, but if the basic logic of the mathematics of factor analysis is understood, the whole technique becomes comprehensible.

There have been many good books on factor analysis but among the best are Harman (1976) and Cattell (1978). Kline (1994a) has written one of the simplest accounts, with the mathematics made as easy as was possible, while at the other end of mathematical sophistication is the excellent book by Krzanowski (1988) which relates factor analysis to other multivariate techniques, some of which will be briefly discussed later in this book where they are particularly relevant.

Since in discussing factor analysis it is necessary to use some technical terms, these will now be set out and defined.

Definitions of factor analytic terms

- *Confirmatory factor analysis.* Here factor analysis is used to confirm a hypothesis. For example, the expected factor loadings (q.v.) are put into a target matrix and confirmatory analysis aims to fit this matrix as closely as possible.
- *Eigenvalues* or *latent roots.* These indicate the size of the factors. Since each variable has an eigenvalue of 1, only factors with eigenvalues greater than 1 are of any interest.
- *Exploratory factor analysis.* This was the original use for factor analysis. A large matrix of correlations is factored in order to account mathematically for the correlations in terms of a smaller number of factors. In the terminology of matrix algebra, factor analysis is a procedure for reducing the rank of a matrix, e.g. explaining the correlations between 100 variables in terms of 10 factors. This is to be contrasted with *confirmatory analysis* (q.v.).
- *Factor.* A factor is a linear sum of variables. These combinations mathematically account for the correlations in the correlation matrix, and may be thought of as constructs, dimensions or vectors.
- *General factor.* This is a factor common to all variables in the matrix. General intelligence, g, is an example of such a factor.
- *Group factor.* This is a factor common to a group of variables in the matrix.
- *Specific factor.* This is a factor loading on one variable only.
- *Factor loading.* A factor loading is the correlation (q.v.) of a factor and a variable. In some circumstances it is also the beta weight (q.v.) for predicting the variable. Factors are identified by their loadings.
- *Factor pattern.* The factor pattern is the set of factor loadings as a whole – the weights on the factors to predict the variables. This, in orthogonal solutions, is the same as the factor structure. However, in oblique solutions the pattern differs from the structure, and the higher the correlations between the factors the greater is this difference.
- *Factor structure.* The factor structure is the set of factor loadings, as a whole – the correlations of the variables with the factors.
- *Oblique factors.* Oblique factors are correlated together. In a graphical representation of factors the correlation is given by the cosine of the angle

between the factors. This definition will be clear after reading the relevant text.

- *Orthogonal factors.* These factors are uncorrelated. In a graphical representation the factors are at right angles. As with oblique factors, this definition will become clear.
- *Principal axes* or *principal factor analysis.* This is the standard factor analysis procedure in which common factor variance is distinguished from *error variance* (q.v., below).This is achieved by inserting into the diagonals of the correlation matrix (the correlation of variable 1 with 1, 2 with 2 and so on) not 1 but some other appropriate coefficients. But see *principal component analysis.*
- *Principal component analysis.* In this 1s are placed in the diagonals of the correlation matrix. Principal components analysis accounts for all the variance in the matrix, including error variance.
- *Primary factors* or *first-order factors.* These are the factors obtained from factor analysis of the correlation matrix. See *second-order factors.*
- *Rotation of factors.* In the graphical representation of factors as axes on a graph, these can be rotated relative to each other. The factor loadings change, after each rotation, but are mathematically equivalent. Thus in factor analysis there is an infinity of equivalent solutions.
- *Second-order factors.* These are the factors of the correlations between the first-order factors. These are necessarily broader factors than first-orders, whose variance they account for.
- *Simple-structure rotation.* Because there is an infinity of possible rotations it is usual to choose the simplest – simple structure being essentially that rotation which yields factors each with a few high loadings and many zero or near zero loadings. Such a structure is easier to identify than less simple rotations.
- *Beta weights.* Beta weights are the optimal weightings for variables to maximise their multiple correlation with the factor. If factors are uncorrelated, these beta weights are the same as the correlations between variables and factors.
- *Correlations.* The correlation coefficient is an index of agreement between two sets of scores. It runs from 1, perfect agreement, to 0, no agreement, to -1, where there is complete disagreement. The set of correlations between variables forms the correlation matrix, which, in psychometrics, is the usual basis for factor analysis.
- *Variance.* Variance is an index of variability in a set of measurements.
- *Error variance.* Error variance is that proportion of the variance which is attributable to random error.

These definitions, some of which may seem obscure, will become clear when they enter our discussion of factor analysis.

Reasons for using factor analysis in psychometrics

The experimental univariate approach

In the standard classical, univariate experimental method, the effects of variables are examined one at a time. For example, if light levels are considered to affect speed of reading, reading speed will be compared at various light settings, all other things being held constant. Any differences in reading speed in the groups will be attributable to differences in light levels. It might also be thought that typeface was a determinant of reading speed and the same text could be read with different typefaces. Analyses of variance allow more than one variable to be compared and it is possible to design an experiment in which the effects of light level and typeface are examined together. With this design, interactions between typefaces and light levels can be investigated.

However, only a moment's thought suggests that even such a bivariate design seriously underestimates the numbers of variables and the complexity of their interactions which are likely to affect reading speed, thus rendering the design weak. For example, in addition to typefaces and light intensity we could investigate spacing of lines of print, margin sizes, quality of paper, width of paper, difficulty of the text, familiarity of the text, experience of reading aloud, intelligence of the subjects, age of the subjects, education and so on. Furthermore, the investigation of each one of these variables on its own is unlikely to be satisfactory. It is likely that there are many interactions and that some variables are more important than others.

Although in principle it might be possible to arrange all these variables into an enormously complex analysis of variance design, the interpretation of significant interactions and, if these are present, the main effects becomes impracticable. A radically different design is required.

Multivariate analyses

Multivariate analyses are statistical methods which can deal with a large number of variables simultaneously. Hence, as Cattell (1957) pointed out, they are ideally suited to psychology, which, unlike the natural sciences, has this problem of the complexity and interactions of the variables within its sphere. It is quite rare for one variable to operate alone. Factor analysis is one of such multivariate methods. It was essentially developed for the needs of psychometrics and is so suited to the subject and has been so widely used that it must be discussed on its own. Once factor analysis is understood, other multivariate methods, of which some will be briefly described, are easy to grasp. As Krzanowski (1988) has demonstrated, multivariate methods are highly similar to each other. In brief, it is argued that the multiplicity of variables affecting most human behaviour makes multivariate methods a necessity for the analysis of data. Of these methods factor analysis is the most widely used in psychometrics and is central to the subject. Thus it will be examined in some detail.

Aims of exploratory factor analysis

The aim of exploratory factor analysis, as it is most commonly used in psychometrics, is to simplify a correlation matrix. Suppose that we have administered 100 tests to a sample of subjects and correlated the scores together. This gives us 100×100 correlations. Even the finest human brain finds that amount of information too much to hold at any one time, thus making it impossible to interpret the correlation matrix. Even the small correlation matrix in Table 3.1 makes it clear how difficult it is to grasp just sixty-four correlations. Although this is an artificial example for explanatory purposes it is not unlike what is frequently obtained in the analysis of school subjects and it illustrates why factor analysis is so useful. A brief inspection of this correlation matrix immediately raises several questions: Why are all the correlations positive? Why are some correlations larger than others? Why do the correlations fall into groups, at least to some extent? Thus the verbal subjects tend to correlate together and so do the science subjects. Geography correlates moderately with most of the subjects while Latin and Greek cut across sciences and arts. Of course this is a deliberately simplified example. It is not difficult to guess that these results could be explained in terms of three factors, intelligence, verbal ability and mathematical ability. Indeed, a factor analysis of these correlations might well reveal such factors.

Table 3.2 is a factor analysis of some personality tests to illustrate the interpretation and meaning of factors. It is taken from a study by Draycott (1996) which attempted to investigate what certain personality tests measured.

Interpretation and explanation of Table 3.2

Two tests, the NEO Personality Inventory (Costa and McCrae, 1992b) and the EPQ-R (Eysenck and Eysenck, 1991), were factored together to test two different claims made by these authors. Costa and McCrae claim that five factors

Table 3.1 A typical correlation matrix

Variables	Eng.	French	Latin	Greek	Maths	Physics	Chemistry	Geography
English	1.0	0.65	0.42	0.41	0.23	0.15	0.18	0.27
French	0.65	1.0	0.51	0.41	0.20	0.16	0.13	0.21
Latin	0.42	0.51	1.0	0.75	0.49	0.38	0.32	0.28
Greek	0.41	0.41	0.75	1.0	0.50	0.34	0.28	0.21
Maths	0.23	0.20	0.49	0.50	1.0	0.56	0.47	0.19
Physics	0.15	0.16	0.38	0.34	0.56	1.0	0.48	0.22
Chemistry	0.18	0.13	0.32	0.28	0.47	0.48	1.0	0.31
Geography	0.27	0.21	0.23	0.21	0.19	0.22	0.31	1.0

Table 3.2 Factor analysis of the NEO and EPQ personality tests (Direct Oblimin rotation)

	Factor 1	*Factor 2*	*Factor 3*	h^2
NEO C	−009	−760	−022	593
NEO A	064	−468	−412	355
NEO E	902	−103	251	003
NEO O	613	175	−171	398
NEO N	−203	064	916	841
EPQ P	221	890	018	819
EPQ E	873	148	−062	780
EPQ N	−191	−005	930	874
Eigenvalue	2.35	1.77	1.42	
Percentage variance	29.4	22.1	17.8	
Cumulative percentage variance	29.4	51.5	69.3	

Note: A decimal point should be read before all the factor loadings

account for the variance in personality tests while the Eysencks argue that three are sufficient. Both agree that extraversion (E) and neuroticism or anxiety (N) are important factors. However, there is controversy over the other three factors, Eysenck claiming that P, psychoticism, includes A, agreeableness, C, conscientiousness and O, openness of the NEO-PI. A factor analysis is a good test of this argument since it will demonstrate whether there are three or five factors and whether the different tests correlate as might be expected. Again, it is to be noted that the sixty-four possible correlations among these scales are too diffuse to answer this question precisely. The aim of this analysis is to simplify the more complex correlation matrix.

Before describing the type of factor analysis or why three factors were selected, details which will be discussed below, I shall identify the factors. Factors are identified by their factor loadings. It is the convention to regard factor loadings as salient or significant if they are greater than 0.3. In this case, as will be seen, these factor loadings are the correlations of the variables with the factors.

FACTOR 1

The two highest loadings on the first factor are with the E scales of the two tests. Thus, regarding the factor as a construct, one asks what construct correlates highly with two extraversion scales. Obviously, this is the extraversion factor. It is interesting to note, therefore, that O, openness, also correlates with this factor. This suggests that openness is not independent of extraversion.

FACTOR 2

This factor loads on NEO C and A and on the EPQ P (the highest loading). First note the negative loadings. This means that *low* conscientiousness, *low* agreeableness and *low* psychoticism correlate with this factor. It would have made no difference to the interpretation if these loadings had been positive. This is because a construct, such as a personality factor, is inherently bipolar. Anxiety, for example, is a construct or dimension of high to low anxiety. It is possible to change the loadings on a factor, from negative to positive or vice versa, provided that all the loadings are changed, without changing the meaning of the factor.

To return to the identification, this factor is clearly psychoticism. Conscientiousness and (to a lesser extent, the correlation being smaller) agreeableness are also related to this factor. It is interesting to interpret the meaning of these loadings but this will be left to a later section of this chapter.

FACTOR 3

The two anxiety or neuroticism scales (the N scales) load on this factor so that it is easily identified as anxiety. However, agreeableness also loads this factor: anxious people tend to be disagreeable.

Thus this factor analysis identifies, from the factor loadings, three clear factors – extraversion, psychoticism and anxiety – in the EPQ-R and the NEO-PI personality questionnaires.

Other important points in this factor analysis

1 *The eigenvalues.* These are calculated by squaring and adding the loadings on each factor. These indicate the size of the factors: the larger the eigenvalues the bigger the factor – in the sense that it accounts for more variance. Each variable has an eigenvalue of 1. Thus a factor must, at least, have an eigenvalue greater than 1 if it is to be of any importance.

2 *Percentage variance.* This indicates the proportion of the total variance in the matrix, which the factor accounts for. It is calculated by dividing the eigenvalue by the number of variables in the matrix. Factors are extracted in both principal components and principal factor analysis in descending order of size.

3 *Cumulative percentage variance.* This is the variance accounted for by all the factors. This gives a good indication of how good the factor analysis is – the more variance the better. Given that a principal factor analysis eliminates error variance the cumulative percentage variance should be about 70 per cent, and again the more the better.

4 *The communality.* This is calculated by squaring and adding the loadings for each variable. It indicates the proportion of variance for each variable which the factors account for. Again the more the better. Thus in our example, the three-factor solution accounts for only 35.5 per cent of the variance in NEO A. This means either that this test measures a variable different from that measured by these three factors or that the test is highly unreliable and

contaminated by error. On the other hand, nearly 90 per cent of the variance in NEO E is accounted for, and this means that we can assert with some confidence what this test measures provided that we can identify the factors.

From this it is clear that the adequacy of a factor analysis can be determined, at least in part, by an examination of the eigenvalues (percentage and cumulative percentage variances are simply indices more easy to grasp) and communalities. However, although this is, in principle, true, other conditions must be satisfied if the factor analysis is to be relied upon. These conditions will now be discussed.

5   *Rotation of factors.* At this point it is essential to illustrate rotation of factors. As has been said, once a factor analysis has been calculated the factor axes can be rotated relative to each other, thus giving an infinity of different solutions which are equivalent, in the sense of being able to reproduce the original

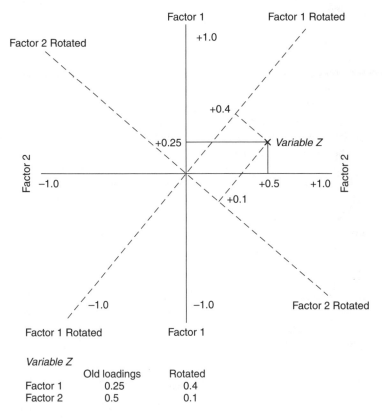

Variable Z		
	Old loadings	Rotated
Factor 1	0.25	0.4
Factor 2	0.5	0.1

Figure 3.1 Two rotated factors and their loadings

correlation matrix equally well. Figure 3.1 shows a simplified rotation which shows how the factor loadings change with rotation of the factors.

As can be seen, the loadings change but the variance explained by the loadings and the correlations computed from the cross-products remains the same. Of course this is a highly simplified example. It indicates how rotation can produce zeros or near-zeros on factors, and in the attainment of simple structure this has to be done for all factors. Each factor is rotated until the best overall position in terms of simple structure is obtained. This example makes it clear why a reason for choosing one position for the axes rather than another is needed. There is an infinity of positions, and simple structure, by definition, is the simplest. Although, as has been said, simple-structure factors are easier to identify than more complex factors, this is not the only reason for rotating to simple structure. In the natural sciences it is accepted that if there are competing hypotheses to explain the observations, it is best to choose the simplest. This is known as the law of parsimony or Occam's razor. Now each different position of the axes in rotation can be seen as a hypothesis to explain the correlations. Furthermore, each position is equally good and thus the simplest should be selected.

6   *Simple structure.* As discussed above, in order to choose among the infinity of possible factor analytic solutions the simplest is preferred. A simple-structure solution essentially demands factors with a few high loadings, the others being zero or close to zero. Simple structure has been shown by Cattell (1978) to provide replicable factors and this is crucial, of course, to the scientific endeavour. However, it should be obvious that a non-simple solution with many high loadings and/or many moderate loadings is bound to yield better communalities and higher eigenvalues. Thus these latter are essential criteria for a good solution provided that simple structure has been obtained. However, examination of Table 3.2. shows that simple structure has indeed been reached, and thus the figures are not misleading. It should also be pointed out that Cattell (1978) has shown that in some instances simple-structure solutions can reveal causal determinants of correlations.

7   *Direct Oblimin rotation.* The description of Table 3.2 indicated that it was a Direct Oblimin solution. Direct Oblimin is a method of rotating the factor axes which has been shown by Hakstian (1971) to be highly effective at reaching simple structure. It provides an oblique solution and in this example the factor matrix shown is the factor structure. Thus the factor loadings are the correlations with the variables. These factor were virtually orthogonal and thus the pattern matrix was almost identical to the structure matrix.

Interpreting the factor analysis

So far I have identified the factors from their factor loadings and discussed some other essential features of factor analysis revealed in Table 3.2. We are now in a position to interpret this factor analysis, to assess the light it throws on these personality questionnaires and on the wider issues of personality and its measurement. In this process factor identification is only a part.

It should be recalled that the problem that this factor analysis sought to solve concerned the number of factors necessary to account for the variance in personality questionnaires — five or three factors, to simplify the question.

This solution showed three factors. It seems adequate in that simple structure has been obtained and a high proportion of the variance in the matrix accounted for. Furthermore, the comunalities of the EPQ scales are all satisfactory, as are two of the NEO scales, the E and N scales. O, A and C (this to a lesser extent) are not satisfactory simply because they fail to load highly on the three factors.

The first clear conclusion is that Eysenck's claim that three factors, E, N and P, account for the main variance in personality questionnaires is correct. These three factors clearly emerge and the relevant Eysenck scales do not load other factors. The second clear conclusion is that there is good agreement between the EPQ and NEO extraversion and anxiety scales.

Thus, as is to be expected, the problems arise with the NEO C, O and A factors. Conscientiousness and agreeableness, as Eysenck has argued, are not independent factors but aspects of psychoticism and they load factor 2 accordingly. This finding strongly supports the three-factor solution.

Two other conclusions may be drawn from this analysis. First I shall deal with openness. Openness loads the extraversion factor quite highly although much of its variance is not explained by these three factors, as is shown by its low communality. This factor is a difficult construct and it is fully discussed in Chapter 9. Here in this section, illustrating the interpretation of factor analyses, it is sufficient to point out that it not an independent factor and is related to extraversion.

The other conclusion is that the NEO A measure is not unifactorial. It appears to measure a mixture of psychoticism and neuroticism, since it loads on both these factors. As has been explained, this is not a good thing. Univariate variables are essential for scientific measurement.

I think enough has been said about Table 3.2. Clearly it shows that three factors account for the variance in these tests and that the Eysenckian claims concerning N, E and P are well founded. However, it must be noted that this example has been used for purposes of explication and demonstration of the interpretation of factor analysis. It happened to yield a solution of unusual clarity. However, it must be stressed that this table is not cited as proof or even as incontrovertible evidence concerning the number and nature of personality factors. This is a highly complex issue, of which this study is but one piece of evidence, and the whole topic is the subject of a separate chapter in this book.

Causes of disagreement among factor analyses

Even a cursory study of factor analysis and the findings which have been obtained from it immediately reveals the huge disagreements among the various practitioners, especially in the field of personality, although as regards abilities there is some consensus. As Cattell (1978), Cattell and Kline (1977) and Kline (1994a) have argued, much of this disagreement arises from technical deficiencies in factor analysis. I shall set these out, and briefly discuss them since they render many studies worthless. This is now particularly important with the rise of meta-analyses, certainly one of the disadvantages of modern computational power. These average out the results of all studies ever carried out with the relevant variables. However, since they fail to distinguish between those with methodological flaws and good studies they can yield nonsense. Thus it is critical that researchers are aware of the pitfalls of factor analysis. Nunnally (1978) was also cognisant of the dangers of factor analysis in unskilled hands, a section of his excellent book being essentially how to fool yourself with factor analysis.

The particular defect which was stressed by Cattell as destroying the value of a factor analysis was the failure to reach simple structure, and he devised procedures for ensuring that simple structure was obtained, of which the most essential will now be described. Studies which are defective in any of these areas are best ignored.

Criteria for sound factor analyses

1   *Sampling of subjects.* It is essential in an exploratory factor analysis that a full range of subjects is sampled. If the sample is homogeneous for a factor, that factor will have little variance and thus not take up its proper place in the factor analysis. If, for example, in a study of personality, all the subjects were bar staff or salespersons, who are likely to be highly extraverted, extraversion would be greatly attenuated.

2   *Sampling of variables.* In an exploratory analysis it is also essential that the full range of variables is sampled. Thus in the field of abilities it is certain that many factors have yet to be identified, especially those of a practical kind, not easily testable with standard, current psychometric tests. Examples of these would be rapport with horses (as in jockeys) and a mason's skill at splitting bricks with a single blow.

3   *Sample size.* Standard textbooks vary on this point. However, there are two issues to be borne in mind. Since one of the aims of a factor analysis is to be able to reproduce from the factor loadings the original correlations it is essential that these are as free of statistical error as possible. For this reason alone, a sample size of 100 subjects is a desirable minimum. However, it is also agreed that the ratio of subjects to variables is important. If there are more variables than subjects the factor analysis is meaningless. There must always be more subjects than variables. However, textbooks vary in their recommendations concerning the ideal ratio, running from 10 to 1 (Nunnally 1978) to 2 to 1 (Guilford, 1956). Barrett and Kline (1981b) carried out an empirical study of this problem with a large sample of subjects using the EPQ test. They found that with a sample size as low as 2 to 1 the main

factors were retrieved and beyond 3 to 1 there were no improvements. A more recent study by Arrindel and van de Ende (1985) claimed that the critical factor was the number of subjects to factors, a ratio of 20 to 1 being required for stability. There is no doubt that the greater the number of subjects, the more stable and reliable the results are likely to be.

4   *Principal factor rather than principal component analysis.* Although Harman (1976) showed that in large matrices there was little practical difference between component and factor analysis, on theoretical statistical grounds factor analysis is to be preferred. This is because, by estimating the diagonals in the correlation matrix, error variance is eliminated from the factor matrix. Furthermore, since the factors are estimates rather than the actual factors in the particular matrix, they are more likely to be generalisable to other matrices. There is some argument as to how these diagonals should be computed, and readers are referred to Harman (1976), Gorsuch (1974) or Cattell (1978) for excellent discussions of this point.

5   *Number of factors to rotate.* Principal components and principal factor analysis produce a series of factors of decreasing size. As each one is extracted it accounts for less variance than the preceding factor. Factors were defined as the linear sums of variables, and since each variable has an eigenvalue of 1, any factor with a smaller eigenvalue than this must be of no significance. Thus some statistical packages choose for rotation all factors with eigenvalues greater than 1. However, it has been shown by Cattell (1978) that such a procedure can, in some instances, overestimate the number of factors. This criterion, therefore, becomes the lowest bound. It is certainly true that no factors should be rotated with eigenvalues less than 1. Cattell (1978) has always argued that selecting the right number of factors is crucial for obtaining simple structure. Rotate too many factors and factors split. Rotate too few and factors run together.

6   *Selecting the right number of factors.* If eigenvalues greater than 1 cannot be relied upon to select the right number of factors, what should be done? Barrett and Kline (1982) investigated various methods of factor extraction with reference to obtaining the correct number of factors. They found that two methods seemed to find the target: Cattell's (1966b) Scree test and the Velicer (1976) method. Although the Scree test can be automated, it is a subjective method, essentially an algorithm which works effectively, and it is sensible to use both methods as a check and, if different, to rotate both sets of factors. Many factor analysts prefer the genuine statistical selection of the number of factors offered by factoring using the maximum likelihood method. However, attractive as this option appears, it is not without its own problems. The main one is that without a large sample the maximum likelihood estimates are not reliable (Krzanowski, 1988).

7   *Choice of rotational procedure.* Cattell (1978) regards this, together with the selection of the right number of factors, as the crucial element in obtaining simple structure. The need to rotate factors to simple structure arises from

the fact that there is an infinity of equivalent mathematical solutions once the preliminary factor analysis has been computed. Orthogonal rotations yield uncorrelated factors and many factor analysts regard these solutions as the best, the uncorrelated set being necessarily simpler than any others. There is no doubt that the best procedure for orthogonal rotation is Varimax rotation (Kaiser, 1958), and this is contained in most computer packages for factor analysis. Cattell (1978) has been one of the main advocates of oblique factors on the grounds that in real life it would be unlikely that causal determinants, as he believes factors to be, would be uncorrelated. Furthermore, in allowing factors to take up any position relative to each other, each factor can be made as simple as possible, using the criteria of simple structure. There are many different procedures for oblique rotation but studies of different methods in relation to simple structure tend to show that Direct Oblimin (Jennrich and Sampson, 1966) is highly effective (see Harman, 1976). Cattell favours his own methods – Maxplane followed by Rotoplot – but these need considerable skill to operate and have been shown by Harman (1976) to be no better than Direct Oblimin, which is now the preferred method of rotation for most factor analysts.

Conclusions

If there has been adequate sampling of subjects and variables and there is a large sample of subjects, relative to the number of variables and factors, and if the correct number of factors, as selected by the Scree or Velicer tests or by statistical tests after maximum likelihood analysis, and if Direct Oblimin rotation is used, then it is likely that simple-structure, replicable factors will be obtained. Such factors are likely to repay further experimental analysis and to be of some psychological significance. Needless to say, all factor structures must be replicated on further samples.

Concluding remarks concerning exploratory factor analysis

It should be clear from this discussion of factor analysis that there are many steps in the procedure where it is possible to depart from the best practices set out above. This is not through ignorance or lack of effort in all cases; it is often difficult to obtain the requisite samples, or to measure all the variables one might desire to clarify the meaning of the analysis. There are limits on the testing time that subjects can endure, and sometimes with hindsight it is obvious that certain measures should have been included. In brief, many factor analyses are far from perfect and the results are dubious.

Factor analysis in test construction

This discussion of factor analysis was instigated originally – although the reader may well have forgotten – so that readers could understand the application of factor analysis in psychometric theory and application and in test construction. I hope that the principles of the method are now clear. To conclude, I shall set out how factor analysis is used in test construction. I shall outline the essence of the method below; full details can be found in Kline (1995, 1999).

1   Items are written which it is hoped measure the relevant variable or variables. It is often convenient with the factor analytic method to construct several tests at once. This allows full use of simple-structure rotations, as discussed above.
2   The pool of items is administered to a large and representative sample of subjects for whom the test is designed. There must be a subject to item ratio of at least 2 to 1.
3   The correlations between the items are subjected to factor analysis and simple-structure rotation. It is particularly in the case of item factoring, where there are a large number of small factors, that it is important to rotate the correct number and obtain simple structure.
4   Items are selected which load only one factor. We want, as was discussed in the previous chapter, univariate scales. Items are checked for content. If items do not seem to cover the field, new ones are written and administered in a further item trial.
5   The new scales are administered to new samples and subjected to new factor analyses. Items are retained which load their respective factors.
6   Reliability of the scales is checked, as is the content of the items, to ensure that there is full coverage of the scale in the loading items.
7   Validation and normative studies are then carried out.

From this it can be seen that the rationale of factor analysis in test construction is precisely that of exploratory analysis in general, as has been described. If a set of items measures extraversion we should expect that set to load on a common factor. If in the course of tests construction items do load a factor, it is not necessarily the case that the test must be valid. It could be that there is some other common factor running through the items. One such is the response set of social desirability (Edwards, 1957), the tendency to endorse socially desirable items. That is why step 7 is so important – the validation of the factored scale. This is particularly true in the case of personality scales, where there are no clear rules determining whether an item measures a variable. Item writing is essentially subjective, even though one can list with great care the attributes one is trying to measure.

Confirmatory factor analysis

The majority of factor analyses in psychometrics are exploratory and, until the advent of high-speed computing and particularly the work of Joreskog and Sorbom (1984), who provided a workable computer package, confirmatory analyses were virtually unheard of. Whereas exploratory analyses seek out the main factors in a matrix of correlations, confirmatory factor analysis aims to see whether a particular set of factors can account for the correlations. If they can, then this set is confirmed. If not, the set is refuted. In this latter sense, the refutation of a set of hypothesised factors, confirmatory analysis resembles the older-style experimental method, as advocated by Popper (1959) (discussed in full in Chapter 1), and gets away from the rank empiricism of some traditional factor analytic studies.

In confirmatory analysis a target matrix of factor loadings is set up, on the basis of previous findings or the relevant psychological theory. The obtained data are then subjected to factor analysis in which, using maximum-likelihood estimates, an attempt is made to match the target matrix as closely as possible. How good the fit actually is to the target matrix can be put to the statistical test. Thus hypothesised factor structures can be confirmed or rejected statistically.

This seems like an ideal procedure and it has been enthusiastically taken up by some psychometricians. However, there are some difficulties and problems with confirmatory analysis which are often ignored, and these must be discussed because it can produce highly misleading results.

Problems with confirmatory factor analysis

The most severe of these problems are set out below. A brilliant discussion and evaluation of these difficulties with confirmatory analysis is given by Loehlin (1987) and a simpler version by Kline (1994a) if more details are required. I shall not deal here with the complexities of the mathematics.

1   *Goodness-of-fit tests.* Essentially goodness-of-fit tests compare the correlations derived from the factor analysis with the target loadings, with the actual matrix of correlations. If these were exactly the same, which they never are, the fit would be perfect. How close do they have to be for one to say that they fit? In fact, there are several indices of fit, and, as Loehlin (1987) points out, on occasion these do not agree. One may accept a target matrix, another reject it. Occasionally, also, if we are testing two different target matrices, the methods may give different results for each target. Obviously, care has to be taken with these tests.

2   *Problems with large samples.* For maximum-likelihood estimates to be accurate, large samples are a necessity – ranging from 500 (Nunnally, 1978) to 1,000 (Krzanowski, 1988). However, with large samples the statistical test of fit, χ^2, is highly sensitive. Target matrices are rejected which fit the correlations, on subjective analysis, quite well.

3   *Problems with small samples.* In addition to the difficulties with the maximum-likelihood estimates, with small sample sizes the statistical tests are highly insensitive. Thus target matrices are accepted which yield correlations that appear to be quite divergent from the actual correlations. Thus with confirmatory analysis it is always necessary to inspect the observed and estimated correlations, to ensure that the statistics are sensible.

4   *The meaning of a statistical fit.* One of the main difficulties with confirmatory analysis is really nothing to do with the statistical problems which have been raised above, serious as they are. There is a more fundamental difficulty with the technique, one concerning its meaning. If a target matrix is confirmed, it does not mean that this is the only matrix which fits the data. It could well be that there many other hypothetical factor structures which could be confirmed. Thus, apart from the philosophical point that a hypothesis can never be proven by an affirmative instance, confirmatory analysis demonstrates only that the hypothesis is not incompatible with the facts – useful but far from proof.

5   *Difficulty of setting a target matrix.* Sometimes it is difficult to set a target matrix because insufficient is known about the field. Then a rather crude target is often used, where a few high loadings are inserted. This is relatively easy to hit and thus the confirmation does not mean much.

6   *Insensitivity of selecting between targets.* Because, as has been argued, confirming a hypothesis means only that this hypothesis has been confirmed, not that only this hypothesis has been confirmed, some investigators try to select between several possible target matrices. Unfortunately, as Loehlin (1987) demonstrates, the statistical procedures often accept more than one of the targets, if not all.

For all these reasons confirmatory analysis, although a useful technique, is not the panacea that many psychometricians have hoped for, doing away with subjective estimates as to the quality of a factor analysis and providing definite proof that a factor structure is correct. Alas, it cannot do this, even though more sophisticated and elaborate tests of fit have been developed.

Conclusions concerning confirmatory factor analysis

Before confirmatory factor analysis was made accessible by Joreskog and the LISREL programs, factor analysts had to use rather *ad hoc* methods to demonstrate that factor analyses were the same, within the bounds of statistical error, and Cattell (1978) gives many ingenious procedures for estimating factor similarity.

Confirmatory analysis is a statistically based variant of these, and when the main loadings of the target matrix can be realistically inserted (for example, based upon previous work), then confirmatory analysis is highly useful. When the targets have to be loosely specified and when there might be many other likely hypotheses, confirmatory analysis is not as powerful or useful a technique. Furthermore, in all these instances it is important to remember the problems with the statistical tests of fit. Certainly more than one test should always be used. Finally, from the viewpoint of test construction a confirmatory analysis on a new sample, with the target matrix the previous factor loadings of the items, is certainly a useful technique. It adds statistical weight to what otherwise is a subjective procedure: simply comparing the two factor analyses or using an index of factor similarity (Cattell, 1978).

Final conclusions concerning factor analysis

I have described factor analysis in some detail because it is the pivotal statistical method of psychometrics. It is regarded as one of the best methods by which to construct tests and, even more importantly, it is and has been used to investigate, by means of tests, the psychology of individual differences in ability, personality and motivation. Further, the results of factor analysis are the basis of both theory and application of this theory to clinical, educational and occupational psychology.

However, as our discussion has made clear, there are severe problems with factor analysis. The main one concerns the fact that there is an infinity of possible solutions and the consequent need to obtain simple structure. Unfortunately, as Cattell (1978) has shown, one of the main causes of disagreement between factor analysts has been the failure to reach simple structure, a failure determined by technical flaws in the factor analytic procedures. Thus it is essential to understand the logic of factor analysis and the artefacts of poor technique. All these matters have been discussed, and a generally accepted approach to obtaining simple structure in exploratory analyses has been described: proper sampling of variables and subjects; a large sample, relative to the number of variables and factors; correct extraction of factors by Scree test or maximum likelihood analysis; oblique rotation, where required, by Direct Oblimin; replication of factors; and validation of factors experimentally and against external criteria.

These criteria have not been introduced as some arcane and pedantic system of rules which has to be known for its own sake. When, in subsequent chapters, we come to scrutinise and discuss the substantive findings from psychometrics in the various fields, then we will be referring to these technical issues, since many purported findings fail when judged against these criteria.

Perhaps even more important than these matters of factor analytic technique is the logic of the method. As has been demonstrated in this chapter, factor analysis essentially reduces the rank of matrices. It accounts for correlations between variables in terms of a few factors or dimensions, and these can be shown to be important determinants in their field. However – and this is where psychometrics can be misleading – factors are not necessarily determinants. They can be trivial, reflecting the fact that items are paraphrases of each other or so similar that a correlation is inevitable. All depends on the nature of the variables in the analysis. One uninformed criticism of factor analysis (e.g. Heim, 1975) is that you only get out what you put in. This is not true, but what is true is that factors depend entirely on the variables in the analysis. This, as will be argued, has led to severe errors in the interpreting of factors, especially in the fields of personality and motivation.

Because factors account for correlations it is clear that factor analysis is an excellent technique of test construction, in principle, because the items of a good test should be measuring a common factor, or the test could not be valid. Again this has led to error in test construction because it does not follow from this assertion that all tests measuring common factors are good tests.

Finally, confirmatory analysis was examined. Here it became clear that this was a useful method of confirming previous results, provided that the target matrix could be properly specified and provided that caution was shown in interpreting the results. The statistical tests are strongly influenced by sample size. In big samples good fits may be rejected and with small samples bad fits may be accepted. Again, as with exploratory analysis, there is a logical difficulty which is perhaps more important than the technical issues. This concerns the meaning of the fact that a target matrix has been confirmed. Such a finding does not imply that other target matrices could not have been confirmed. These features of confirmatory analysis must never be forgotten when interpreting the findings.

Factor analysis is a powerful method of determining the most salient variables in a field and of constructing a univariate test. However, it is also a method which is open to grievous misinterpretation when the logic of its calculation, and the nature of the variables in the research, are neglected – and, unfortunately, many such errors have been perpetrated in psychometrics over the years.

4

MULTIVARIATE ANALYSES AND TEST CONSTRUCTION

Other methods

In Chapter 3, I described factor analysis in some detail – sufficient, I hope, for readers to be able to evaluate the arguments in the second part of this book, where the substantive findings in psychometrics are discussed and examined. This was especially important because factor analysis has been widely used in psychometrics and the great majority of the best psychometric tests have been developed using factor analysis. Furthermore, since one of the main aims of the book is to determine whether psychometric testing is scientific measurement in any sense at all, factor analysis has to be carefully scrutinised.

Other methods of test construction are also used in psychometrics, however, and these must also be subjected to scrutiny. In addition, other multivariate analyses are performed and these also require some brief consideration. In this chapter, therefore, I shall describe and discuss the most important and commonly used of these procedures, with the same aim as that of the previous chapter: to evaluate their utility for a genuinely scientific, psychometric psychology.

Methods of test construction

In addition to factor analysis there are various other methods of constructing psychological tests. These will be examined to see whether they come at all close to scientific measurement as described in Chapter 2 or to the highest standards of psychometric measurement, using the classical model of test error. The methods to be considered are set out below:

- item analysis;
- criterion keying;
- Guttman scales;
- Thurstone scales; and
- item characteristic curves and models.

Item analysis

Item analysis is still used in test construction because it is a far simpler procedure than factor analysis, not requiring as many subjects, and in certain circumstances it can be highly efficient. Nunnally and Bernstein (1994) go so far as to suggest that item analysis can be used as a preliminary to factor analysis, getting rid quickly and efficiently of unsatisfactory items.

Procedures of item analysis

1   Administer a pool of items to a representative sample of subjects for whom the test is intended. This sample need not be as large as is necessary for factor analytic tests since item analysis uses correlations. Thus a sample of 100 is sufficient to reduce standard errors, although, as always, the more the better.

2   In item analysis two indices are computed: the correlation of each item with the total score, and the proportion of the sample putting the correct or keyed response (e.g. 'Yes' to an extraversion item).

3   Items are selected which correlate with the total score greater than 0.3 and which also are endorsed by between 80 per cent and 20 per cent of the sample.

4   Checks are made that the selected items fully represent the variable and new items are written as required.

5   The new pool is administered to a new sample and items reaching the two criteria are selected for the final test.

6   Reliability is computed, norms set up and validation studies of the test are executed.

Comments on item analysis

The rationale of item analysis is remarkably simple. If a test is measuring a variable, then it must be the case that each item is also measuring that variable. Thus the first criterion of item analysis, the correlation of the item and the total score, makes good sense. An obvious objection concerns the circularity of this procedure since there is no a priori way of knowing what the items in the pool measure. This, of course, is a reasonable objection, and if the selection is wrong, the whole test is wrong. This problem is countered by step 6. Of course, item analysis only demonstrates that a test, the set of items, is measuring a variable. It is necessary to show what that variable is, just as was the case in factor analytic tests.

There used to be considerable discussion as to what the best correlation coefficient was to measure the item total correlation (e.g. Anstey, 1966). However, generally the Pearson product moment coefficient is used in computing packages. In short scales the influence of the item itself on the total score is usually removed since that will inflate the correlation.

The rationale for selecting only items endorsed between the 20 per cent and 80 per cent levels is to maximise the discriminating power of the test. If an item were endorsed by 100 per cent of the sample, or 0 per cent, the test would be making no discriminations whatever.

From this it can be seen that an item analytic test selected according to the criteria above must be discriminating and measuring a variable common to all the items. For this reason it is bound to be reliable.

Disadvantages of item analysis compared with factor analysis

The qualities adduced above make it clear why the procedure was advocated by Nunnally and Bernstein (1994) as a preliminary to factor analysis and why some test constructors are content with this method alone. Indeed, the correlations of the items with the total score are obviously highly similar to factor loadings, the correlations of the items with the underlying factor, and with univariate tests the correlation between loadings and item total correlations is almost perfect, as was found by Barrett and Kline (1981a).

However, the term 'univariate' gives the game away. In many tests, items and scales are not univariate. Thus if we had a set of items which measured extraversion and sensation seeking, for example, clearly correlated factors, an item analysis would produce a test with both sets of items. Furthermore, a factor analysis of items reveals those items which load more than one factor, and these can be excluded from the final scale, which cannot be done with item analysis.

For all these reasons item analysis is not satisfactory as a sole means of test construction. As Nunnally and Bernstein (1994) advocate, if it is used it must be followed by factor analysis. From this brief description it is clear that in respect of scientific measurement item analysis and factor analysis are highly similar. Item analysis, it is certain, cannot be superior to factor analysis as a method of test construction.

Criterion-keyed test construction

In this method of test construction a pool of items is administered to various criterion groups. If an item can discriminate one group from the other groups it is selected for the relevant scale. An example from the most famous test constructed on this procedure, the Minnesota Multiphasic Personality Inventory (MMPI) (Hathaway and McKinley, 1951), will clarify the method. The MMPI was designed for the diagnosis of psychiatric conditions, such as depression and schizophrenia. Originally there were nine clinical scales but these were extended, by using the item pool with many other groups, into more than 200 (Dahlstrom and Welsh, 1960). Thus if an item discriminated depressives from all the other clinical groups and the normal control group, it was inserted into the depression scale.

Elsewhere (Kline, 1995) I have set out in detail the many objections to this form of test construction but the main points can be summarised here.

- *Problems with the criterion groups.* There is often a general problem in the formation of criterion groups. This is in addition to the specific difficulty associated with psychiatric classification (Beck, 1962), which is notoriously unreliable. The point concerns the reality of the groups, *qua* groups. For example, are accountants different from other professional groups in any significant degree, such that one might generalise to accountants in other countries? Obviously this affects the generalisability of criterion-keyed tests.
- *Empiricism in item selection.* Criterion-keyed tests are genuinely empirical. A huge battery of items has to be tried out in order to obtain a set of discriminating items. Items are selected simply because they discriminate. Often there appears to be no clear reason why particular items work and others do not. This does not matter to the test constructor whose sole aim is a discriminating set of items. It does, however, have two evil consequences, as set out below.
- *Lack of homogeneity of test items.* Because it is possible, indeed likely, that groups will differ on a number of variables, an empirical, atheoretical set of items, selected because they will discriminate, lacks homogeneity. Thus its internal consistency reliability is usually low. This means that, by the standards of the classical model of test error (see Chapter 2), it is unclear from what universe of items the items are derived.
- *Lack of psychological meaning.* This lack of homogeneity, the fact that items have been selected simply on the grounds of their discriminatory power, leads to the creation of scales empty of psychological meaning. This is, perhaps, the most serious defect of criterion-keyed scales as scientific measures. Eysenck, in his preface to a book on the MMPI (Friedman *et al.*, 1989), pointed out that this was the most cited personality questionnaire in the world, with more than 12,000 references. Unfortunately, the psychological inanity of the scales, on account of their method of construction, means that this huge number of studies has held up the development of the science of clinical psychology. Because the scales have no meaning, it is impossible to construct theories or hypotheses about the results of such studies. This is in contrast to factor analytic tests, where the tests must be measuring a definite variable. All that one can say about a criterion-keyed test is that it does or does not discriminate a particular group. This is far away from any kind of scientific measure, as defined in the sciences.

For all these reasons it is difficult to advocate either the construction or the use of criterion-keyed tests in the scientific study of human behaviour. Since the MMPI has been so widely used it seems a reasonable question to ask why this is so, if my arguments are correct. The only possible rational use of this type of test is where mass screening is the sole aim of the testing. For example, if it is known that highly neurotic individuals could not do a particular job with any success and would be a public danger in such a post, the use of a criterion-keyed scale which could reliably discriminate such neurotics would be in order. This, however, is practical psychology, not science or applied science (exactly, in fact, as described by Michell (1997)).

One possible manoeuvre to improve the use of criterion-keyed tests, it might be argued, is to factor analyse the scales, both the total scores with other tests and the correlations between the items. This, however, will not do. It is far more efficient to factor analyse at the beginning. If a particular scale turns out not to be univariate, the scores are impossible to interpret or compare. In fact, with the MMPI, factor analyses have not been clear-cut except that extraversion and anxiety may be found. Generally factors tend to be sets of items with similar meanings (Johnson *et al.*, 1984). However, this is a substantive, not a general methodological, issue, and discussion of the factor structure of the MMPI will be found in Chapter 9.

Conclusions concerning criterion-keyed tests

From all these arguments it clear that, whatever their practical uses, criterion-keyed tests cannot be considered to be scientific measures. This is the case according to the usage of the notion of scientific measurement in the natural sciences and in psychology, where the concept of true score and error has been introduced in an attempt to render measurement scientific.

Guttman and Thurstone scales

Two of the most distinguished psychometricians, Thurstone and Guttman, both developed scales which have been used in social psychology and which require only brief analysis since neither measures up to the requirements of scientific measurement.

Guttman scales

Suppose that we have a Guttman scale of 10 items, arranged in order of difficulty. If a subject gets the first four items correct and item 5 wrong we know that that subject will get all subsequent items wrong. This will be true of all subjects. This means that each item is correlated perfectly with the total score, using a biserial correlation.

The construction of Guttman scales is essentially a sorting procedure such that items are arranged into levels of difficulty so that failure at any one level implies failure at all higher levels and success at all lower levels. These sorting procedures, for which computer programs are now available, require large samples and large numbers of items (of which the majority have to be rejected) if the characteristics of Guttman scaling are to be preserved in other administrations of the test.

Apparent advantages of Guttman scales

Nunnally (1978) has pointed out that Guttman scales appeal to common sense. In the first place, this perfect ordering of items can be seen in the everyday measures that we are all familiar with. If I weighed 114 pounds, I could also say that I did weigh all lower weights than this and that I did not weigh all higher weights However, it must be noted that with this example there is a clear unit of measurement (pounds).

Another obvious point is that when we know the score of a subject on a Guttman scale, then we know what items the subject got right and what wrong, This is not the case for most tests, especially in the field of personality and motivation. However, these advantages are more than outweighed by the problems and difficulties with Guttman scales.

Disadvantages of Guttman scales

There are really three problems with Guttman scales which render them of little scientific value.

1 *The underlying measurement model.* The first concerns the fact that items correlate perfectly with the total scale score or the attribute being measured. This is unlikely of any variable in the real world. In general terms, as Levy (1973) has pointed out, it means the measurement model does not fit what is being measured. This is not dissimilar to the difficulty raised by Michell (1997) and discussed in Chapter 2, namely that in psychological measurement it is simply assumed that the attribute is quantitative.

2 *Unidimensionality of the scale.* It has been argued that all valid measuring instruments must be unidimensional. Now the construction of a Guttman scale does not ensure unidimensionality. It would be perfectly possible to take items from different scales, each item of a considerably different level of difficulty, and these would form a Guttman scale. This is because the scaling characteristics of Guttman scales are dependent only on difficulty levels. Thus Guttman scales may not be unidimensional. The only practical way round the problem is to factor the items first, but then it may prove difficult to make a Guttman scale with so restricted an item pool.

3 *Ordinal measurement.* Nunnally (1978) points out that the construction of Guttman scales permits only ordinal measurement. This severely restricts the kinds of statistical analyses which can be used with Guttman scales. Far more importantly, it means that Guttman scales are quite different from scientific measurement as it has been defined in our earlier chapters. Guttman scales cannot be scientific.

Conclusions

For all these reasons it is clear that despite their appeal, Guttman scales cannot form part of a scientific system of measurement.

Thurstone scales

Thurstone scales were widely used in the measurement of attitudes. However, the practical problems involved in the necessary data collection, if they are to be properly constructed, and some more theoretical difficulties are such that they are difficult to recommend for scientific measurement.

Construction of the scales

There are three steps in the construction of Thurstone scales:

1   Statements relevant to the attitude to be measured, in newspapers and books, for example, are collected together.
2   These statements are rated by judges on an 11-point scale, from 'strongly favourable' to 'strongly unfavourable'.
3   Statements, where there is good agreement by the judges, are selected for the test. Agreement is measured by the standard deviation of the ratings for the statement; the smaller, the higher the agreement. Usually from 10 to 20 statements are included in the final test. Of course these statements must reflect the full range of the attitude (1–11).

A Thurstone scale can be scored in one of two ways:

1   The subject's score is the mean rating of the items with which he or she agrees.
2   The subject's score is the highest scale rating of any item with which he or she agrees.

There are severe objections to Thurstone scales of which two deserve special mention since they preclude their use. The first is practical. Edwards (1957), in his study of social desirability, a response set which affects rating scales and personality questionnaires, showed that reliable rating required 100 judges. Furthermore, it is essential that the judges be drawn from the population for whom the test is intended. Otherwise ratings will not be accurate. For example, the ratings given by students concerning Doc Martens boots and business suits, in a study of attitudes to clothes, would differ greatly from those of top executives. That is why only items with small standard deviations can be chosen, but this may well limit the test, the most salient items being unusable.

There is a theoretical objection raised by Nunnally (1978). In the model underlying Thurstone scaling, each item should receive the keyed response only at a particular point on the attitude dimension. For example, the item 'Abortion should be permitted but only with good reasons' is certainly not at the extreme end of attitudes to abortion but it would also be endorsed by those believing abortion should be allowed in any circumstances. Most attitude items are of this kind, and the scaling model does not fit the real world of attitudes.

Sufficient has been said to make it clear that, even if the practical objections could be overcome, Thurstone scaling could not be considered to be a scientific test in the sense of those terms in the natural sciences.

Likert scales

Mention must be made of Likert scales because these are now the most commonly used attitude measure. Likert (1932) introduced these scales, which are characterised by having statements to which subjects have to indicate their degree of agreement on a 5- or 7-point response scale. The score a subject receives is the sum of that subject's responses on the total number of items. A few points need to be made about Likert scales. The first is that items are usually balanced, so that in a scale about, say, attitudes to abortion, favourable attitudes are not simply endorsed by agreement. Some items are reversed so that agreement is registered by disagreement with the statement. To some extent this overcomes the response set of acquiescence, agreement with an item regardless of content (Cronbach, 1946), a distorting feature of personality questionnaires as well as attitude scales.

From the viewpoint of scientific measurement Likert scales are no different from tests developed by factor analysis or item analysis, both of which are used in their construction. They have all the problems and difficulties in respect of scientific measurement which we have already discussed. They have no units of measurement and no true zeros so that their validity, such as it is, comes from the classical model of test error with its dependence on the concept of the true score.

Conclusion concerning attitude scales

It is evident from this discussion of three kinds of attitude scale that none of them could be called scientific. The Guttman scale is only ordinal and is not necessarily homogeneous. The Thurstone scale is based upon a scaling model which is inappropriate for attitudes even if the practical difficulties of obtaining judges are ignored. Finally, Likert scales were shown to be no different from standard psychometric tests developed by factor analysis or item analysis. Of these types of scale, only Likert scales even come close to being capable of providing scientific measurement.

Item characteristic curves and theory

There is an approach to the development of psychometric tests which is independent of factor analysis and the classical theory of test error, but is based upon models of item response and item characteristic curves which describe these responses. Much of this work is highly complex statistically and it has been well discussed by Lord (1974, 1980), Hambleton *et al.* (1991) and Embretson (1996). I intend here to discuss only what is strictly relevant to scientific measurement rather than give a full description of the theory and its applications.

However, before the discussion can begin it is necessary to define a few terms.

Item characteristic curves

In Figure 4.1 I set out two typical but hypothetical item characteristic curves. There are several points to note about these curves relative to the classical psychometric test theory which has been discussed in this book and which is the basis of most psychological ability tests and virtually all other tests. Practical tests using item characteristic curve theory are very rare and have been restricted to the field of abilities.

- The attribute (what the items measure) is hypothetical and can only be inferred from the items. It is usually referred to as a latent trait. In Figure 4.1 for purposes of discussion we might label this latent trait intelligence. The abstraction of the latent trait is not that different from the notion of the true score.

- Latent traits are clearly similar to factors. However, there is one theoretical difference which in practice may not be important. In the latent trait model it is assumed that if the latent trait is fixed, then items are uncorrelated. Of course, in any group of subjects, the latent trait differs and thus items can be correlated. Thus the latent trait explains entirely the correlations between items.

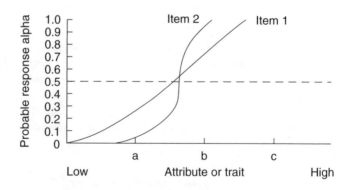

Figure 4.1 Two typical item characteristic curves

- Item characteristic curves present a stochastic or probabilistic account of the response to items. Thus in Figure 4.1 the probability of subject a, who is of low intelligence, responding to item 1 correctly is low 0.2. For item 2 it is even lower: 0.05. There is an interesting aspect to these item characteristic curves, namely that while item 2 is more difficult than item 1 for those low on intelligence, for those of moderate ability and above it is actually easier. Subject b, on the other hand, who is of average ability, has a probability of 0.5 of getting both item 1 and item 2 correct.

- In these curves the difficulty of an item is defined as that point on the attribute where the curve crosses the line at the 0.5 level of probability of response. This is similar to the level of difficulty indexed in classical test theory by the proportion getting the item correct. However, it is not the same, since in these item characteristic curves the difficult level refers not to the average of the population but to a group of subjects at any particular level of the attribute; that is, at a particular intelligence quotient, in this example.

- The steepness of the slope of the curve reflects the discriminability of the item. The steeper this slope, the more discriminating this item is at the level of attribute where the item crosses the 0.5 probability line, this latter being a function of the shape of the normal ogive curve.

- In classical psychometric theory it is assumed that the total score is the number of responses correct or, in the case of personality and attitudes, the number of keyed responses. No assumptions are made about the shapes of these item curves. In item characteristic curve theory it is assumed that curves form normal ogives. Not every item has to assume this form exactly, but it should approach it. In this theoretical work it is further assumed that these normal ogive curves are actually logistic curves (which are highly similar but have useful mathematical properties). Thus both the item characteristic curves in Figure 4.1 are approximations of logistic curves.

- In item characteristic curve theory, various models have been put forward to account for these item response curves. As Levy (1973) and Nunnally and Bernstein (1994) point out, these are highly similar, and essentially variants of each other. One model has proved popular, that of Rasch (1960). The simplest form of the Rasch model claims that the probability of a subject responding correctly to an item is a function of two variables: (a) the facility of the item for eliciting the trait among subjects; and (b) the status of the subject on the latent trait.

There are several points to notice about this model. First, the facility for eliciting the trait is equivalent to the difficulty level of an item in classical test theory. Second, it is almost certainly an incorrect model. Thus guessing must be an important parameter of response and so is item discrimination. However, more complex forms of the model have been developed to deal with these extra complications (Waller and Reise, 1989). The model devised by Birnbaum (1968) exemplifies this type. Finally – and this is of crucial significance to this book – the Rasch model is claimed by Wright (1985) to be an example of additive conjoint measurement, which was shown by Krantz *et al.* (1971) to be a form of fundamental measurement, as was discussed in Chapter 2. This is because the response to a Rasch scale is held to be a function of two independent variables, which is a necessary condition of additive conjoint measurement. If this is true, then Rasch scaling is the answer to the problems of psychometry as posed by Michell.

Advantages and problems with item characteristic curve theory in psychometric testing

I have already mentioned the fact that there are few tests developed using this item-based approach to testing. Its main use, at present, is in the development of tailored testing in which subjects are tested on brief subsets of items especially designed for them. It is interesting to note also that Cattell and Johnson (1986) make no mention or reference to item characteristic curves – and this is intended as a definitive text on psychological testing by one of the world's leading factor analysts over more than fifty years. Jensen (1980) similarly includes little on this topic. Yet Lord (1980) and most who work in this field claim that any other methods of test construction are essentially a waste of effort.

Compared with the standard testing methods there are certain advantages in using item characteristic curve theory in test construction. The first is that the item statistics are sample free, at least in the Rasch model. In factor analytic tests, in contrast, this is not the case. If the homogeneity of any set of subjects is different from that on which the test was constructed, the factor loadings will be different. However, as is argued by Nunnally and Bernstein (1994), although the loading might differ it is highly likely that the rank order of the loadings will be the same and that the items will still be effective. Where they might change is the case when extreme groups are used, but testers are aware of this and no competent tester would use a test with extreme groups which had not been designed for that purpose.

This may not, therefore, be a striking disadvantage of classical tests. However, these tests yield scores which are not sample-free, a failing which is corrected in tests based upon item characteristic curves, at least for the Rasch model. With standard tests, as we have seen in Chapter 2, scores have to be interpreted in the light of the norms for the particular test. However, this entails that the same items are used in every application. Where subjects have to be retested, as, for example, in studies involving child development or in monitoring the progress of educational or therapeutic procedures, this creates an obvious difficulty. In tests where the characteristic curves of items are known it is possible to estimate the scores of subjects on items which they have not taken from the scores on other items. This assumes that from the subset of items which subjects have taken, their position on the latent trait is known. Of course, if the position is known it adds little to score them on the new items, although doing so may be useful for normative purposes.

This, then, is the great advantage of tests which are devised from item characteristic curves and the Rasch model. Accurate scores for any group of subjects (regardless of ability level) can be obtained with any set of items (regardless of difficulty level). This would seem to be so clear an advantage that it is curious why there are so few such tests.

If population-free scaling is to be achieved, huge samples have to be used. Lord (1974) claimed that a sample of 10,000 subjects was required. Furthermore, Chopin (1976) found that it was difficult to obtain items which actually fitted the Rasch (1960) model and that other models are no easier to fit. Furthermore, the measures of fit are themselves subjects of disagreement. In addition to these difficulties, Wood (1978) fitted random data to the Rasch model, which is the model most used by practical test constructors as distinct from specialist researchers into the theory of item characteristic curves. Certainly fitting the Rasch model does not imply unidimensionality, as Barrett and Kline (1981a) showed in their attempt to Rasch scale items from the EPQ.

Nor is this all. It should be clear from the description of item characteristic curves and the location of subjects on the latent trait that the method implies a real dimensionality; that being on a higher position on the trait involves knowing everything that those lower on the trait know. This may well be true of simple abilities in a very general sense such as vocabulary. Yet even here, although few low on the trait would know the meaning of, say, 'grisaille', it is still possible that there are words known by some low on the trait, yet unknown to those above them. Thus these models are not very good fits to real-world data even in abilities. As regards personality traits they would appear somewhat dissonant, although attempts have been made to produce Rasch-scaled personality tests. This last objection was raised to Guttman scales, and Levy (1973) has shown that Rasch scaling is a probabilistic form of Guttman scaling.

Relation of item characteristic curve theory and classical psychometric test theory

An obvious difference between the two theories is that the item characteristic curve theory is probabilistic whereas the linear model of correlations and factor analysis underlies psychometric theory. However, there are considerable similarities between these theories, which I shall briefly set out.

- Roskam (1985) showed that the factor loadings of the items in a test were good estimates of the slopes of the item characteristic curves, provided that the latent trait was normally distributed.

- De Gruijter (1986) has argued that from the correlation of the item with the total score and the proportion putting the keyed response it is possible to estimate the parameters of item response models: difficulty, discriminability and guessing.

- As has been previously mentioned Levy (1973) has shown that Rasch scales are probabilistic versions of Guttman scales.
- Finally, and perhaps more powerful than these theoretical points, as Nunnally (1978) argued, there is a high correlation between Rasch scales and those constructed using standard psychometric methods.

Hambleton and Jones (1993) summarise a number of other similarities and differences between item response theory and classical test theory but these are more relevant to practical test construction than to the problems of developing scientific measures and will not be further discussed here.

Conclusions concerning item characteristic curves and tests derived from them

The conclusion from this discussion of item characteristic curves and their theory and models seems clear. They are little different from standard psychometric scales. For certain simple abilities they may have certain practical advantages for retesting and using short versions of scales. However, all this ignores the point we have noted earlier in our discussion, namely that Rasch scaling is an example of additive conjoint measurement and is thus fundamental measurement, scientific in the sense used by Michell (1997). This must now be examined. For if this were indeed the case, it would be essential for scientific measurement in psychology that Rasch scales were immediately adopted, provided that the problems which we have already discussed do not rule them out.

Additive conjoint measurement and the Rasch model

Wright (1985) demonstrates that the Rasch model is a unit-maintaining process, which enables the construction of additivity and hence fundamental measurement. Following Luce and Tukey (1964), Wright argues that conjoint additivity is as good for measurement as physical concatenation (as in the case of the 12-inch rule), as we have fully discussed in Chapter 2. Conjoint measurement can be obtained from test items provided that the responses to the items are dominated by a linear combination of person measures and item calibrations. All these conditions are fulfilled by Rasch scales. This is the nub of his arguments, as we have seen.

However, even if it is accepted that it can be shown that Rasch scaling provides units of measurement and additivity, and is thus an example of conjoint measurement, it does not follow, unfortunately, that Rasch scaling is the answer to the scientific needs of psychometrics. I think that, like factor analysis, Rasch scaling is one of the easier roads to self-delusion. The arguments are set out below. For the sake of simplicity I shall restrict myself to intelligence tests, but the arguments will apply, of course, to all other psychological variables, perhaps with even more strength.

If we think of a typical item curve, as set out in Figure 4.1, we see that the horizontal axis consists of the latent trait. Although the latent trait is truly latent and cannot be known, it is defined by the total score on a set of items. Given the equations of Rasch scaling, what has been done is to show that the scales provide a set of equal-interval measurements for the scores derived from those items and an equivalent set of items, as calibrated in the Rasch analysis, instead of simply totalling the number of items correct, as in, for example, a standard intelligence test.

However, this is far different from jumping to the claim that these are unit-maintaining measures of intelligence. In other words, the problem turns on the identification of the latent trait with intelligence. One difficulty with the Rasch model, as has been stated, is that it assumes that correlation between items is entirely accounted for by the latent trait. Factoring of items suggests that there are many other sources of variance and covariance as well as error. It is simply incredible to imagine that, however scaled, the items of an intelligence test (and Rasch-scaled intelligence tests would use some of the items from standard intelligence tests – those which fitted the Rasch scaling) could constitute units of intelligence. The efficacy of standard intelligence tests was deemed to be based on the fact that the items were a sample of the kinds of problem which required intelligence to solve. They indicated the capability of the subject for reasoning. They were not thought to represent units of some variable.

In fact, what the Rasch scaling does is to index with high precision, and independently of the trial sample, the difficulty level of the items. The unit-maintaining quality, and thus the ability to obtain additivity, is derived from this characteristic. Wright (1985) writes, 'What item j will make the performance of person A appear the same as the performance of person B on item 1?' Clearly this can be answered only when the difficulty level of the items is calibrated using sample-free estimates, as is done in Rasch analysis.

However, this scaling of items by difficulty level, while mathematically allowing additivity and creating units of measurement, does so only among the Rasch set of items. To attempt to jump from this to intelligence, even if there is a good correlation between the Rasch scale and intelligence tests, is to go far beyond the data. Rasch scaling can produce scales with improved measurement characteristics, although, as Nunnally (1978) points out, there are high correlations between Rasch scales and their factored equivalents, so this improvement is not very large.

OTHER PROBLEMS WITH RASCH SCALES

There are yet other problems with Rasch scales: the poor fit of the Rasch model to most psychometric variables and to the psychology of responding to tests; the difficulty of fitting items to the Rasch model; and the problems of unidimensionality. All these problems have been briefly discussed earlier in this chapter but they are particularly pertinent here.

I shall deal first with unidimensionality. It is perfectly possible to produce a Rasch scale from items that are known to be from different factors. Thus the production of a Rasch scale does not guarantee that there is a meaningful latent trait. However, even if the items are factored first and thus are shown to be unidimensional, this does not totally solve the problem. First, it will ensure that there is little difference, in items, between the Rasch and the original scale, and Nunnally (1978) pointed out that there is a high correlation between scales thus produced. Second, factored items are not assumed to measure only the factor, unless the loadings are 1.0. This is not so with the latent trait model. Thus factored items are not really suited to Rasch analysis. Furthermore, Rasch analysis assumes that there is the same difficulty level for all items, which is manifestly not the case with scales developed by factor analysis. In addition to this, there is no place for guessing in Rasch analysis. Although a guessing parameter can be introduced, as Wright (1985) shows, the resulting scale is no longer an example of additive conjoint measurement. This is also true if a parameter of discrimination is introduced because this means that the ordering is not the same for individuals of different levels of the trait (Cliff, 1992). Finally, with any but the simplest variables it is often not possible to find items which fit Rasch scales when strict criteria are used.

Conclusions

For all these reasons, I still maintain that Rasch scales are not the psychometric answer to the measurement problems posed by Michell (1997). The problem is that response to the items is not simply, as the additive conjoint measurement model requires, a function of subjects' position on the latent trait and the facility of the item for eliciting the trait. This is the case because the items do not correlate perfectly with the latent trait and because the latent trait itself, which is notional, does not fit any real psychological variable. In addition, other parameters, such as guessing, and other response sets clearly affect responses to scales.

At most, Rasch scales make minor improvements to the precision of measurement of standard psychometric tests, improvements so minor as to be of little psychological significance. This is not, however, to deny their importance in practical, applied psychometrics. Here they can be useful where frequent testing needs to be done with alternative and parallel sets of items. For the production of equivalent item sets Rasch scaling is useful.

Importance of additive conjoint measurement in scientific psychology

I have shown that Rasch scales exemplify additive conjoint measurement but that they are insufficient for the task of scientific measurement in psychology. I shall now examine the efficacy of conjoint measurement as used in the example discussed in Chapter 2, the work of Stankov and Cregan (1993). Here conjoint measurement was applied to a putative test of intelligence, letter series, in order to show that the measure was additive and that the variable was quantitative. There are several points that can be made about this investigation which are also generally applicable.

- Stankov and Cregan (1993) investigated three scores: number correct, time to complete the test and rate of performance. Even had they established that the number correct was an additive scale and a variable with quantitative structure, this is not to establish that intelligence has quantitative structure, although the scale has a correlation with Raven's Matrices of 0.53. This is similar to the problem raised with Rasch scales. To show that the number of series items correct constitutes an additive scale does not say much of psychological interest. The psychologically interesting question is why? That the scale is additive means that it might be used as a useful variable in some scientific study of intelligence. However, as a measure of intelligence, the fact that it is additive does not make it valid.
- There is a further point about this approach to conjoint measurement. This concerns the fit of the conjoint model to variables such as intelligence or trait anxiety. Thus if a measure of intelligence varies with motivation it cannot be an adequate measure of the variable since intelligence is not thought to vary within individuals.
- This does not mean that conjoint measurement is worthless. It enables us, if the conditions are met, to create additive scales and to show that the variable is quantitative.
- In Chapter 2 we saw that scientific measures were fundamental or derived measures, quantitative and with clear units of measurement. Fundamental scales allow powerful mathematical treatment, as do conjoint measurement scales. However, from the viewpoint of scientific utility there appears to be a crucial distinction. This concerns the units of measurement. Thus in the example I have given, the unit, number of series completed, cannot be regarded as of great psychological significance, even if its intervals are equal. With Rasch scales there was a similar problem. Thus the similarity between fundamental and conjoint scales is one of mathematical properties; there is still a distinction between them of units. What we need in psychometrics are scales which employ units of intelligence, verbal ability, extraversion and so on – fundamental scales of these variables. The development of Rasch and other conjoint scales of psychological variables deals with the mathematical

shortcomings of psychometric tests, where the conditions can be met, but does not address the real scientific problem, namely that we have no scientifically meaningful units of measurement. A powerful psychometrics would utilise such units and thus, before scientific measurement can begin, precise theories of the nature of personality and intelligence must be developed and tested.

From this one can conclude that Rasch scales and conjoint measurement are not the answers to the scientific shortcomings of psychometric measurement, although the methods of conjoint measurement are useful in establishing the quantitative nature of a variable.

Other multivariate methods

As scrutiny of any statistical or psychometric text will show, factor analysis is not the only multivariate statistical analytic procedure. However, factor analysis has been described in detail because it is *the* psychometric method. Not only are many of the substantive findings in psychometrics derived from it (the basis of the discussions in the second part of this book) but, as has also been shown, factor analysis is an important method in the construction of psychometric tests themselves.

Many other multivariate analytic methods have been developed for various different purposes and many of these are used in the analysis of psychometric data. However, there is nothing distinctively psychometric about them. These methods include:

- *Multiple correlation or regression.* In this method the aim is to maximise the correlation between a set of predictors and a criterion variable. A typical example was provided by Cattell and Butcher (1968), who predicted academic success from a battery of ability, personality and motivation tests. For this purpose beta weights are produced for each variable, and the larger these are, the more important is the variable in the prediction. The problem here is that beta weights capitalise on sample error and tend to drop on replication.
- *Canonical correlational analysis.* This is the method for maximising the correlations between sets of variables. Canonical variates are produced indicating the correlations with the variate for each variable. Draycott and Kline (1995) utilised this technique, together with factor analysis, to establish how much common variance there was between the NEO and the EPQ personality questionnaires.
- *Discriminant function analysis.* In this method a set of discriminant functions is developed which maximises the differences between groups. Each function contains the optimum weighting for each variable to maximise such differences. However, as was the case with multiple regression, these weights are

sample dependent and replication in new samples is essential. It should be noted that these functions are highly similar to multiple analyses of variance which check whether the differences between groups are significant. Where distributions differ markedly from the normal, logistic analysis is to be preferred to discriminant analysis, and this is now available on many computer statistical packages. For more details of these methods readers must be referred to Krzanowski (1988).

These standard methods of multivariate analysis are useful when the questions which they were designed to answer arise in the study of psychometric data. They are by no means specifically psychometric and I shall not discuss them further.

The work of Guttman

Guttman, whose work in psychometrics is highly original, in addition to scaling procedures also developed a variety of analytic methods for psychometric data including least-space analysis and image factor analysis, which is an ingenious method of attempting to deal with the problems of error variance. However, as Cattell (1978) has argued, image analysis has its own difficulties and provides results little different from those of more standard factor analyses. In addition to all this, Guttman developed some other ingenious ways of examining correlation matrices, which have sometimes been used and advocated as superior to factor analysis (Romney and Bynner, 1992), and these must be discussed. Guttman (1992), for example, suggested that factor analysis is too much influenced by the idiosyncrasies of the sample, although this is easily remedied by replication and factor identification, and Romney and Bynner (1992) argue that factors are too static to be useful in psychological theory.

Guttman's alternative methods are known as the simplex, the radex and the circumplex. These are based on the rank ordering of correlations. A simplex structure (Guttman, 1955) can be found in correlation matrices in which correlations decrease from the principal diagonal to the corners. In the circumplex (Guttman, 1966) the correlations decrease and then increase. Finally, the radex (Guttman, 1954) is a mixture of circumplexes and simplexes. Simplex structures follow a linear sequence and in circumplex structures variables are located in a circle (hence the names). It should be pointed out that hierarchical factor models can be represented by the circumplex and the radex and some ability structures by the simplex. Romney and Bynner (1992), who are strong advocates of these methods, argue that they allow for a more dynamic conception of the variables than do factors and they prefer them sometimes because they appear to give more hope to teachers that change is possible, compared with the fixed traits of factor analysis. For more details, readers should refer to their book, but in my view optimism is not a relevant consideration in the sciences.

There is no doubt that these three patterns can be neat ways of encapsulating the information in correlation matrices, However, as Cattell (1978) has argued, there is a distinction between these structures and factors. Simple-structure factors, as has been shown, are replicable, and reflect, in some cases, the determinants of the correlations. At the least they are the simplest account of the correlations. These Guttman structures have no other status than being descriptive accounts. One can study them and comment on them but there is little more that can be done with them. Indeed, Fabrigar *et al.* (1997) have shown that there are complex conceptual and methodological issues surrounding the definition of circumplex structures and that often there are no formal procedures for testing whether the data really form a circumplex.

Structural equation modelling

Discussion of these Guttman methods leads on to the final topic of this chapter: structural equation modelling. Just as the circumplex is a different account of the correlation matrix from that supplied by factor analysis, and one implying a different model, so structural equation modelling deliberately sets out to test the fit of data to different models.

Factor analysis is a linear model and thus its use implies linear relationships among the variables. Although this may be questionable, as Cattell (1981) has argued, this is the simplest assumption, and until it is shown to be wrong it makes little sense to postulate more complex models. Certainly the fact that in the field of abilities good predictions can be made suggests that the model is not far out. On the other hand, in the fields of personality and motivation high predictability has not been generally found and structural equation modelling makes more sense.

Boyle *et al.* (1995) have a useful discussion of some aspects of structural modelling and I shall summarise some of their points. First the definition. Structural equation modelling involves the application of two models simultaneously: the measurement model (factor analysis of the variables) and multiple regression analysis of the latent traits, the factors, on each other (the structural model). Structural modelling allows statistical testing of the fit of hypothesised models to data. For example, causal models can be tested, as with path analysis, but structural equation modelling is not forced to assume that error terms are zero, and poor variables which do not contribute to valid variance can be eliminated.

LISREL is the best-known computing pack for structural equation modelling but, as Boyle *et al.* (1995) point out, it is important that various assumptions are met if the results are to be trustworthy, and these can cause problems. Thus although large samples are required to eliminate sampling bias the tests of fit are size sensitive, and with large samples hypotheses are easily rejected, a criticism that is applicable to confirmatory analysis. Similarly, even if a model is fitted, it does not mean to say that other models could not be fitted. Furthermore, it may not be easy to specify a plausible theory in the first place.

However, in summary, it may be said of structural equation modelling that it can be useful where adequate theories can be tested and where samples can be chosen that are large enough to be representative and reliable yet not so large as to cause rejection. However, the specification of such theories is difficult and, given that support of a theory is not proof, merely not disproof, structural equation modelling needs to be used with care.

Final conclusions

In this chapter I have described methods of test construction and multivariate data analysis which are different from factor analysis in order to investigate whether these would solve any of the problems of psychometric measurement which render it unscientific in the most strict sense. Conclusions can be stated clearly:

- None of the five methods of test construction discussed – item analysis, criterion keying, Guttman scaling, Thurstone scaling, methods using item characteristic curves – could be considered as capable of producing scientific measures.
- Rasch scales, a particular form of scale developed with item characteristic curves, have been claimed to be additive and unit maintaining, that is, examples of conjoint measurement. This was shown to be true but in so limited a sense that they could still not be considered scientific measures, and in addition it was clear that their underlying model did not fit most psychological variables.
- Conjoint measurement itself was scrutinised. Although conjoint measurement can demonstrate that scales are additive and that variables are quantitative, as with Rasch scales there are difficulties over their psychological importance because the units of measurement are still those used in psychometric scales.
- Some other multivariate statistical methods were briefly examined and found to answer useful questions but not to be specifically psychometric. These included multiple regression, canonical correlation, discriminant functions and logistic analysis.
- Some specific psychometric analytic methods, the simplex, radex and circumplex, were shown to be descriptive accounts of correlation matrices, but to have no special status.
- Structural equation modelling was found to be useful but to be treated with caution, much as confirmatory analysis.
- It has to be concluded that none of these methods or procedures remedies the problems of scientific measurement discussed by Michell (1997), although conjoint measurement allows powerful statistics to be used.

5

SUMMARY, CONCLUSIONS AND OVERVIEW OF PART 1

First I shall summarise the argument of this book. In Part 1 I have shown that the scientific method is not an instant recipe for discovering the truth, even in the natural sciences. In fact it is beset with philosophical difficulties, and its true rationale as a method is that it has worked so well. However, this is not the case in psychology, where there is no agreed and established body of knowledge. Thus it is necessary to examine the nature of the scientific method and the nature of psychology, especially the field of measurement, which is an essential of the true sciences. I then demonstrated that psychological measurement is unlike scientific measurement in a number of ways. In Part 2 the book I shall scrutinise the substantive findings of psychometrics in the light of these criticism of its measurement techniques and suggest how psychometrics must proceed in the future.

I now want to summarise and clarify the arguments and the thesis which have been proposed in the first part of this book. This is absolutely essential, since in the second part, as I have said, these arguments will be used to evaluate the findings in the different fields of psychometrics, and, what is perhaps of greater importance, to suggest new approaches in measurement and theory.

For maximum clarity the arguments will be set out briefly in list form. Obviously for full details and justification readers must turn to the relevant chapters.

- It is accepted that the huge advances in the natural sciences have arisen through the application of the scientific method.
- It is accepted that it is desirable that the scientific method be applied in psychology, and necessary if the subject is to become scientific.
- Examination of the scientific method shows that essentially it involves the statement of hypotheses and their testing.
- Science, therefore, is provisional. It is always liable to change as hypotheses are refuted. This distinguishes scientific knowledge from dogmas and beliefs.
- However, further examination of the scientific method shows that it is not a universal nostrum for the advancement of knowledge. There are some difficulties associated with the method.
- The first concerns the meaning of 'testable', as applied to a hypothesis.

Ultimately it means no more than that an investigator, or Popper, cannot think how it may be tested. This is clearly unsatisfactory.

- More serious is the fallibility of inductive reasoning, which is an integral part of the scientific method. Indeed, the claim that the scientific method is effective is itself an example of induction.

- Thus the defence of the scientific method must be pragmatic, rather than methodological, namely that it works. This is fine for the natural sciences but less impressive in psychology, where there is no clear body of established knowledge.

- There is a further, more serious objection, often raised in the social sciences, namely that there is no such thing as truth and that the hypotheses of science are no different from any other set such as those of religion or mysticism.

- The scientific method is dependent on the notion of an external reality (which it seeks to discover) and on the correspondence theory of truth, both of which have been attacked in much modern philosophy.

- From the arguments of Searle (1995) and others it was demonstrated that the notion of an external reality is philosophically viable. It is reasonable to conceptualise brute facts, kinds, essences and primary qualities as constituting an external reality and to accept that many other aspects of the world are socially constructed.

- The scientific method claims that its formulations of the external world are true. However, what is meant by the claim that a statement is true has been the subject of considerable philosophical analysis and dispute. Yet it is essential for the viability of the scientific method that the correspondence theory of truth implied in it is also viable.

- On the basis of the arguments of Searle (1995) it was demonstrated that the correspondence theory of truth is viable and that facts state the conditions in the world which would render any statement true or false.

- Thus there is no philosophical objection to the scientific method as a means of searching for the truth about the external world. Claims that such a world is simply a construction of the human mind were shown to be false.

- A distinction between the subject matter of the natural sciences and psychology was noted. The natural sciences are concerned with the brute facts of the external world.

- Psychology is concerned, in part, with an internal world of emotions, feelings and thoughts. However, other aspects are clearly more amenable to the scientific method.

- Thus some parts of psychology may become genuinely scientific and others may remain beyond the sphere of science. Which parts these are depends on the precision and nature of psychological measurement, the subject matter of psychometrics, and this must now be examined.

- The variables of psychological tests appear to be different from those measured in the natural sciences. These latter are data in the public domain rather than abstract concepts.

- Psychometrists, aware of their problems of measurement, have aimed to construct tests with certain clear characteristics which they regard as the hallmark of scientific measurement. These are set out below.
- Tests must be of high reliability, with respect both to internal consistency reliability and stability over time.
- Tests must be highly discriminating, yielding as much variance as possible.
- Tests must be valid; that is, measuring what they claim to measure. Validity is defined in terms of correlations with other similar tests, predictive power, and the test's ability to fit hypothesised patterns of scores (construct validity).
- The best psychometric tests meet all these criteria.
- These characteristics of good psychometric tests are based on a theory of test error, namely that any score obtained on a test consists of two components: true score and error.
- The true score is a notional concept, consisting of the score a subject would make on all the items in the universe of items relevant to the test variable. It is assumed that any test consists of a random set of these items. Hence in theory, the more reliable a test, the more its items must be drawn from the universe of items and the less the error.
- Because psychometric tests have no true zero, the meaning of a test score has to be relative to the scores of other individuals. Psychological tests, therefore, have to be standardised; that is, normative scores for various groups must be set up so that the score of any individual subject can be interpreted.
- Thus a good psychometric test is internally consistent, reliable over time, discriminating and of demonstrated validity in respect of its correlations with other tests, its predictive power and the performance of various criterion groups. It also has good norms.
- Tests with these qualities are used in the psychometric study of intelligence and other abilities, motivation and personality both to construct theory and in the applied settings of educational, clinical and occupational psychology.
- These characteristics, however, are quite different from those of the measures used in the natural sciences, as Michell (1997) has pointed out.
- Michell argues that scientific measurement entails first that it be shown that the attribute to be measured has a quantitative structure.
- It is further necessary to discover the additive structure of the attribute in order to calculate the ratio between magnitudes.
- Thus scientific measurement is defined as the estimation or discovery of some magnitude of a quantitative unit to a unit of the same attribute, after it has been shown that the attribute is quantitative. Conjoint measurement was suggested as a form of measurement suited to psychology and this is entailed in Rasch scales.
- As Michell argues, these definitions are quite different from those in

psychology, where measurement is generally defined as a procedure to assign numbers to events (other than in conjoint measurement).

- Stevens (e.g. 1951), as Michell points out, is the most notable defender of psychological measurement, and his views are simply accepted as standard in the majority of modern psychology texts.

- Michell demonstrates a logical incoherence in the arguments of Stevens which seems to refute them. Thus Stevens utilises operational definitions of variables. This entails that the meaning of a concept arises from the operations which identify it: intelligence is what intelligence tests measure.

- However, this definition is antirealist. Normally one would say that measuring a as longer than b depended upon a's being longer than b. However, on Stevens' definition all that is meant by saying that a is longer than b is a statement about measurement. Thus any measurement can be seen as defining and representing the relation, and it follows that measurement is the assignment of numbers according to rules.

- However, science, as has been argued, entails a realist view of the world and thus Stevens' definition is incoherent with a scientific position.

- Nevertheless, since we have seen that the arguments in favour of the scientific method are ultimately pragmatic, these philosophical problems with standard psychometrics are not completely devastating. It could be that, even with imperfect procedures, some scientific progress has been made.

- To investigate this possibility I examined factor analysis, the statistical method favoured in the construction of psychometric tests and in the analysis of their results. Although this assumes a normal distribution for variables in the analysis, I argued that such assumptions for the main factors identified were not untenable.

- It was shown that many exploratory factor analyses were flawed on account of technical deficiencies.

- However, the problem that there is an infinite number of equivalent factor analytic solutions can be solved if there is rotation to simple structure, this being defined as a set of factors each with a few high loadings and the rest zero. Simple structure, as Cattell (1978) has demonstrated, yields replicable, meaningful factors which, in some cases, are important determinants of the correlations.

- Simple structure can be obtained if there is proper sampling of variables and subjects; a subject to variable ratio greater than 2; principal factor analysis; the correct number of factors rotated, selected by Scree test or by statistical tests after maximum likelihood analysis; and Varimax or Direct Oblimin rotation, as the case may be.

- Confirmatory analysis can be valuable but caution has to be shown since the fact that a target matrix has been confirmed does not mean that other hypothetical matrices could not be fitted. There are also problems over fit:

with large samples good fits may be rejected and with small samples poor fits accepted. Indices of fit do not always agree.

- Thus technically adequate factor analyses are worthy of careful consideration.
- As a method of test construction, it is clear that factor analysis is highly useful (given the standard psychological definition of measurement). Factor analytic tests must be univariate and reliable, and are a sound instantiation of the true-score model of error, the theoretical basis of psychometric tests. However, they are not similar to scientific measures, in the sense of Michell (1997).
- Other methods of test construction were briefly examined to see whether they approached better the ideals of scientific measurement.
- Item analysis was shown to be highly similar to factor analysis as a method of test construction.
- Criterion-keyed tests were shown to fall far short of what is required for scientific measurement.
- Thurstone and Guttman scales were also demonstrated to be flawed.
- Tests constructed using item characteristic curves were also examined. These were shown to have many problems despite their statistical sophistication. They were clearly valuable for developing parallel sets of items for use in tailored testing and in applied work. However, their underlying models made them suited mainly to achievement testing and abilities, and even here the fit of model to data was dubious.
- One particular model, the Rasch model, was claimed to possess additivity and be capable of fundamental measurement, in the sense of conjoint measurement. However, this model, even if these arguments could be maintained, holds that item difficulty and subjects' ability are the only determinants of item response. This is manifestly wrong since guessing is clearly one other factor. Models which included this or any other parameter unfortunately are no longer additive. There are other problems with the model. It does not ensure unidimensionality and, with indices of fit, it is difficult to find items to fit the model in many cases.
- Conjoint measurement, as applied to variables, was shown to be useful in demonstrating that a scale was additive and that the attribute was quantitative. In this, conjoint measurement resembled scientific measurement but there is a difficulty over its lack of meaningful units of measurement.
- It was concluded that, for most psychometric variables, it had to be accepted that tests failed to meet the criteria of fundamental scientific measurement.
- Some other multivariate techniques were examined, such as multiple regression, canonical correlation, discriminant function and logistic analysis. These were shown to be useful for certain questions but they were quite general methods and not specific to psychometrics.
- Finally, some specific methods used in psychometrics were scrutinised. Guttman's radex, simplex and circumplex were shown to be interesting

descriptions and structural equation modelling was found to be of value for testing hypotheses, but a method to be used with caution.

- It was concluded that the measurement methods of psychometrics were, indeed, different from those of the natural sciences and this would have to be taken into consideration in the evaluation of psychometric findings concerning ability, personality and motivation.
- This was particularly important because I had previously demonstrated that the scientific method, *per se*, was no absolute guarantee of arriving at the truth, given the problems of falsification and induction. Thus if the scientific method in psychometrics is not actually scientific at all because of measurement problems, there is further reason to scrutinise psychometric results with especial care.

This, therefore, is the task in the second part of this book, to answer the following two questions:

1 Are the psychometric findings in the fields of ability, personality and motivation of any scientific value, given the problems of scientific measurement?
2 Can scientific measures be developed in these fields?

Part 2

THE NEW PSYCHOMETRICS
The scientific measurement of personality
and ability

6

INTELLIGENCE AND ABILITY

Definition of intelligence and ability

Intelligence and ability are widely used terms in normal, conventional English usage and there ought to be little difficulty in defining them. Carroll (1993), however, in his exhaustive study of human cognitive abilities, which involved the reanalysis by the best factor analytic methods of all factor analytic studies of human abilities, devoted a long first chapter to the topic. Yet his abstract and precise definitions seem to convey little of what is normally intended. For example (p. 8):

> ability refers to the possible variations over individuals in the liminal levels of task difficulty (or in derived measurements based on such levels) at which, on any given occasion in which all conditions appear favourable, individuals perform successfully on a defined class of tasks.

This definition, difficult as it is, involves yet another complex definition, that of 'task', with which I shall not weary the reader. Precision without clarity is not useful.

By the term 'human abilities' I refer to those attributes of individuals which are involved in the solution of problems. In the main these are cognitive abilities, the term 'cognitive' referring to use of mental information processing. Of course, in any task other attributes play some part, such as persistence if the task is lengthy and tedious, but the trait of persistence, because it is not cognitive, in the sense defined, would be regarded as a personality trait.

Thus it is useful to make a broad distinction between cognitive traits, involving the processing of information, and personality traits, which will be fully discussed and defined in Chapter 8 but which refer, in general, to the way we do what we do. Motivational traits, it might be added here for completeness, including moods and transient states, refer to why we do what we do. Indeed, the full power of the psychometric model of human behaviour (Kline, 1980; Cattell, 1981) is that it attempts to predict real-life behaviour precisely in a regression equation utilising the major factors from these three spheres of ability, personality and motivation.

If the term 'abilities' refers to those traits which are involved in the solution of problems through information processing, then the status of intelligence becomes clear. It is one of such traits – probably, given its common English usage, the most important. As Kline (1991a) demonstrated in his study of intelligence, there have been numerous definitions of this variable and there is no ready agreement. However, the broad, general definition which I prefer is that intelligence refers to the general reasoning ability which is useful in the solution of problems. I do not want to go beyond this definition. This is because the verbal analysis of concepts and notions is the province of philosophy, valuable in itself, but by no means destined to arrive at the truth.

As I argued throughout the first part of the book, the whole point of the scientific method is that it appears, in general, in many spheres of human knowledge, to approach the truth more closely than does any other procedure. Psychometrics is an attempt to apply this method to the study of individual differences. Hence I shall rely upon psychometric procedures to establish any more precise definition of intelligence.

Thus we can say, in summary, that 'intelligence' and 'abilities' refer to those traits involving information processing and used in the solution of problems and that intelligence itself refers to a general reasoning ability. It is highly likely, on the basis of human experience, that there are other, less wide-ranging abilities such as verbal or mathematical ability, and many highly specific ones, such as, for example, in music, sight-reading or chord perception. This is the concept of human abilities which is held in psychometrics. Psychometricians, ever since the first paper by Spearman (1904) on the factor analysis of human abilities, have been concerned with such empirical analyses. It is to their results that we must now turn.

The main ability factors

In this section of this chapter I shall set out in Box 6.1 the most important ability factors which have emerged after more than ninety years of factor analysis. There are several criteria which have to be met if factors are to be included in this box (and in subsequent tabulations in other chapters):

- Factors must be of some importance. Factors may be considered important if they account for a substantial proportion of the variance in human abilities. The factors must be derived from technically sound analyses. The discussion of factor analysis in Chapter 3 made it clear that many published factor analyses suffer from technical faults which render them of little scientific value. It is pointless to discuss or investigate such flawed factors, although this is regularly done in meta-analyses.
- Factors must be replicated. It was also made clear there that factors need to be replicated. Replication is essential, as in any science, and it is preferable that the factors be replicated in different laboratories.

- Factors must be validated. In Chapter 3 it was made clear that validation is also critical, since it is perfectly possible to produce technically sound, replicated but scientifically worthless factors – bloated specifics or tautologous factors.

Provenance of Box 6.1

There have been numerous attempts to provide a definitive list of ability factors, for example by Ekstrom *et al.* (1976), Cattell (1971), Hakstian and Cattell (1974) and the present writer (Kline, 1979, 1991a, 1993). However, since the publication of Carroll's reanalysis of virtually all the factor analytic studies in the psychometric literature, this task of selection, using the criteria mentioned above, has been greatly simplified. It is fortunate that the factor analytic methods favoured by Carroll (1993) closely resemble those advocated here and by Cattell, so that there is no technical controversy concerning the findings. It is also reassuring that the factors in the Carroll list and those in the other lists are so similar that there can be little doubt about their identity. The fact that Carroll's careful reanalysis of all previous work supported so clearly the original work of Cattell (1971) on abilities confirms the correctness of Cattell's rigorous approach to factor analytic research. In the field of human abilities it is a fair summary to say that Cattell's position has been entirely vindicated. My Box 6.1 represents a synthesis of all the work cited above and is not identical with that of Carroll.

Primary and higher-order factors

The elucidation of the structure of human abilities through factor analysis has utilised, until the past few years, exploratory factor analysis, and the factors set out in Box 6.1 were thus derived. Exploratory analysis depends for its efficiency (see Chapter 3) on adequate sampling of all variables in the field of abilities. Such sampling is a difficult problem, and it is admitted by Cattell (1971) that undoubtedly some classes of abilities are under-represented in any list or, perhaps, not represented at all. The further distant a task is from the typical problem to be found in the sciences and arts curriculum, the more likely it is that it has not been adequately tested and thus there will be no clear factor or factors embracing the ability required to perform it. Horse-riding ability, as evinced by leading jockeys, and the ability to communicate well with animals are two abilities that have never been subjected to any kind of factor analysis, for example.

The consequence of this is twofold:

- There can be no definitive list of primary ability factors. In the first place any list of primary factors, the factors derived from the correlations between tests, is almost certainly incomplete. It is bound to be so unless every possible test were to be included in some absolute factor analysis.
- A list of primary factors which in any way attempts to cover the range of

abilities is inevitably lengthy. If we were to take verbal ability as an example, it would be odd if what we think of as its constituents – vocabulary, grammatical ability, appreciation of the rhythm of a sentence, comprehension – were all separate. It is highly likely that such primary factors are themselves correlated.

- There is a problem of bloated specifics. In addition, what constitutes a factor is to some extent arbitrary, which accounts for the emphasis that we place on the validation of factors. Thus if we wrote enough items in a test of mathematical ability which all had in common a particular operation, perhaps the elucidation of π, it is conceivable that these would form a separate small factor. This would be a bloated specific of no interest whatever, but it highlights the difficulty of producing a definitive list of primary factors.

In summary, with primary factors, all that can be done is to show those which regularly occur as accounting for substantial proportions of the ability variance.

Higher-order factors

For this reason it is sometimes preferred, and it is certainly a neater solution, to list the higher-order factors, almost always the second-orders. Second-order factors are derived from the factor analysis of the correlations between the first-order factors (primaries) (see p. 54). These load, therefore, on the primary factors. These are broader factors than primaries, accounting for more variance, and a small number of second-order factors do indeed account for much of the variance in human abilities. Second-order factors are highly effective in providing an economical account of a complex field. It should be noted that there are factor analytic techniques for computing the factor loadings on the higher-order factors of the original variables, the tests, as well as the primary factors. This is valuable in identifying the factors and ensuring that the concepts remain close to the original data (see Cattell, 1978).

Of course, if there is a large matrix of variables, covering the widest possible range of abilities, it is possible that there will be a sufficient number of second-order factors to make it worthwhile to extract the third-orders. This is sometimes done in the case of ability factors, and the results will be discussed on pp. 103–4. Here it is sufficient to say that any third-orders are obviously very broad factors of ability. The main proponents of the extraction of higher-order factors are Undheim and Gustaffsson (e.g. Undheim, 1981; Undheim and Gustaffsson, 1987).

Comments on Box 6.1.

Before I describe the factors in terms of their factor loading and discuss their psychological meaning a few points are worthy of note.

Box 6.1 The largest higher-order ability factors

1　g (third-order). In Carroll's analyses, this factor occurred in around 150 of the data sets.
2　Fluid intelligence. This is a second-order factor which emerged from most of the sets of data, as did all the other second-orders listed in this box.
3　Crystallised intelligence.
4　Visual perception.
5　Auditory perception.
6　Cognitive speed.
7　Retrieval ability.
8　Memory ability.

- Carroll includes a factor additional to those in this list: a mixture of crystallised and fluid intelligence which sometimes occurred in his analyses. In general, however, the emergence of this factor appears to be an artefact of the variables in the matrix. As Cattell (1978) has shown, third-order factors can occur at the second order in certain conditions and it is unlikely that this factor is of any psychological substance other than to demonstrate that fluid and crystallised intelligence are highly correlated.
- As I stated earlier, Carroll's factors are based upon virtually all data sets, and factor analyses without technical flaws. Five of his factors are identical to those of Cattell (1971) and Hakstian and Cattell (1978). These are fluid ability, crystallised ability, visualisation, cognitive speed and retrieval capacity.
- There were some other, smaller factors, notably cognitive speed factors, and these will be discussed in Chapter 7, where an attempt will be made to suggest how a new psychometrics, with scientific, fundamental measures, might be developed from these factor analytic results.

Description and identification of the factors

Factors are identified initially from their factor loadings. This identification is then validated against some external criterion. Only when this has been done can any confidence be placed in the identification of the factor. As I have previously demonstrated (Kline, 1993), careful examination of the factor loadings, even of well-known tests, indicates that the identification of the factors is dubious. First, therefore, I shall scrutinise the loadings on each of these ability factors. Carroll (1993) gives the median loadings for tests from all his data so there can be little doubt that the tests do load the factors.

Factor 1 (g)

The four highest-loading variables are: I (induction); Vs (visualisation); RQ (quantitative reasoning); and V (verbal ability). Flexibility of closure, numerical facility, associative memory, word fluency, speed of closure, sequential reasoning and spatial relations all load beyond 0.4. Ideational fluency, originality, lexical knowledge, perceptual speed, memory span and sensitivity to problems all load beyond 0.3.

There are several important points concerning this factor:

- · Note the number and heterogeneity of the variables loading on it. It is evident from the description of the variables loading this factor that it must be considered a general factor of cognitive ability.
- It would be interpreted as an ability underlying all these diverse, different abilities. Thus it makes sense to call it intelligence or general reasoning ability. It is noteworthy that three of the highest-loading factors involve reasoning: induction; verbal ability, which is essentially comprehension; and quantitative reasoning, the reasoning required for the solution of mathematical problems. Visualisation, the other high-loader, involves the manipulation of the orientation of shapes in your mind. It loads highly on chess and some kinds of spatial, mathematical analyses.

The emergence of this factor supports the notion of a general intellectual capacity, general reasoning ability, which might be called intelligence, although, as Cattell (1981) and Carroll (1993) have argued, it would be better to drop that term with its enormous number of everyday connotations which are not precisely matched by this or any other factor. This is almost certainly the factor identified originally by Spearman (1904), as has always been claimed by Undheim (Undheim 1981; Undheim and Gustaffsson, 1987). Factor analysis, therefore, it can confidently be asserted, has identified a broad, general factor of reasoning ability, namely intelligence, which accounts for a substantial proportion of variance in human abilities (slightly more at lower than higher levels of ability (Deary *et al.*, 1996). If we wanted to measure this factor, tests of inductive reasoning, verbal comprehension, quantitative reasoning and visualisation would be effective.

Factors 2 and 3 (fluid and crystallised intelligence)

Factors 2 and 3 are second-order factors which account for the correlations between the primary factors. Before I identify them from the loadings found in the analyses of Carroll (1993), it is necessary to point out that these intelligence factors are the critical features of the work of Cattell (1971). His analyses and those of Hakstian and Cattell (1976) indicated clearly that the old g factor, measured by traditional intelligence tests, on proper rotation split into two correlated factors: fluid and crystallised intelligence. To simplify somewhat

Cattell's investment theory, it was argued that fluid intelligence was the basic reasoning capacity of the brain, dependent upon (though not, of course, entirely) its neurological structure. It was thus expected to have, and was shown to have (Cattell, 1982), a considerable genetic determination. Crystallised intelligence, on the other hand, was conceptualised as the sets of skills, usually those valued in a culture, in which fluid intelligence is invested. In the West these are often scientific and technological subjects and high culture, for those less gifted in respect of fluid ability. These factors were highly correlated early in life but less so later for obvious reasons, in that they depend upon individuals' life experiences and educational opportunities.

Finally, before we examine the nature of fluid intelligence and crystallised intelligence, as revealed in the factor analyses, it should be pointed out that the great advantage of this split lies in the fact that these factors can be measured separately. As has been mentioned, old-fashioned intelligence tests, such as those of Wechsler (1958), measured a combination of these two factors, and, as we have seen, bivariate tests are not good. Often it is revealing, especially for children, for example, who are doing poorly at school, to have separate measures of both these factors. The child from a disadvantaged home who yet reveals a high fluid intelligence is clearly a different case from a child from a good home whose crystallised ability suggests a higher fluid intelligence than in fact he or she has.

NATURE OF FLUID INTELLIGENCE

Fluid intelligence is characterised by four variables which have median loadings greater than 0.6. These are: I, induction; Vs, visualisation; RQ, quantitative reasoning; and FI, ideational fluency. Just as was suggested by Cattell (1971), this factor, fluid intelligence, does appear to be involved in reasoning. Ideational fluency, although it loaded highly, did so only in three studies.

THE NATURE OF CRYSTALLISED INTELLIGENCE

In contrast, the variables loading crystallised intelligence are somewhat different. They are verbal ability, language development, reading comprehension, sequential reasoning and general information. Ideational fluency sometimes loads this factor. It is clear from these loadings that this is a factor involved in verbal ability and reasoning. In any culture, this is a sensible way to invest one's basic intelligence. These are the skills essential for and basic to any culture.

In some data sets a mixed factor of intelligence at the second order was observed loading on a mixture of the variables in these two factors. Where this occurred there was usually a clear third-order factor which could be extracted from the matrix – the one which we have discussed above as the factor of general ability.

CONCLUSIONS

Although of course this survey by Carroll (1993) contained no studies later than that date, the clear replicability of the findings which I have discussed above and the quality of the factor analyses make it unlikely that any dramatically new findings will be reported in later work, and indeed none have been as yet. It can be said that there is a consensus over the nature of intelligence, as defined in factor analysis. It is essentially as it was conceived by Spearman and explicated by Cattell.

In human abilities there appears to be a large general factor which accounts for a considerable proportion of the variance in human abilities and for the fact that they are positively correlated (the positive manifold). This broad, third-order factor appears to be concerned with basic reasoning capacities. However, it is very broad. At the second order it splits into two correlated factors, crystallised and fluid intelligence. The latter loads on basic reasoning abilities and is highly similar to the original Spearman's g factor, while the former consists of those more verbal abilities which, in the work of Cattell (1971), are conceived as arising from the investment of fluid intelligence in the skills valued in a culture.

What is certain from the analysis of well-known intelligence tests (see Kline, 1991a, 1993 for examples), is that many load on both these factors. It makes good sense, in my view, to see intelligence as composed of the fluid and crystallised intelligence factors. Fluid intelligence would appear to set an upper limit to intellectual performance which is often well predicted by crystallised intelligence. For individuals who have been exposed to a good education and a stimulating environment (whatever that may be; it is by no means self-evident) their crystallised intelligence may fully reflect their fluid ability. In other, less fortunate individuals there may be more room for improvement.

Such, then, is intelligence as revealed by factor analysis: essentially two correlated factors involved with reasoning ability. They are general because reasoning is required in the solution of almost all problems.

More precise analysis of crystallised and fluid intelligence

Factors, I have argued, are identified from their factor loadings. This is what has been done in the preceding paragraphs. The identification and descriptions which have been discussed are the accepted views of the leading psychometricians, and, as has been seen, they are well founded.

However, this book is concerned with a critical analysis of the field. For this purpose it is instructive to forget the identification of these factors and look at the actual items of the test variables which load on them. In subsequent chapters I shall do this for all the personality and motivation factors claimed to be important.

Fluid intelligence

The three critical factors were induction, visualisation and quantitative reasoning.

TYPICAL INDUCTION TASKS AND ITEMS

The test loading most highly on fluid intelligence and whose variance is most accounted for by that factor is Raven's Matrices (Raven, 1965a), as is clear from Woliver and Saeks (1986), although the test was produced before the Second World War. Matrices items are excellent examples of inductive reasoning items and thus of what is required of subjects to score highly on fluid intelligence.

Each item is of the same kind but, as we shall see, it is easy to vary their level of difficulty. A matrix item is a series of diagrams or patterns and the subject is required to complete the series, from a set of alternative patterns. The correct solution demands that from the series shown the subject works out the rule of the series (induction) and then applies the rule to the possible responses.

Another excellent test which loads the fluid intelligence factor is Cattell's Culture-Fair Test (Cattell and Cattell, 1959). This was designed to overcome a problem with the Raven's Matrices, namely that the test contains only one kind of item. From the model of test measurement discussed in Chapter 3, in which scores consist of the general factor plus a specific factor and error, it is evident that the specific factor on a test in which items are similar is bound to distort the general-factor score. This, indeed, happens occasionally with the Matrices, and subjects are found who score much higher or much lower on this test than on other tests of fluid ability. The Culture-Fair Test, which uses non-verbal items, overcomes this problem by using items of more than one kind, the specific error thus cancelling out or being of negligible size. The item types are:

- *Series*. In series a set of diagrams is shown and the rule of the series has to be induced. For example, a set of heads is shown in various positions and the next position from a set of positions has to be chosen. Again the rule has to be induced.
- *Classifications*. Items in this test consist of five diagrams or patterns and subjects are required to induce the classification rule which makes two of them different. Which two has to be indicated.
- *Matrices*. These are similar items to those in Raven's Matrices.
- *Conditions* (topology). Items of this kind consist of a set of diagrams in which are various configurations of, say, circles and squares, or triangles and rectangles. Subjects are required to choose the diagram in which it is possible to place a spot according to a rule, such as outside a circle but in a square.

The ability to score highly on items of this type typifies the person high on fluid intelligence. All these items, as is clear from the descriptions, necessitate the ability to induce rules and to apply them to new contexts. I think this also clarifies why this is so general a factor of human abilities. Much problem solving is of this kind.

VISUALISATION

Visualisation is the other primary factor which loads this flexible intelligence highly and distinctively. An examination of typical visualisation items will clarify the factor. In fact, it is tests of spatial ability which load the visualisation primary factor. Many of the test which load most saliently involve the mental rotation of shapes in two or three dimensions.

Thus in the Wechsler tests we have *block design*. Subjects are shown a design that may be constructed from a pile of blocks by placing blocks such that the top surface represents the design. *Block counting* is a not dissimilar task with a high loading on visualisation. This involves counting how many blocks appear in a picture of blocks in which some are occluded, or how many blocks touch certain other blocks in a pile. Eliot and Smith (1983) drew up a compendium of published spatial tests from which it is clear that the majority of visualisation tests are essentially variants of the typical tests which I described. All require subjects to match shapes in different orientations.

It is highly interesting that this visualisation factor, so clearly defined by its prototypical tests as requiring subjects to be able to carry out mental rotation, is so salient to fluid intelligence. Whereas everyday notions of intelligence would be likely to include inductive reasoning as essential, this is probably not true of visualisation.

QUANTITATIVE REASONING

It is certainly the case that most people would think that the ability to reason quantitatively is an important aspect of intelligence – as, indeed, the evidence indicates. The tests or items which load this factor are those mathematical tasks (involving arithmetic, algebra or geometry) which demand reasoning, either inductive or deductive. Good mathematicians are almost always highly intelligent because ability at mathematics depends so greatly on mathematical reasoning, which is an important component of intelligence. Some other forms of academic learning may not require much reasoning ability at all (the social sciences and many arts subjects spring to mind), and even if they do, they require, further, considerable amounts of knowledge. The idea of an uneducated, natural, historian is not meaningful. There have been cases of such brilliant mathematicians, notably the Cambridge mathematician Srinivasa Ramanujam, a shipping clerk from Madras.

CONCLUSIONS CONCERNING FLUID INTELLIGENCE

Careful examination of the items most highly loading this factor suggests that its identification is reasonable. The question we ask is this: what would account for the fact that there is a correlation between the skills demanded by matrices items, mental rotation and mathematical reasoning? A basic reasoning ability would appear to be a supportable identification.

Two points are worth noting here. Writers opposed to the notion of a general intelligence have tried to explain the large g factor away by arguing that is a factor of attention or the motivation to do tests and that it is why it correlates with academic success. However, were this the case, all tests would load the factor about the same. Another claim is that the factor demands the same skills as academic success and that the common factor is not just reasoning ability. However, scrutiny of the items, as is now obvious, other than in the quantitative reasoning factor, destroys that argument. That is precisely what this factor is not. It is loaded by items with which subjects are not familiar from their education. This is in contrast to crystallised intelligence, and I shall now look the items loading that factor.

One further study needs consideration. Kyllonen and Christal (1990), in four researches with large samples and using tests of reasoning and working memory (Baddley, 1986), found the reasoning factors correlated with working memory capacity between 0.8 and 0.9. Their paper was thus entitled 'Reasoning ability is (little more than) working memory capacity'. However, this interpretation seems false. It may be the case that some reasoning tasks are closely linked to working memory capacity, as measured by Baddley, because failures of such memory preclude reasoning. However, this does not mean that reasoning ability is working memory. In any case, most studies separate memory factors from those of intelligence (Cattell, 1971; Carroll, 1993), and no factor of working memory has ever been found (Carroll, 1993). One must be careful, therefore, in accepting the claims of Baddley (e.g. 1986) and colleagues at the Applied Psychology Unit in Cambridge that these tasks do indeed measure working memory capacity. The work of Embretson (1995) is also relevant here. Embretson found that working memory (as measured by the Baddley tasks) was related both to reasoning ability and to processing speed. However, the same comments pertain. It is clear that to reason at all, working memory is essential. This was recognised in the Wechsler scales, where digit span is one of the tests.

Items loading crystallised intelligence

The three most salient and prototypical factors defining crystallised intelligence are verbal ability, general information and reading comprehension. This makes good sense if we remember the definition of Cattell (1971): that crystallised intelligence represents the investment of fluid intelligence in the skills valued in a culture. In most Western cultures, at least, education is essentially verbal and thus we would expect crystallised intelligence to be predominantly verbal.

Typical verbal ability test items are: vocabulary, analogies, synonyms, meaning of proverbs and, for older children and adults, the comprehension of passages of English, or any other native language.

Vernon (1950) showed that the single best indicator of crystallised intelligence in children is the vocabulary test, and if a brief intelligence test is required, a combination of vocabulary and matrices (fluid and crystallised intelligence) is highly effective. Sternberg (1977) in his study of analogies made it clear that the reasoning demanded to work out analogies is central to intelligence in general. Indeed, verbal analogies load crystallised intelligence, and non-verbal analogies, fluid intelligence. The solution of analogies involves, of course, the induction of the rule which relates the two components.

From these items it is clear that verbal ability is, in reality, the ability to reason in words rather than in symbols. Middle-class children with educated parents who read and talk more, it is presumed, than their working-class counterparts are likely to develop their crystallised intelligence to a greater extent than those children from less verbal backgrounds.

From this description of the items of verbal ability it is hardly surprising that the other salient factors were general information and reading comprehension. General information is always high in the highly intelligent and educated person. This is because, in part, highly intelligent individuals can find structural links in the material they come across, making retention easier. It is also true that retention depends in part upon interest. But things are more interesting if they can be linked to other information. Tests of general information, therefore, simply tap knowledge. Similarly, reading comprehension, which is a particularly good test of crystallised ability for children, is measured, as would be expected.

CONCLUSION CONCERNING CRYSTALLISED INTELLIGENCE

These items make it clear that verbal reasoning and an ability with words are central to crystallised intelligence. Crystallised intelligence is essentially reasoning ability verbally instantiated.

The factor analytic picture of intelligence

Whether we see intelligence as a broad third-order factor or a combination of two correlated second-order factors, fluid and crystallised intelligence, makes little or no difference to our conception of intelligence. Study of the items in these factors indicates that reasoning ability is common to both. In crystallised intelligence the essence is on verbal reasoning and ability, cognitive activities encouraged in the education system. Fluid intelligence appears in new and unfamiliar tasks requiring reasoning, where experience and practice play less part. Possibly in an egalitarian society such that all were educated to their full intellectual potential, these two factors would merge.

So much for the factorial description based on factor loadings. I shall now examine external evidence for the validity of these intelligence factors.

The validity of the intelligence factors

Because it has been shown (e.g. Jensen, 1980; Cattell, 1971; Carroll, 1993), that crystallised and fluid ability are correlated factors and that traditional intelligence tests load on both, I shall deal with their validity together. My brief survey – and it will be brief because there is such considerable agreement over the findings – will scrutinise the evidence for the validity of these g factors. I shall deal with the evidence under a number of headings.

Intelligence and academic achievement

- There is a substantial correlation between intelligence and academic performance at all ages. The exact size of the correlation varies on account of the unreliability of some measures of academic achievement and the homogeneity of samples in the case of studies of college students, both factors which lower the correlations. Nevertheless, at the primary school the correlation between intelligence and attainment is of the order of 0.6 (Vernon, 1960). If we want to predict the future educational achievement of a 5-year-old, the intelligence test is the best single test we could give. The work of Terman (Terman and Oden, 1959) and his gifted sample is striking support for this claim. Jensen (1980), summarising much of this work, claims that the child of high intelligence simply learns more quickly and easily the necessary scholastic knowledge, and scores more highly on tests of achievement than do children of lesser ability. All these facts are supported in a recent issue of the journal *Intelligence* in which the first chapter consists of discussion of findings concerning mea- sured intelligence which are agreed by leading authorities in the field (Gottfredson, 1997a).

- The correlation between intelligence and educational attainment is not caused by some third variable or variables affecting all learning ability. Egalitarian opponents of intelligence testing (e.g. Pedley, 1953) have attempted this argument, claiming that poor environments affect both school achievement and intelligence test scores, conceptualised as measures of having learned to reason. This point will not stand scrutiny. In the first place, as Vernon (1960) demonstrated, coaching on intelligence tests pro- duces only small gains in IQ, and these are achieved after five or six hours' coaching. Furthermore, such gains do not much generalise to other intelli- gence tests, even parallel forms. Reasoning ability is not really teachable. Attainment, on the other hand, clearly can improve with practice. This is commonplace knowledge, and is supported empirically by, for example, the work of Ericsson (1988).

- Intelligence tests do not simply measure some motivational or personality variable that affects both educational and test performance. This claim again is easily refuted. First, as was made clear by the work of Cattell

111

and Butcher (1968) in the prediction of school performance, motivational and personality variables are largely independent of g and other ability factors, and account for different aspects of the variance in educational achievement. Furthermore, if this argument were true there would be virtually the same correlation between different school and university subjects and intelligence test scores. But this is not so. The correlations are highest with those which, a priori, would appear to demand reasoning ability and lowest with those in which success demands little more than rote learning, the classics and mathematics being examples of the former, sociology and history of the dance in Africa, the latter (see Jensen, 1980). As Gottfredson (1997b) points out, the more complex the task, the higher its correlation with g.

- The correlation between intelligence test scores and academic success cannot be explained away by the fact of some common content in intelligence tests and educational measures. In fact, the best predictor of how a person will do in an entirely novel sphere is an intelligence test (see Jensen, 1980 and Kline, 1991a for a full discussion of this point).

CONCLUSIONS

All these facts, about which there is almost no disagreement, even among opponents of intelligence tests, support the notion that what is measured by intelligence tests is the ability to reason. Only this sensibly accounts for the observations discussed above.

Intelligence and occupational success

- In a survey of more than 10,000 investigations, Ghiselli (1966) showed that the single best predictor of any job was an intelligence test. The average correlation with success at a job was 0.3. No other test approaches this predictive power. Gottfredson (1986) confirms these findings, as does Furnham (1995). Given that there are considerable problems in providing a good criterion for occupational success, these results are remarkable. Furthermore, it has been shown (Cattell and Kline, 1977) that there are differences in the level of intelligence among different occupational groups, as would be expected. For example, theoretical physicists score more highly than elementary school teachers. There can be no doubting the conclusion that these intelligence factors are implicated in occupational success. The recent survey by Gottfredson (1997b) simply confirms all these claims as do Schmidt and Hunter (1998).

Heritability of fluid and crystallised intelligence

A few preliminary points need to be made about the results which I shall report here.

- Although this is a highly contentious area, particularly since the realisation that the twin data of Burt (1966) were not reliable, in fact there is a high measure of agreement between studies. It is an irony that Burt's results are virtually identical to the weighted average of all twin studies up till 1993 (Bouchard, 1993)

- The results to be discussed are taken from a variety of intelligence tests, which, as has been argued, measure a combination of crystallised and fluid ability. However, it should be remembered that the heritability of fluid intelligence is higher than that of crystallised intelligence, as is to be expected from the hypothesised nature of these factors (Woliver and Saeks, 1986).

- Most findings are obtained from biometric studies of intelligence which involve the study of the variances and covariances of intelligence test scores between individuals of varying degrees of consanguinity. Usually this involves monozygotic (MZ) and dizygotic (DZ) twins, reared together and reared apart, siblings, parents and adopted children and their adoptive and natural parents. Such biometric methods assume that the phenotypic variance of a trait may be broken down into genetic and environmental sources. The latter may themselves be split into shared and non-shared sources of variance (see Fulker (1979) for a clear account of these methods).

- The proportions of variance claimed to be genetically or environmentally determined refer to population variance. Thus such proportions are bound to differ in different populations, depending upon the diversity of the environmental influences.

- There is no doubt that intelligence test scores are highly heritable. Heritability coefficients vary from 0.5 to 0.8, this latter being obtained from a careful sampling of all separated twins in Sweden. This study (by Pedersen *et al.*, 1992) is revealing. The correlation for MZ twins reared together was 0.80 and for MZs apart was 0.78. For DZ twins these figures were 0.32 and 0.22. It should be noted that these were adult samples.

- The heritability of intelligence increases with age. By adulthood the influence of the shared family environment on intelligence is close to zero. In this sample of separated twins, there was no relation between within-pair differences in environment and the within-pair correlations for intelligence. These results are supported by studies of adoptive children, in which, as the children grow older, the correlation of intelligence between children and adoptive parents drops to zero (Phillips and Fulker, 1989).

- The shared environment contributes little to the determination of intelligence. This is a general finding in studies of the heritability of intelligence, although it runs counter to sociological accounts of the development of intelligence (Brody and Crowley, 1995). These authors, however, demonstrate that this simple dichotomy, although useful, is probably too simple. There are genetic influences on the environment and genetic and environmental interactions.

Nevertheless, this basic claim that the shared environment is not influential still holds.

- It can be concluded that these g factors, crystallised and fluid intelligence, are highly heritable. Again it should be noted that the most recent survey of this work, that by Plomin and Petrill (1997), supports all these claims.

- Finally it should be pointed out that, in addition to this biometric work, the search is on for the DNA markers of intelligence (Plomin *et al.*, 1994, 1995; Skuder *et al.*, 1995; Petrill *et al.*, 1996), with already the first signs of success. However, it is interesting that it was mitochondrial DNA rather than nuclear DNA which was involved. No doubt as the genome map is completed, this field of investigation will become clearer but see Plomin *et al.* (1998).

Conclusions

From this examination of the relevant evidence it must be concluded that the factors measured by intelligence tests, fluid and crystallised intelligence, are well identified as involved with a basic reasoning ability which is influential in academic and occupational achievement and which is largely heritable.

There is considerable agreement in the literature of testing that the best intelligence tests – Raven's Matrices, the WAIS scales, the Cattell Culture-Fair test and the Stanford–Binet, for example – load clearly on these factors (Kline, 1995; Cattell and Johnson, 1986). Thus it can be argued that current traditional intelligence tests measure intelligence with psychometric efficiency (high reliability and validity) and that they yield clear quantitative information concerning intelligence.

Hence, it can be claimed that the psychometric corpus of knowledge concerning intelligence and ability is, indeed, well founded in terms of psychometric measurement. From work with these tests, as has been shown above, a coherent account of the nature of intelligence has emerged, an account, furthermore, which enables real-life predictions to be made. This then raises the critical issue of this chapter: how can the clear validity of psychometric intelligence tests and their predictive power in many different spheres be reconciled with the criticisms of Michell (1997) that these measures are not scientific because they have no additive structure and no units of measurement? Perhaps, as most psychologists and psychometrists have assumed, Stevens was right: the strict mathematical rigours of scientific measurement are not necessary.

Psychometric and scientific measurement of intelligence

For the sake of clarity I shall set out the arguments point by point:

- The fact that a consistent, meaningful and applicable set of results can be obtained from intelligence tests means that it would be folly to abandon them and jettison their findings because they do not conform to the criteria of scientific measurement, as I have argued elsewhere (Kline, 1997).

- Nevertheless, the fact remains that if intelligence tests had clear units of measurement and additive structures, they would be superior.
- The way forward, therefore, in the measurement of intelligence is to attempt to construct such measures. In my view the standard approach to the measurement of intelligence is about as good as it can be. Further development of such tests may marginally improve reliabilities and validities but their scientific defects will remain.

The new psychometrics of intelligence

One attempt to improve the measurement of intelligence, which has already been scrutinised, I shall discuss briefly. This is Rasch scaling. As Wright (1985) demonstrated, Rasch scales, through their careful scaling procedures, maintain equal-interval measurement. However, there are several objections to the techniques which render these scales less than satisfactory. These equal units apply to the items in the scale provided that items can be found which fit the Rasch model. Provision of such equal units is not the same as providing equal units of the latent trait.

Furthermore, since Rasch scaling does not guarantee unidimensionality and since it is inconceivable that the items could be error free, or that guessing does not occur, the Rasch model is not a satisfactory fit to the notion of intelligence. If the Rasch model fits any set of data it would be that of achievement tests, where achievement can be conceived as the accretion of knowledge. Yet even here, unless the knowledge were entirely hierarchically structured, the model would not be in good concordance with the actual constructs. For all these reasons, and the fact that extra parameters seem necessary which destroy the unit equality, Rasch scaling is not going to be the way forward to a new psychometrics. Support for this pessimistic notion comes from the fact that it is now almost forty years since its birth and there are still few Rasch scales.

Relation between experimental psychology and the measurement of intelligence

Cronbach (1957) deplored the split between psychometrics and experimental psychology. Within the past twenty-five years, however, there has been a gradual *rapprochement*, especially with experimental cognitive psychology, and this is highly relevant to the proposed new psychometrics. Cattell (1971) recognised this point. The main difficulty even with a factor as clear as fluid intelligence is that it is too broad. Even if we know that fluid intelligence is involved in complex problem solving, it is not a precise description. It would be interesting, and necessary if we were to claim full understanding, to know exactly how the solution was obtained. This is what computer simulations and studies in artificial intelligence attempt to do, but from another viewpoint.

Hunt (1976) was one of the first psychologists to attempt to investigate the cognitive processes underlying intelligence and verbal ability. In so doing he argued that it was possible that problem solution may not be a linear function of a fixed set of cognitive processes. Since factor analysis is a linear model, it follows that it may be an unsuitable technique for the study of cognition and hence intelligence. However, as Cattell (1978) argues, it is best to accept the simplicity of the linear model until the data compel its abandonment, and the success of the factor analysis of abilities in the applied field suggests that that time has not yet occurred.

Carroll (1980), in an attempt to elucidate the cognitive processes underlying intelligence, carried out detailed studies of what are referred to as elementary cognitive tasks (ECTs), examples of which, taken from cognitive psychology, are:

1   lexical decision tasks, in which words or phrases have to be judged true or false;
2   reaction times to stimuli with and without priming; and
3   shape comparison in which subjects are presented two shapes, two names of shapes and a name and a shape. The task is to decide whether members of the pair refer to the same shape.

In all instances the measure is speed of reaction time. Carroll subjected the results to factor analysis, and it is possible to link the scores on these ECTs or ECT factors to the main ability factors.

The work of Sternberg (1977) on componential processes must be noted. For non-verbal analogies Sternberg claimed that he could compute five processing parameters: encoding; inference; mapping; application; and preparation and response. According to Sternberg, from estimates of these process times it is possible to predict total solution times for analogies. These processes, it should be added, are likely to be involved in the solution of many other problems since, as we have seen, the perception of analogies is one of the main tests loading fluid intelligence.

Finally, the work of the Erlangen school must be briefly examined (Lehrl and Fischer, 1988, 1990). They developed the basic information parameter (BIP), a measure of the capacity to process bits of information, based upon the speed of reading letters and on their processing model of how this is done. According to these writers, the BIP correlates highly with the WAIS and provides a basis for the claim that intelligence itself is simply a function of the speed of information processing in the brain.

Significance of these methods for the new psychometrics

This chapter has concentrated upon the two intelligence factors, fluid and crystal-lised intelligence, which account for much of the variance in human ability. However, as was made clear, they load on the primary, more specific factors, and there are, in addition, some other second-order factors such as visualisation and cognitive speed.

The significance of this work for the new psychometrics is clear. The ECTs represent basic cognitive processes. If these could be shown to account for the variance on the intelligence factors, then we would have an account of intelligence in terms of such processes. We might know precisely what was going on when individuals were using their intelligence. This is to conceive of ECTs as small primary factors. One reason they have not appeared in the main list of such primaries is that until recently such variables were not included in factor analyses.

However, from the viewpoint of the new psychometrics, these measures have the advantage of being reaction times with true zeros, equal intervals and units of measurement. Intelligence measured thus would conform to the rigours of scientific measurement and provide an insight into the nature of intelligence.

A similar argument can be used in favour of the Erlangen school. Their work has claimed to show the speed of information processing of individuals of given WAIS IQ. Again such a measure is scientific in the terms of Michell (1990), and if it could be shown to be valid it would be a considerable improvement over standard intelligence tests. Similar arguments apply to the measurement of componential processes, as advocated by Sternberg (1977), although his more recent work on intelligence has rather abandoned this approach (Sternberg, 1985).

Two features should be noted about these tentative proposals for a new psychometrics of intelligence. The first concerns the fact that all employ measures which, because they are reaction times, meet the criteria of scientific measurement. That they are reaction times suggests that speed is implicated in intelligence, if these tests are to be valid.

Measures of speed and intelligence

Popular conceptions of intelligence, if they do not equate it with speed, certainly consider that intelligent people are quick, fast-thinking and fast-reacting in contradistinction to the slow-witted country bumpkin – or this was so before the onset of political rectitude.

Indeed, it has been claimed that inspection time, the time a subject reliably takes to discriminate two almost equal lines, is a superb measure of intelligence (Brand and Deary, 1982), with correlations with intelligence test scores beyond 0.9. However, more recent work has shown that the correlation is in fact, considerably smaller, although positive (Nettelbeck, 1982), and a study I carried out with Cooper (Cooper *et al.*, 1986) indicated that inspection time loaded on perceptual speed and visualisation.

Jensen, over many years, has studied the relation of speed of reaction time to simple and complex stimuli to intelligence test scores (Jensen, 1987a) in the hope of establishing that intelligence reflects the speed of neural transmission. Nevertheless, correlations are low, in the order of 0.3. Actually the correlations between intelligence test scores and the variance of reaction times are slightly higher, reflecting, it is claimed by Jensen, the fact that intelligence is related to the integrity of information processing through the brain.

There are two important points here, from the viewpoint of the proposed new psychometrics. First, since reaction times and inspection times have only low correlations with fluid ability, it seems clear that cognitive speed is distinct from intelligence. However, the possible new measures of intelligence which have been mentioned all depend on speed. This is clearly a difficulty. Furthermore, as was made clear at the beginning of this chapter, cognitive speed is an important factor in its own right, as found by both Cattell (1971) and Carroll (1993). Any new psychometrics would have to ensure, therefore, that speed was not confounding any putative measures of the intelligence factors, even if these were scientific in the sense of Michell (1990).

From all this discussion it is clear that these new, scientific measures of the intelligence factors need to be discussed in the light of the other ability factors, particularly cognitive speed and the primary factors which, as has been argued, may be close to some ECTs. This, then, is the task of Chapter 7.

Summary

In this chapter I set out the main factors in the ability sphere and examined in considerable detail those which have been identified as intelligence factors:

- the third-order intelligence factor;
- fluid intelligence; and
- crystallised intelligence.

It was demonstrated that there is a good consensus among factor analytic studies that intelligence may be regarded as a mixture of the fluid and crystallised intelligence factors and that it is these that many intelligence tests measure. These appear to be factors of reasoning ability: fluid, a basic ability, a function of one's neurology; and crystallised, ability resulting from the investment of that ability in culturally valued skills.

Examination of the actual tests and items loading these factors supported this identification, as did studies of their external validity. These demonstrated that these factors predict educational and occupational success and have a considerable genetic determination. However, despite their efficiency in prediction, it was undeniably the case that the best tests of intelligence, such as Raven's Matrices and the Cattell Culture-Fair Test, fail to meet the criteria of scientific measurement.

It was argued that the results are too consistent and too powerful in prediction to allow the psychometric measurement of intelligence to be jettisoned. However, attempts to improve the measurement by improved scaling, such as Rasch scaling, were also shown to be unlikely to succeed. A possible new approach to the psychometric measurement of intelligence was briefly outlined; it stems from the experimental study of cognitive processes, componential analysis, and the work of the Erlangen school. However, further work on the relation of cognitive speed to intelligence and the obvious relationship of some cognitive processes to primary factors raised some problems with such possible new measures of intelligence. The discussion and scrutiny of such new measures of intelligence will be examined in more detail in the next chapter.

7

PRIMARY FACTORS, COGNITIVE SPEED AND NEW MEASURES OF INTELLIGENCE

At the end of Chapter 6 it became clear that attempts to measure intelligence on scales which fit the criteria of scientific measurement, as discussed by Michell (1997), are already in existence, and I shall examine these in this chapter. With the exception of Rasch scaling, which I have shown is unlikely radically to improve the measurement of intelligence, all these new methods involve techniques and methods developed from experimental psychology. However, because some of the variables which are measured might, in principle at least, be considered to be rather narrow primary factors and because they also involve speed, it is necessary first to open this chapter with an examination of the best-established primary factors and the speed factor. It should be said, in connection with this last point, that the disentangling of speed from ability factors of any kind, let alone intelligence, is a complex issue, as Carroll (1993) has argued.

Primary (first-order) ability factors

As was discussed in Chapter 7, there is a surprisingly good consensus concerning the main primary factors of ability, given that a definitive list is impossible. Scrutiny of the most careful surveys (Cattell, 1971; Ekstrom *et al.*, 1976; Carroll, 1993) indicates not only that the primaries are similar, even if the names given are not identical, but that the second-order factors are virtually identical. This is good support for the agreement among primaries since if these were different, the second-orders could not be the same. Second-order factoring is a recognised method of identifying primary factors (Cattell, 1978).

The factors in Box 7.1 are considered by Cattell (1971) and Hakstian and Cattell (1974, 1976) to be the most important in the ability sphere. With the exception of O1 they are measured in the Comprehensive Ability Battery (Hakstian and Cattell, 1976). Cattell (1971) also suggests that on re-rotation of data sets which were imperfectly factored, a few other factors would be likely to be found, including general motor coordination, deductive reasoning and a number of musical ability factors such as sensitivity to pitch and a factor connected to rhythm

---

Box 7.1 The main primary factors of ability

V   verbal ability: understanding words and ideas;

N   numerical factor: facility in the manipulation of numbers, not arithmetic reasoning;

S   spatial ability: ability to visualise figures in different orientations;

P   perceptual speed and accuracy: involving rapid assessment of differences between pairs of stimuli;

Cs   speed of closure: the ability to complete a pattern with parts missing;

I   inductive reasoning;

Ma   rote memory: memory for pairs within which there are no mediating links;

Mk   mechanical ability;

Cf   flexibility of closure: ability to find stimuli embedded in distractors;

Ms   memory span: the ability immediately to recall digits or letters;

Sp   spelling;

E   aesthetic judgement: the ability detect the basic principles of good art;

Mm meaningful memory: the ability to learn links between pairs of linked stimuli;

O1   originality of ideational flexibility: the ability to generate many different and original ideas;

Fl   ideational fluency, similar to O1 and O2: the ability to generate ideas on a topic rapidly;

W   word fluency: rapid production of words conforming to letter requirements;

O2   originality, marked by the test of combining two objects into a functional object;

A   aiming: hand–eye coordination;

Rd   representational drawing ability;

Au   auditory ability: the ability to differentiate between tones and to remember a sequence of tones.

---

and timing. He also argues for a factor of motor speed which Guilford also claims (Guilford, 1967). These factors have been essentially confirmed by Carroll (1993).

Comments on Box 7.1

As I have argued, there is general agreement that these are important primary factors in the field of abilities. It is not intended as a complete list. Such a list would be enormous, as the work of Carroll (1993) indicates, but it is presented for reference in our subsequent discussions of measures of intelligence which conform to rigorous scientific criteria.

One further point needs to be made. Guilford (1967) and Guilford and Hoepfner (1971) have proposed a 'structure of intellect' model of human abilities which in its early form implied 120 human abilities and denied the force of general intelligence. This stressed the difference between convergent abilities, those required for the solution of intelligence tests, and divergent abilities, those useful in the solution of problems without fixed answers. There was always the implication in this work that divergent thinkers were more creative and more valuable than the conventional uninspired individuals with a high IQ.

Guilford and colleagues presented massive evidence in support of this model, which is, of course, quite different from the structure of abilities described in this and the previous chapter. However, much of the support for this model came from factor analyses of tests using Procrustes rotations. These involve factoring tests to attain target matrices, in these studies targets implied by their model. This work appeared to confirm the structure of intellect model and it can still be found in modern textbooks of psychology. Unfortunately, Horn and Knapp (1973) showed that Procrustes would fit any target. It could fit random data and even data with a structure which was antithetical to the target.

Although this work means that the model proposed by Guilford is quite untenable, it does not mean that his work in human abilities was worthless. On the contrary, a number of the factors in the Guilford list have been carefully measured and studied in his laboratory, notably those factors concerned with flexibility and fluency – those loading the second-order retrieval factor.

Elementary cognitive tasks and reaction times

It was pointed out that experimental psychologists, for example Hunt (1976), had attempted to elucidate the nature of ability factors by studying them alongside elementary cognitive tasks, and it is now necessary that we examine these in more detail. This must be done because the scores obtained from such tasks are, in many cases, times, and these conform to the criteria of scientific measurement. Thus if a series of measures derived from cognitive tasks could be developed which correlated highly with a well-established and validated factor, such as fluid intelligence, and which also showed high validity in their own right, then we would have a scientific measure of that factor. Indeed, it could be the case that differences from the psychometric factor were attributable to the measurement weaknesses which have been pointed out.

Carroll (1993) lists the following ECTs as those most frequently studied in the research literature up to that date. It should be noted that, with the appropriate experimental apparatus, reaction times may be broken down into decision time and movement time. It is also not uncommon to use means of scores over trials and standard deviations, it having been argued (e.g. Jensen, 1982) that the variance of reaction times might reflect the efficiency of the information processing.

1 *Simple reaction time.*
2 *Choice reaction time.* This involves experiments in which Hick's law (Hick, 1952), that reaction time is a function of the bits of information implied in the number of alternatives, plays a part. However, as Barrett *et al.* (1989) point out, it is unfortunate that not all subjects appear to conform to the law, a result which complicates some of the findings.

3   *Categorisation paradigm.* This is a variant of task 2, in which the signal for the choice is contained in the stimulus, e.g. G for a green light.

4   *Odd-man paradigm.* This another variant of task 2, in which subjects have to move to the most distant of three lights.

5   *Posner paradigm* (Posner, 1970). Here subjects have to decide whether two stimuli are the same or different according to various criteria.

6   *Visual search.* In this ECT a visual stimulus is presented, followed by a series of further stimuli. The subject has to decide whether the initial stimulus is present or not.

7   *Scan and search.* This (much used by Neisser (1967)) is similar to task 6. Many different target sets of stimuli are presented and the subject has to say whether the original stimulus is present in each set.

8   *Memory search.* This is the task which S. (not R.J.) Sternberg has investigated. Many stimuli are presented, then a single stimulus which subjects have to indicate as being present or absent initially – essentially a variant of tasks 6 and 7.

9   *Inspection time.* This is the threshold amount of time required for the detection of the difference between two stimuli, visual or auditory.

10   *Sentence verification.* This is the time taken to decide whether a sentence correctly describes a pattern, terms of position and negation affecting mean response times.

Before we examine the evidence adduced by Carroll (1993), as well as evidence from other studies, it is interesting to compare these ECTs with the primary factors listed in Box 7.1.

The first primary factor to note is P, perceptual speed, defined as the ability to discriminate rapidly between pairs of stimuli. It is clear from the descriptions of these ECTs that inspection time, especially visual search and scan and search, are highly similar to the P factor. Carroll (1993) points out that some tests for P are identical with the ECTs for scan and search. In other words, it can be argued that these three ECTs are essentially measures or tests of the primary factor of perceptual speed. Actually, a study of inspection time which I carried out with my colleague Cooper (Cooper *et al.*, 1986) demonstrated this case since in the factor analysis inspection time loaded the perceptual factor.

It is possible that these tasks might also load the factor Cf, flexibility of closure, since in these tasks stimuli have to be found embedded in lists of irrelevant stimuli. There is certainly a prima facie case that some of these ECTs are nothing more than tests of these primary perceptual factors.

The only other ECT which at all resembles any of these primary factors is, of course, memory search, in which a stimulus is presented and the subject has to decide whether he or she has seen it in a previous presentation. This is obviously similar to Ma, rote memory. In conclusion it can be argued that some of these ECTs are highly similar to some of the well-established primary factors. This suggests that the other ECTs may be similarly primary factors but even more narrow and specific and thus encapsulating less variance than those in Box 7.1.

As Carroll (1993) argues, although there have been numerous factor analytic studies of these ECTs it has not proved possible either to establish a clear factorial structure or identify with any certainty what any of the factors might be. This is because, unlike psychometric tests, these experimental techniques are not absolutely fixed. One can vary the stimuli, the number of stimuli, the intervals of presentation and so on, and these variants tend to give different results. Of course, this fact alone suggests that any resulting factors must be highly specific and thus of little general psychological interest.

Furthermore, many of the variables extracted from these ECTs are of low reliability and thus fatal for factor analysis, which attempts to fit a matrix of correlations. If this is errorful, the analysis is bound to be so. For example, as in the Hick paradigm, slopes and intercepts are calculated, since reaction times are regressed on the number of possible choices. As Jensen (1987b) argues, the intercept is interpreted as the best estimate of the total processing time: attention, sensory registration of the stimulus, transmission of the signal to the brain, reception and encoding, transmission of the response signal and muscle lag in execution. The slope is interpreted as the required time for discrimination and choice. Yet slopes and intercepts have been reported to be of low reliability (Dunlap et al., 1989).

Technically one of the best studies in the compendium of Carroll (1993) was the dissertation by Kranzler (1990). In this study decision and movement times were orthogonal. They appeared on different second-order factors. At the first order, decision times appeared on different factors depending on the particular ECT, and movement times appeared on two factors. This suggests that whatever ECTs measure, there is a considerable amount of specific variance, which is not of general psychological interest. It is also noteworthy that mean and standard deviations of reaction times loaded on the same factor. The same was true of intercept variables and their corresponding means.

However, the two second-order factors in this study are of particular interest to the thesis of this book. Thus the second of these factors is easy to identify. It seems to be a factor relating to movement time, and loading on the two first-order factors of movement time, as measured by ECTs. It was independent of psychometric variables. From this second-order factor it can be concluded that movement times in ECTs are not related to the ability factors measured by psychometric tests. I should point out that this is my own conclusion. Carroll (1993) simply reports his reanalysis.

However, it is the first second-order factor that is particularly pertinent to the arguments of this chapter. Thus this factor loaded decision-time variables on odd-man tasks, memory and visual search tasks, Hick tasks, inspection time (all ECTs) and, from the Multidimensional Aptitude Battery (MAB) (Jackson, 1984), the performance tests (0.519) spatial, object assembly and picture arrangement tests, together with Raven's Matrices. The MAB verbal tests also loaded this factor (0.425) vocabulary, information and comprehension.

In my view (I say this because, again, Carroll (1993) studiously avoids mention of this interpretation) this first second-order factor is good evidence that decision-time variables are related to general intelligence. The performance scales of the MAB are typical of those loading and measuring fluid intelligence (see Chapter 6). Similarly, the MAB verbal scales typify those loading crystallised intelligence. Thus this first factor is the usual mixed intelligence factor, and odd-man tasks, memory and visual search, and Posner tasks load highly on it. The Hick tasks and inspection time load positively but lower. These high-loading ECTs appear to measure a factor which is a combination of fluid and crystallised intelligence.

However, it must be pointed out that these ECTs load more highly on the factor than the two intelligence factors. It could be, given the measurement problems and the fact that intelligence tests could not be pure measures of a basic intelligence simply because their items are culturally constrained, even the performance scales, that these ECTs are superior measures. However, this remains to be seen. What is required is careful studies of the ECTs, not with other intelligence tests, but with criterion scores. If they could predict these better than standard psychometric tests, we would be able to argue that these are, indeed, superior measures and are, in addition, scales which meet the criteria for scientific measurement.

The different factors emerging from the other studies analysed by Carroll (1993) were confusing and no clear pattern was evident. There were various reasons for this, including the fact that some studies fail to distinguish between movement and decision time, thus confounding two factors. In addition, some designs were of the kind that confounded choice and simple reaction times.

There is, perhaps, a more fundamental difficulty in the factor analysis of ECTs which is discussed by Carroll (1993). This concerns the fact that the tasks are not entirely independent, having successive processing component stages, some requiring one stage, others all of them. The stages are: response component; decision component; encoding component; and comparison component.

Kyllonen (1985) computed from the ECTs times for these various components, on the basis of differential performances at tasks thought to require more or fewer of these components. These were then factored and six factors were identified: reaction time (response component); choice reaction time (decision component); categorisation time (encoding component); sequential matching (comparison component); a component associated with word matching; and a component associated with letter matching.

Since these parameters were derived by relating the scores on different ECTs it is difficult to argue that they can be truly independent. Furthermore, the fact that there were different factors associated with letter- and word-matching tasks suggests that these factors may be highly specific and of little generality. This lack of independence was further confirmed by the high correlations between the factors: all were significant except that between factors 1 and 6. Four were greater than 0.6, and 0.33 was the lowest of them. Carroll (1993) claims that the pattern was a quasi-simplex and that multidimensional analysis showed two dimensions: amount of perceptual processing and amount of memory required. However, these correlations suggest that a general speed factor might account for much of this variance, but in view of the derivations of these parameters (mentioned above), the meaningfulness of these correlations and any subsequent analyses is dubious.

One further point should be noted. Many ECTs are novel tasks which are likely to improve with practice. However, although in some studies practice is given, as Carroll (1993) points out this is rarely long enough for optimum performance to be reached. Thus it could be argued that the relationships between intelligence and ECT performance, at the second-order factor structure, reflects not that these ECTs are measuring intelligence or aspects of intelligence but that they measure learning ability or speed of learning. As Jensen (1980) has shown learning ability is best predicted by intelligence.

This survey of the factor analytic work on ECTs is accurately but disappointingly inconclusive. It is not possible to state clearly what are the factors in ECTs, or their relationship to the intelligence factors. The study by Kranzler (1990), however, despite these difficulties, does suggest tentatively that decision times on ECTs are related to intelligence, both crystallised and fluid. However, the problem then arises that this correlation may itself be a function of speed, since intelligence tests are themselves speeded, and it is necessary to examine the relationship of speed, intelligence and these ECTs.

Since the publication of Carroll's (1993) book, and partly in response to the problems and obscurities which have been pointed out, two investigations have been aimed directly at these difficulties: a study by Roberts (1997) of the factor structure of ECTs and the relation of these factors to fluid and crystallised intelligence, and a similar investigation by Draycott and Kline (1996).

The work of Roberts (1997)

Roberts factored 11 ECTs (all of the kind in which difficulty could be scaled into bits) measuring separately both decision time and movement time, as has been shown to be necessary. Particularly interesting is the fact that he included two measures, inspection time (Nettelbeck, 1982) and information flow (Lehrl and Fischer, 1988), which have both been claimed to be highly correlated with intelligence and which, for this reason, are dealt with separately, later in this chapter.

In fact there were three movement factors: speed of limb movement, multi-limb coordination and a more tentative recognition/articulation speed. These have been noted before in the summary by Carroll (1993) and in the original work of Fleishman and Quaintance (1984) on the factors in motor skills.

The three decision-time factors were DT to a light-key code; DT to a pictorial motor code; and DT to a semantic verbal code. Although, from the viewpoint of this book, seeking fundamental measures of intelligence, the existence of six factors is initially disappointing, it was interesting to note that at the second order there were two factors – decision time and movement time – which define a third order, despite the problems of accurate location of the factor at this order: general response speed or 'chronometric t'.

This first part of the study by Roberts (1997) does clarify the field with the two second-order ECT speed factors of movement and decision time. In the second part these factors were correlated with the factors from a battery of psychometric tests which included many standard measures of the factors described in Chapter 6. Fluid intelligence correlated 0.42 with chronometric t, 0.40 with decision time and 0.25 with movement time. Crystallised intelligence correlated only with decision time to semantic–verbal code. Highly interesting were the correlations of the ECTs and clerical/perceptual speed. This perceptual speed factor correlated 0.6 with the general speed factor, 0.46 with movement time and 0.43 with decision time. The actual perceptual speed tests were number comparison, stroop colour, string search and digit symbol.

Conclusions from this study by Roberts (1997)

The conclusions which I discuss below are mine rather than those of Roberts, whose interests in this paper were to some extent different.

- It is quite clear that none of these factors derived from ECTs is a possible measure of crystallised ability. Since crystallised ability is essentially verbal, this is perhaps not surprising. However, if these factors measured any process basic to cognition one would have expected some more positive relationships with crystallised ability.
- The salient factor with fluid intelligence is decision time rather than movement time. However, a correlation of 0.40 is not enough to allow it to be used as a possible measure of fluid ability. Indeed, its highest correlation is with perceptual speed.
- Perceptual speed correlated 0.6 with chronometric t, the third-order factor. It is possible these perceptual speed tests are essentially measuring chronometric t but are overlain with variance connected with the actual materials, letters and words of the test items.
- It is possible that some development of ECTs might allow measurement of fluid ability but these results rather suggest that ECTs are essentially measures of perceptual speed. On measurement grounds they would be preferable, and it would be worth further investigating them as tests of this factor.
- In summary, this paper by Roberts supports the claims of Carroll (1993) that decision time is the crucial ECT variable that is likely to be related to fluid intelligence. It more strongly suggests that ECTs essentially measure perceptual speed, as was argued previously. However, this study still leaves the problem of the relationship of speed and intelligence untouched, for it is argued by Carroll that the relationship between decision time and intelligence

may be the result of the fact that speed is implicated in the measurement of intelligence.

Speed and intelligence

The relationship between speed and inteligence is a complex issue and I shall begin by making a number of clear points.

- It is customary in psychometric tests to distinguish between speed and power tests. A power test is given untimed, while a speeded test is given under time limits. In fact, there is usually a high correlation between tests given under these two conditions (Vernon, 1961). A power test is sometimes said to indicate the level of performance of a subject.
- Most ability tests are speeded. Thus, *inter alia*, a score must represent speed and power variance. Ideally, as Carroll (1993) argues, these should be separated out.
- The correlation, according to this argument, between a speeded and an unspeeded test is artefactually high because the former measures level plus speed and the latter level. The level variance in both tests distorts the correlation. However, this argument of Carroll's is not convincing. Since there is a correlation, either the speed variance is small or it is correlated with the level variance.

Actually, examination of the items in a good intelligence test often indicates that extra time is not worthwhile since some items are simply too difficult for subjects, almost regardless of time. Nevertheless, there is some force in these points made by Carroll (1993), and it is possible that speed could create or influence a general factor among ability tests.

Carroll (1993) suggests that research into this problem of speed and intelligence testing should evaluate test performance from the viewpoint of both speed and accuracy or quality of response, following the advice of Hunt and Pellegrino (1985).

A study by Draycott (1996) and Draycott and Kline (1994b, 1996)

We decided to put these hypotheses of Carroll's (1993) to an empirical test by factoring together a set of tests: the AGARD tests (AGARD 1989), which are essentially ECTs (see below), and the Hakstian and Cattell (1976) Comprehensive Ability Battery (CAB), which, as has been argued (Cattell and Johnson, 1986; Carroll, 1993; Kline, 1993), covers the main ability factors. It should be noted that this research bears on several of the topics of this section: the relationship between speed and intelligence; the utility of ECTs in the prediction and measurement of intelligence and the relationship of ECTs and primary ability factors. It is, indeed, similar to the study by Roberts (1997) discussed in the previous section, although the ECTs of the AGARD are claimed to measure simple cognitive processes. Furthermore, we factored the ECTs and the psychometric test, rather than relying on correlations, on the grounds that this would reveal more clearly the implication of speed in intelligence tests. It should be pointed out, at this juncture, that this research was part of a large-scale investigation into the validity of the AGARD battery supported by the Defence Research Agency.

The AGARD tests (Reeves et al., 1991)

The AGARD battery is not well known, being a battery of performance tests developed by NATO for use in the assessment of fatigue in operatives of machinery, with special reference to space and flight. It consists of seven subtests all administered on IBM PC-compatible computers with responses on the serial mouse. The following subtests make up the AGARD battery.

1   *Reaction time.* There are three tasks, each variants of the other. In the first, one of four numbers appears on the screen. Subjects have to press the appropriate mouse button. In task 2, the stimuli are degraded. In task 3, the inter-stimulus duration varies at random. This is a test derived from the additive processing model of S. Sternberg (1969).

   Scores: For each task speed and accuracy are recorded.

2   *Mathematical processing.* A series of mathematical problems involving additions or subtractions is displayed on the screen. Subjects press button A on the mouse if the answer is less than 5, B if more than 5. This test is claimed to tap four processes: retrieval from long-term memory; updating information in working memory; execution of arithmetical operations; and numerical comparison.

   Scores: Speed and accuracy are recorded.

3   *Memory search.* This is the standard ECT described on p. 123 in the list of ECTs, testing the ability to search items in memory for the presence of a probe item. Sets of letters (2, 4, 6 in length) appear on the screen, to be memorised, followed by the probe letters. Subjects respond with the mouse, indicating whether the probes belonged to the set or not.

   Scores: Speed and accuracy are recorded for each of the sets.

4   *Spatial processing.* A single, four-bar histogram is presented briefly on the centre of the screen and then disappears. Then another histogram appears oriented at 90 or 270 degrees to the first presentation. Subjects have to record via the serial mouse whether the histogram is the same or not. It should be noted that this AGARD test is highly similar to measures of the visualisation second-order factor and the primary spatial ability.

   Scores: Speed and accuracy.

5   *Unstable tracking.* A short, vertical target line appears in the middle of the screen. This then moves left or right. Subjects are required to keep the target as close to the centre of the screen as is possible by moving the mouse

in the opposite direction to the motion of the target. As the target approaches the edge of the screen its speed increases. If it reaches the edge it reappears in the centre.

Scores: RMS error score based upon the deviations per second from the centre of the screen.

6   *Grammatical reasoning.* This is similar to Baddley's (1986) test of working memory. Pairs of statements appear on the screen such as * BEFORE & AFTER + accompanied by three symbols, e.g. *&+. The statements describe the order of symbols and subjects decide whether they are correct or not.

Scores: Accuracy and speed.

7   *Dual task performance.* This test combines tracking task and memory search. As the tracking proceeds, subjects have to respond to memory probes.

Scores: These tasks are scored as described above.

It must be noted that for six of these AGARD tests speed and accuracy measures are obtained separately. Only in the tracking task is this not the case. To investigate to what extent speed was a confounding variable for intelligence and to assess what factors the ECTs might measure, it was necessary to factor the AGARD with tests of the established ability factors. For this purpose the CAB (Hakstian and Cattell, 1976) was selected. This measures the following factors:

- verbal ability;
- numerical ability;
- spatial ability;
- speed of closure;
- perceptual speed and accuracy;
- inductive reasoning;
- flexibility of closure;
- rote memory;
- memory span;
- meaningful memory;
- spontaneous flexibility;
- ideational fluency;
- word fluency;
- originality;
- aiming.

Subjects: One hundred and thirteen subjects were used in this study, mean age 20.94 years. They were university or college students, of whom 75 were female.

Results: The correlations between the AGARD and the CAB were subjected to principal components analysis, and four factors selected by the Scree test (Cattell, 1966b) were rotated using Direct Oblimin to simple structure.

Factor 1 was clearly a speed factor, loading highly on all the AGARD speed measures. Only one of the CAB primary factors loaded this speed factor. This was Cs, speed of closure.

Factor 2 was clearly fluid intelligence, loading on the CAB primaries N, S, P and I, factors which are typical of fluid intelligence (see Hakstian and Cattell, 1976; Kline and Cooper, 1984a). Only one speed measure, that from mathematical processing, loaded this factor.

Factor 3 loaded the tracking tasks of the AGARD and was clearly the tracking factor. There were moderate loadings on some of the speed and accuracy scores, and both are involved in tracking, together with some moderate loadings on some of the CAB factors.

Factor 4 was clearly the crystallised intelligence factor, loading on the verbal, meaningful memory and word fluency factors. None of the AGARD speed tests loaded this factor.

The factor analysis is set out in Table 7.1.

Conclusions

This factor analysis enables us to draw some clear conclusions concerning the problems which are subject of this section of the chapter.

1   Speed is not related to either fluid or crystallised intelligence. This factor analysis, with separate speed, crystallised intelligence and fluid intelligence factors, demonstrates this. It answers Carroll's (1993) argument that speed might confound measures of intelligence because these were speeded. It might, in principle, but on this evidence it does not.

2   There is a separate cognitive speed factor. This is important. Factor 1 is clearly a speed factor loading on all the AGARD speed measures and Cattell's Cs. This primary factor loads the cognitive speed factor (Cattell, 1971). This suggests that the AGARD speed measures would also load this cognitive speed factor. It is interesting to note here the differences from the study by Roberts (1997). There perceptual speed was related to the ECTs. Here it is cognitive speed. Presumably this results from the different selection of ECTs.

3   ECT speed measures are unlikely to be useful, therefore, despite their measurement properties, in the measurement of intelligence. Mathematical processing speed did load this factor but this is an ECT which resembles a traditional intelligence test. It does not seem strange that ability to process arithmetic rapidly is, in part a function of intelligence. However, it would not be a good measure since it loads also the speed factor.

4   The AGARD battery of ECTs (accuracy measures) measure, in part, fluid and crystallised intelligence. Examination of the two intelligence factors shows that some of the AGARD accuracy scores load these factors. This suggests that ECT accuracy measures might, in principle, be developed to

Table 7.1 Four factor structure matrix – Direct Oblimin rotation

	Factor 1	Factor 2	Factor 3	Factor 4	h^2
CAB V	−0.052	0.221	−0.329	−0.649	0.510
CAB N	0.078	0.743	−0.184	−0.302	0.582
CAB S	−0.177	0.643	0.243	0.107	0.582
CAB Cs	−0.430	0.532	−0.100	−0.343	0.495
CAB P	−0.149	0.722	−0.043	−0.108	0.540
CAB I	−0.119	0.588	0.180	−0.186	0.396
CAB Cf	−0.158	0.427	−0.066	−0.176	0.205
CAB Ma	0.030	0.224	−0.097	−0.369	0.156
CAB Ms	−0.163	0.268	−0.372	−0.075	0.235
CAB Mm	0.062	0.156	−0.144	−0.575	0.342
CAB Fs	−0.138	0.308	−0.382	−0.368	0.331
CAB Fi	−0.024	0.337	−0.506	−0.367	0.444
CAB W	−0.088	0.601	−0.325	−0.518	0.572
CAB O	0.182	0.342	−0.391	−0.220	0.291
CAB A	−0.140	0.364	−0.056	−0.193	0.157
MTH acc	0.423	0.350	0.049	−0.355	0.407
MTH spd	0.423	−0.490	0.071	0.287	0.427
STN2 acc	0.149	0.304	−0.171	−0.251	0.164
STN2 spd	0.763	−0.176	−0.393	0.063	0.697
STN4 acc	0.148	0.327	−0.048	0.077	0.137
STN4 spd	0.850	−0.180	−0.179	0.109	0.755
STN6 acc	0.066	0.312	−0.067	−0.586	0.371
STN6 spd	0.781	−0.150	0.048	0.167	0.662
SPA acc	0.143	0.573	0.097	−0.206	0.390
SPA spd	0.725	0.007	−0.092	−0.066	0.533
PROB acc	0.524	0.296	0.113	−0.307	0.487
PROB spd	0.723	−0.154	−0.405	0.075	0.647
PROC acc	−0.134	0.111	−0.352	−0.074	0.153
PROC spd	0.749	−0.087	−0.436	0.008	0.686
PROU acc	0.464	0.192	−0.022	−0.301	0.327
PROU spd	0.701	−0.168	−0.404	0.163	0.642
GRM acc	0.056	0.329	−0.042	−0.736	0.560
GRM spd	0.498	−0.032	−0.066	−0.389	0.403
TRK	0.272	−0.136	−0.803	0.055	0.707
DUL	0.288	−0.262	−0.743	−0.014	0.678
DUL acc	−0.018	0.179	−0.127	0.586	0.500
DUL spd	0.304	−0.021	−0.427	0.539	0.600
Eigenvalue	6.603	5.385	2.504	2.278	
Pct. var.	17.8	14.6	6.8	6.2	
Cum. pet.	17.8	32.4	39.2	45.4	

measure these psychometric factors with improved precision. The AGARD was developed entirely independently of the structure of abilities but was based upon the claims of cognitive psychology (Reeves *et al.*, 1991).

5   ECTs, if they are to measure intelligence, either fluid or crystallised, must

employ accuracy measures, separate from speed. However, it must be noted that these accuracy measures in some cases are little different from those in psychometric tests and thus suffer from the same problems of measurement. For example, the accuracy score in the arithmetical processing test is the number correct. This is also the case with grammatical reasoning.

In an attempt to explore the implications of this work in more detail, two other studies with the AGARD were carried out (Draycott and Kline, 1994b, 1996). In the first study the performance of the subjects in GCSE was measured, with separate scores for arts, social studies and science. These scores, together with the speed scores from the AGARD and the CAB fluid intelligence and crystallised intelligence scores, were subjected to a Direct Oblimin rotated, simple-structure factor analysis. This indicated that school examination performance was virtually independent of the speed factor but could be predicted from the combined CAB intelligence factors. Note the 'virtually'. This refers to the fact that the maths processing tests did load the intelligence and attainment factor. However, as discussed previously this is an ECT which resembles intelligence test items, as are used in the WISC, for example. We also inserted the EPQ (Eysenck and Eysenck, 1975) measures of neuroticism, extraversion and psychoticism. It was interesting to note that the AGARD speed tests were related to N. Anxious individuals did less well.

In the second study, which used a smaller number of university students, we examined the predictive ability of the AGARD for university performance. In this investigation the AH6 (Heim et al., 1970) was used to measure intelligence since this is a test designed for university students. Since the AGARD tests were clearly loading a single speed factor, only one was used: SN4. This is the memory search task with four-letter strings. Both speed and accuracy scores were put into the analyses. EPQ scores were also included since they had loaded the speed factor in the previous study.

Although this was a small sample ($N = 56$) for a factor analysis, the simple-structure Direct Oblimin rotation made good sense, although caution needs to be shown in the interpretation of the factors. Factor 1, loading on all examination performance and the three AH6 scores, indicated that, as expected, intelligence was important in these examinations. It was interesting that the ECT speed variable also loaded this factor. This may be because in university examinations speed of writing, the sheer amount produced, tends to increase marks. However, its highest loading was on factor 2. This also loaded age, neuroticism, introversion and poorer performance in arts subjects. This is worrying from the viewpoint of using this ECT as an alternative measure of intelligence, since it is thus confounded by personality and age. The ECT accuracy variable loaded the third factor, which was hard to identify since its only other loading was on AH6D. This last factor, given the sample size, is difficult to interpret.

Conclusions from the three AGARD studies

1   ECT speed variables do not appear likely to be good measures of intelligence. This is because there appears to be a speed factor accounting for much of the variance in these AGARD tests, which, as has been seen, are typical of ECTs. If anything, these ECT speed variables measure the second-order factor cognitive speed, while those of Roberts measured perceptual speed.

2   ECT speed variables are confounded by N, neuroticism. This again, from the nature of neuroticism, is not surprising (Eysenck, 1967). One of the studies showed that performance on the speed ECTs was negatively correlated with age. If this turns out generally to be the case, again it would not be surprising (Stankov *et al.*, 1995).

3   The fact that a general factor appears to account for most of the variance in these ECTs is not good support for the cognitive theories underlying their development. It is evident that until there is good agreement on the cognitive processes underlying intelligence, it is going to be difficult to develop powerful ECTs.

4   ECT accuracy scores might be more useful in the measurement of intelligence. However, it is essential, if these are to be used, that they are not just mini-psychometric tests. The whole point of using ECTs was to put the tests used in the assessment of intelligence on to a more scientific footing.

5   ECTs, to be useful in the measurement of intelligence, require better cognitive theories for their theoretical basis.

Further work on reaction times and intelligence

Most of the AGARD tests which were discussed in the previous section were typical ECTs, and they also involved reaction times. However, it should be stressed that while many ECTs attempt to measure (although probably do not) particular cognitive processes, reaction times, which it is claimed follow Hick's law (that reaction times increase as a linear function of the number of choices), have been intensively investigated as an index of speed of information processing. Jensen (1987a, b), Barrett *et al.* (1989) and Vernon (1987) have published extensively in this field.

Before we briefly discuss this work, the reasons for studying reaction times and ECTs at all as possible measures of intelligence need again to be emphasised. This is necessary because in the light of our definition of intelligence as a basic reasoning ability it is somewhat odd that reaction times should correlate at all with intelligence. However, as Jensen (1987a) makes clear, it could be that differences in intelligence reflect differences in rates of information processing. While such differences are tiny, over years they could, the theory goes, build up into substantial intellectual differences. In the case of ECTs, measuring cognitive processes, the principle is similar, but here a more detailed account of intelligence is implicit, involving, for example, the transfer of information from short-term to long-term memory and subsequent retrieval, along with other putative processes.

Their relevance to the new psychometrics is clear. If these ECTs or reaction times could be shown to be related to intelligence then we would have far better measures, from the scientific point of view. Real measurement would become a possibility. With current ECTs, as has been shown, this is at present not possible, but there is a clear way forward for research.

Concerning the Hick paradigm, it is also clear that this will not provide an alternative, more precise measure of intelligence. This is for two reasons. The first is that, as Barrett *et al.* (1989) showed, not all subjects fitted Hick's law. Of Barrett's subjects about 30 per cent failed to conform. This means that the interpretation of the correlation between reaction time and intelligence as being due to rapid processing of information, thus enabling more complex problems to be handled, is untenable. Such a hypothesis must be universally true, not simply for a sample.

It was pointed out earlier that the intercept calculated from Hick's law represents the best estimate of the processing time involved in reaction times. If the processing time were related to intelligence there would be a high correlation between the intercept and IQ scores. However, the correlation is on average only 0.25 (Jensen, 1987a). This is far too low to sustain such an interpretation. Actually Jensen found that the correlation between reaction time and IQ was 0.2 and between the standard deviation of reaction times and IQ 0.48. This is interesting although difficult to interpret, given that the correlation with the intercept is so low.

Longstreth (1984) has argued that Jensen's findings may be the upper limit of the correlations to be expected between reaction times and intelligence. This is because it can be shown that practice and order effects, response bias effects and attentional factors can all influence results. Barrett *et al.* (1989), in their detailed study of reaction times and intelligence, factored all the reaction time variables with the WAIS. The rotated analysis was revealing. WAIS scores, mean reaction times and variances all loaded on three separate factors. This is not dissimilar, it should be noted, to the study of the AGARD tests by Draycott and Kline (1996), in which the AGARD variables were separate from measures of intelligence. Finally, it should be noted that a recent study by Miller and Vernon (1996) showed that in children between the ages of 4 and 6 years the relationship between the g factor, measured by the WPPSI-R, and reaction time and working memory was different from that found in adults. However, this difference may well be attributable to the difference in the g factor as measured by infant and adult tests.

Conclusions

It can be concluded that reaction times cannot be used as alternative measures of intelligence. Nor can the fact of their correlations with intelligence be interpreted as evidence for a limited-channel processing system influencing intelligence, a point stressed by Rabbitt (1996) in his study of global and local effects with Cattell's Culture-Fair Test and measures of 15 reaction-time tasks.

Inspection time

A similar argument was used by Brand and Deary (1982) to account for their claim that intelligence test scores correlated highly with inspection time (IT), the time taken to discriminate reliably two lines of similar length briefly exposed in a tachistoscope or on a computer screen, or two sounds of similar pitch. Inspection time was said to be an index of mental speed. This is, of course, an ECT and was measured in the study by Roberts (1997).

Brand and Deary (1982), summarising their studies in Edinburgh, claimed that the correlation between IT and intelligence as measured by Raven's Matrices was -0.72. The verbal IQ correlation was almost the same: -0.69. Here, they claimed, was a culture-free intelligence test, exactly of the kind which we have been seeking in this book. These authors fell into several psychometric traps: small numbers of subjects with huge ranges of IQ. These authors even subdivided samples into Ns of 6. As Mackintosh (1986) argued, these results should be treated with caution.

In fact, the correlation for proper samples, and excluding subjects with very low intelligence, is only about 0.3 (Nettelbeck, 1982), and Cooper et al. (1986), in a study with only 20 subjects, showed that the IT correlated most highly with perceptual speed, a finding which makes excellent sense in the light of our previous section on ECTs. A recent paper by Deary and Stough (1996) which surveys a large number of studies of inspection time concludes that although the correlations with intelligence are small, they are consistent. However, with correlations of less than 0.6 it is difficult to see how inspection time could be used, on its own, as a measure of intelligence, even though, from the viewpoint of scientific measurement, it is superior to a psychometric score. Finally, it might be pointed out that these somewhat gloomy conclusion concerning ECTs, reaction times and inspection time as possible measures of intelligence or indices of salient cognitive processes are all supported by Stankov et al. (1995).

Frequency Accrual Speed Test (FAST)

Before we leave inspection time, mention must be made of the FAST developed by Vickers et al. (1995), which is not dissimilar. Here the speed of discriminating relative frequency of stimuli is the measure, and the tests showed that this speed was immune to practice and was of satisfactory reliability. The results appear to indicate that FAST is not a measure of cognitive speed and is unaffected by motivation (although subjects must be willing to take the test). The correlation with Raven's Matrices is 0.5, and Vickers et al. (1995) argue that FAST is a measure of the integrity of information processing. This is a promising measure which deserves further investigation, although its correlation with Raven's

Matrices is too low to suggest that it could be used as an alternative measure of fluid ability.

The BIP

Members of the Erlangen school of psychology, of whom the best-known exponents, in the UK at least, are Lehrl and Fischer (e.g. 1988, 1990), approach intelligence from the viewpoint of information psychology. Their studies of human information processing utilise measures involving time and information units (bits). These measures, therefore, conform to the scientific criteria of measurement discussed throughout this book. In their work they have utilised the BIP, the basic period of information processing. According to Lehrl and Fischer (1990), the BIP is a basic psychological parameter, a physiological and general determinant of intelligence, which is measurable at the ratio level and which correlates highly with the WAIS at −0.60. The BIP, therefore, would appear to come close to what we have been seeking. The question, therefore, immediately arises: the BIP, holy grail or chimera?

DEFINITION OF THE BIP

The BIP is the shortest possible time during which a subject can process 1 bit of information.

THEORETICAL RATIONALE OF THE BIP

The BIP is derived from a sequential, binary model of information processing developed by Frank (1959, 1969). This postulates that to process one bit of information requires one step, two bits two steps and so on. The processing demands in terms of bits, according to this model, are fixed not by the stimulus but by the expectations of the subject. For example, if a subject was required to read vowels and was presented with 'I', the information content of the stimulus would be 2.32 bits since $5 = 2^{2.32}$. However, if the subject were expecting any letter of the alphabet, the information content of 'I' would be 4.70 bits since $26 = 2^{4.70}$.

Frank's model of information processing postulates a number of parameters related to the BIP which need to be described. Lehrl and Fischer (1988) assert that information bombards us at a high rate; according to the model, 10^{11} bits/sec. However, this is beyond human capacity, and thus it has to be filtered to accommodate what is significant. This accommodation rate, C_k, is claimed to be, for average adults, 15 bits/sec. Frank (1959) claims that this C_k reflects the information flow to short-term memory. This definition of C_k makes it clear that it is highly similar to the BIP.

The filtered information resides for a finite time in short-term memory, the duration of its presence being T_r. There is one further parameter in this work of the Erlangen school. This is K_k, the total capacity of short-term memory, which is estimated from the product of C_k and T_r.

This discussion makes it clear that the BIP, if it really could be shown to measure intelligence, as the model of Frank (1959, 1969) suggests is the case, not only provides what is essentially a measure of biological intelligence, free of cultural and educational bias, the bane of even the best psychometric intelligence tests, but yields, in addition, a ratio scale, conforming to the criteria of scientific measurement.

MEASUREMENT OF THE BIP AND OTHER PARAMETERS

Lehrl and Fischer have shown that the reading of numerals and letters is the most reliable method for measuring the variable C_k. Subjects have to read a line of 20 letters, printed on a card, as quickly as possible. There are 8 cards and the times are measured by stopwatch. As shown, the information content of each letter is 4.7 bits (rounded to 5 since it is argued that humans make only whole binary decisions). Thus each card contains 100 bits of information. Then $C_k = 100/t$, where t is the time taken to read the card. It is possible to take the mean time over the 8 cards, which is the most reliable measure, or the fastest time, which is necessary for the BIP, as it is defined. Eysenck (private communication) prefers the longest time.

BIP is accordingly defined as $1/C_k$, the fastest time being taken. BIP is thus simply the reciprocal of C_k, but Lehrl and Fischer prefer to discuss the BIP on the grounds that it is more related to basic information processing and its neural physiology. From the viewpoint of this book, the search for scientific measures, the BIP is also preferable.

T_r is measured using the well-known digit span test (forwards) and is followed by a similar version using letters. T_r is the mean of the two versions, each having been corrected for the tendency to use clustering.

K_k is given by the relation $K_k = C_k \times T_r$. Three values for K_k can be produced by using the mean, fastest and slowest C_k respectively.

STUDIES OF THE BIP BY KLINE AND DRAYCOTT

Kline *et al.* (1994) and Draycott and Kline (1994a) decided to investigate these information processing parameters by locating them in the factor space of abilities, a powerful method of establishing what they measure (see Kline, 1979, 1993, for a full rationale). In a number of related studies these parameters, including the variants of C_k and T_r, were subjected to simple-structure Direct Oblimin rotated factor analyses with the CAB (Hakstian and Cattell, 1976) for primary factors, AH6 (Heim *et al.*, 1970) with highly intelligent subjects, Raven's Matrices (Raven, 1965a) and the Mill Hill Vocabulary Scale (Raven, 1965b) as good measures of fluid and crystallised intelligence, and, finally, measures of academic performance, based on examination grades. EPQ scores were also included in some of the studies. Although readers must be referred to the original papers for full details of this research, or to the doctoral thesis by Draycott (1996), the main findings can be briefly set out.

- There were virtually no differences in factor loadings between the variants of C_k, depending on whether the fastest, slowest or mean time was used. Although the fastest time corresponds to the BIP, I report the findings with the mean time because these are the most reliable.
- In the study with Raven's Matrices and the CAB P scale, the BIP loaded both the fluid intelligence (0.591) and the crystallised intelligence (0.622) factors. This supports the original work by Lehrl and Fischer, although the actual correlations of the BIP with the tests were far lower than they reported: 0.216 Raven's, 0.437 CAB P and 0.387 Mill Hill vocabulary. The correlation with P is interesting because this is perceptual speed, and the intrusion of cognitive speed into ECTs as measures of intelligence has been discussed.
- In the first study the BIP was independent of E, P and N as measured by the EPQ, although N had a small loading on the crystallised intelligence factor.
- T_r, based on memory span, loaded moderately the fluid ability factor. This is not surprising given that the memory span test is part of the battery of tests used in the WAIS, and in WISC, the Wechsler Intelligence Scale for Children (Wechsler, 1958).
- In the study with the AH6 test on 106 subjects, the previous results and those of Lehrl and Fischer were not replicated. A three-factor solution produced a general intelligence factor, a personality factor and a third factor loading on the variables C_k and T_r, although this latter moderately loaded the intelligence factor as well.
- With examination performance in the analysis, the BIP again failed to load the g factors but, contrary to intuition, loaded an attainment factor on which only V (crystallised ability), of the AH6 scores, had even a moderate loading.
- This study did not support the validity of the BIP as a measure of intelligence, despite its superior scale characteristics.
- In the study with the CAB, the BIP correlated positively only with CAB V, a measure of verbal ability and a marker for crystallised ability. The simplest interpretation of this correlation is that reading speed, the basis of the BIP, is simply related to how much a person has read. There were no significant correlations with the fluid intelligence primaries I, S or P.
- T_r correlated significantly with the two CAB memory factors, as was to be expected: Ma 0.205 and Ms 0.258.
- The rotated factor analysis was a model of clarity. The BIP loaded the crystallised intelligence factor (0.568), with negligible loading on fluid intelligence and the other factors. T_r loaded the memory factor. Both information processing measures were independent of personality. The composite measure K_k, when

put separately into the analysis, loaded only on the crystallised intelligence factor.

CONCLUSIONS

It must be concluded from these studies that the BIP does not measure fluid intelligence, as claimed by Lehrl and Fischer (1988). It does, however, load on the crystallised ability factor. This is perhaps sufficient to account for the correlation with the WAIS found by the Erlangen school. The correlation with the CAB V factor is interesting. It suggests that scores on the BIP are influenced primarily by verbal ability. It is possible that the BIP score reflects sheer experience of reading. Since intelligent people tend to read more than the less intelligent, this may confound the apparent correlation with g. It should be noted that a replication of this work by Roberts *et al.* (1996) came up with essentially the same results. They argue, indeed, that the BIP may be nothing more than a measure of reading speed, which is a recognised primary ability factor (see also Vigil-Colet *et al.*, 1997).

Theoretically the fact that the BIP correlates with crystallised ability rather than fluid intelligence casts doubt on the claim that it measures a process funda-mental to intelligence. Any such basic measure of processing ability would be expected to correlate more highly with fluid intelligence, measures of which are less distorted by factors such as education, experience or practice. Finally, it must be pointed out that the size of the correlations of the BIP with these other intelligence tests is not large enough to support its use as an alternative measure.

Nevertheless, three points are worth making before dismissing the BIP:

1 First, it is remarkable, to this writer, at least, that such a simple measure should correlate at all with an intelligence test which, as we have seen, measures reasoning ability.

2 Its scale qualities must not be forgotten. This is the reason that we are examining the BIP. It is noteworthy that the factor loadings on crystallised intelligence were higher than the correlations with the individual tests. Certainly the BIP deserves further investigation.

3 With ECTs it was shown that one of the problems lay in the underlying cognitive models. It is possible that this is a weakness of the BIP, since the quantification depends on the model espoused by Frank (1969). It is inter-esting to note that this model could be quite wrong, and yet these findings could be obtained from the BIP provided that reading speed correlated with crystallised intelligence, and this is the simplest explanation of all the find-ings reported in the literature. Indeed, Stankov and Roberts (1997) argue that speed is not fundamental to intelligence. We might conclude that the BIP is the holy grail *and* chimera.

Componential analysis

In 1977 R.J. Sternberg published an analysis of analogical reasoning which involved five components or processes which yielded good prediction of performance on analogies. (See also Sternberg 1985, 1986). Since analogies load highly on both the g factors, it could be argued (as Sternberg did) that these components gave insight into the nature of intelligence. Furthermore, if it could be shown that combinations of the measurement of the times of these processes could predict intelligence, in effect we would have a scientific measure of intelligence.

The five components were:

- *Encoding.* This involves the translation of the stimulus into its mental representation.
- *Inference.* Here the rule relating the terms of the analogy has to be worked out.
- *Mapping.* Mapping refers to finding the rule which relates the two halves of the analogy.
- *Application.* This applies the rules to obtain the solution.
- *Response.* This is relatively trivial. It refers to the communication of the response and varies according to the form of the analogies, and may involve speaking, writing, pushing a button or operating a computer keyboard.

These processes can be timed by allowing subjects to see some of the terms before the analogy is shown. By comparison of the different times under different conditions of pre-viewing, the component scores can be calculated. Responding is clearly a different type of component from the others and I shall not consider it further. However, Sternberg (1986) claimed that high scorers on intelligence tests were faster on inferring, mapping and application while Sternberg and Gardner (1983) showed that component scores derived from three different tasks (analogies, series completion and classifications) had an average correlation with intelligence tests of 0.61. However, high scorers on intelligence tests were slower at encoding. Nevertheless, these componential processes do not seem to be genuinely universal to all problem solving since May *et al.* (1987) found no relationships between them and divergent thinking tests.

In his original studies Sternberg (1977) showed that multiple correlations between these component scores and times to solve analogies were beyond 0.9. Yet this is hardly surprising since, in effect, these components are components of these times. However, there are some problems with these components which must be pointed out.

First, these are non-contingent concepts (Smedslund, 1978); pseudo-empirical, as I argued (Kline, 1991b). From the nature of language they must be true. Thus without mental representation there could be no mental activity. Mental representation is a *sine qua non* of mental life. It is banal if not vacuous to posit such a process as underlying analogy solution. The fact that highly intelligent people spend longer on this process is interesting, although the explanation may be quite straightforward. Thus those who are rapid encoders may encode badly, thus making the problem insoluble, or they may not be trying, and this would account for low scores on the intelligence test. However, whatever the explanation, encoding is a necessity for all problem solving. Inferring and mapping are open to the same logical criticism of being non-contingent. Unless rules are worked out, analogies are insoluble.

Despite these philosophical infelicities, might not the fact that these components are capable of predicting scores on intelligence tests mean that they could form a scientific measure of intelligence since they have true zeros? Unfortunately, this is not the case, for the following reasons.

- These components predict solution times. Now speed and ability are only positively, not perfectly, correlated, and even allowing for the fact that encoding was slower in the highly intelligent, this means that this speed-based measure would not be successful
- Some complex problems in real life require considerable and lengthy study to elucidate the rules. Again, a speed-based measure of reasoning would not be likely to be successful – although this does not rule out speed-based measures of more fundamental processes such as those of inspection time. The objection here is that a measure based on speed of reasoning, although this is undoubtedly correlated with power of reasoning, would not be a good measure of power of reasoning, which is the essence of intelligence.

Conclusion concerning components

I shall not examine componential analysis further since from the viewpoint of this book, despite its interest, it is clear that from such components no scientific measure of intelligence could be constructed. It is noteworthy too that Sternberg has, over the years, gradually abandoned componential analysis in his studies of intelligence, not because they would not form scientific measures with true zeros, but because ultimately they tell us little more about intelligence than can be inferred from the well-established relevant factors.

Final conclusions

Some brief conclusions from this long and complex chapter can be drawn.

- Speed measures have true zeros and equal intervals, and so at least in principle could form the basis of scientific measures of intelligence.
- However, speed measures from ECTs seem to measure the perceptual speed and cognitive speed factors rather than simply fluid intelligence.
- Since intelligence is defined in terms of reasoning, any speed measures should be concerned with underlying fundamental processes involved in

information processing. Speed measures of reasoning, as in componential analysis, are likely to be too superficial.

- Since ECTs are supposedly measuring basic processes, we should not expect a high correlation with intelligence for each measure. Rather, each should add in new variance to achieve a high multiple correlation.
- Inspection time, on its own, cannot form a scientific measure of intelligence.
- Choice reaction times, means or standard deviations, cannot be used to form scientific measures of intelligence.
- Sternberg's components are not suited to be developed as possible scientific measures.
- The BIP correlates most highly of all these ECT measures with intelligence, but this may be explained by its relationship with reading, rather than its being a basic parameter of intelligence.
- Work along the lines of the Erlangen school could well prove fruitful, but better cognitive processing models are required to underpin the work.

8

PROBLEMS IN THE MEASUREMENT OF PERSONALITY AND MOTIVATION

Introduction

First the terms 'personality' and 'motivation', as they are used in this chapter, need briefly to be defined. Personality refers to temperamental traits, the traits which determine how we do the things we do. Motivation refers to dynamic traits, the causes of our behaviour. Actually, the measurement of motivation is far less advanced than is the case with personality, and since tests of motivation are highly similar to those of personality I shall refer simply to personality and personality tests in this chapter, which is concerned with testing.

In Chapter 6 I set out the structure of ability, as it had been revealed in factor analysis. This was possible because there was agreement concerning the structure and there was little question as to the validity of the psychometric tests, at least within their own terms, although, of course, it was clear that these did not measure up to the strict criteria of scientific measurement. In the field of personality and motivation, matters are different.

Until the past few years there was little consensus concerning the structure of personality. Although this is no longer the case, I shall argue, in Chapter 9, that the current agreement is spurious. Furthermore, there is some uncertainty concerning how personality should be measured. Thus there are three radically different types of personality test – personality questionnaires, projective tests and objective tests – and these do not always yield congruent results, despite the ambitious claims of Cattell (e.g. 1957) that his personality factors can be obtained from any type of test, regardless of indicator.

In fact, the structure of personality has been largely derived from personality questionnaires supplemented by ratings. However, as I shall argue, there are considerable problems with questionnaires and ratings which are conveniently forgotten by many of the users. These are sufficient to cast doubt on many, but not all, of the findings obtained from personality questionnaires.

Projective tests were famously described by Eysenck (1959) as nothing but the vehicles for the riotous imagination of clinicians. This was attributable to the fact that, in the majority of cases, subjects' responses to the projective test have to be interpreted by the tester. Certainly these responses are highly subjective and do not stand psychometric scrutiny. However, modern scoring schemes, such as that of Exner (1986) for the Rorschach test (Rorschach, 1921), perhaps the most famous personality test, often known as the inkblots, attempt to overcome these problems. Advocates of projective testing argue that it is far richer than simplistic personality questionnaires and gives rise to data which could be obtained in no other way; see, for example, Semeneoff (1971).

The third category of personality tests comprises objective tests. This term, 'objective', is used in the sense of Cattell and Warburton's (1967) compendium of objective tests. Here they were defined as tests which could be objectively scored and (more importantly) tests whose purport was hidden from the subjects, thus eliminating, it was hoped, deliberate distortion. Although these authors listed more than 600 objective tests of personality, from which more than 2,000 variables could be derived, they have not been much used, and have to be regarded, thirty years later, as still at the experimental stage. Nevertheless, a battery of the best of these tests, the Objective Analytic Battery (Cattell and Schuerger, 1976), has been published and the tests have been investigated by Kline and Cooper (1984b). As we shall see, these objective tests have considerable potential and they deserve considerable further study.

Measuring personality

As already mentioned, the attempts to elucidate the structure of personality have mostly utilised personality questionnaires, and the main findings in the field are questionnaire factors. Objective tests have hardly been used, despite their potential, while projective tests have contributed little to this field. For this reason I shall begin my discussion of the problems of testing personality with projective tests. I shall follow this with a study of objective personality tests and the main section of the chapter will be a scrutiny of personality questionnaires.

Projective tests

Most projective tests consist of ambiguous stimuli which subjects are usually asked to describe or explicate. Since the stimuli are ambiguous, it is usually considered that the responses must indicate something about the individual responding rather than the test. This is the origin of the term 'projective'. The individual, it is believed by the projective tester, projects himself or herself into the responses. It is also considered that the tests tap the deeper layers of personality, thus indicating that there is a concept of personality derived from psychoanalytic theory (in its broadest sense) underlying projective tests. However, it must be noted that this use of the term 'projective' is quite different from the 'projection' of psychoanalytic theory. There projection is a defence mechanism: the individual defends his or her ego from repressed or painful material by unconsciously projecting the material on to others (Freud, 1911). Finally, it should be pointed out that some projective tests do not simply require subjects to describe ambiguous stimuli. Some have them complete sentences. Others have them draw.

Brief description of some well-known projective tests

In order that the problems with projective testing as scientific tests, in the sense of Michell (1997), can be understood I shall describe those most frequently used.

RORSCHACH TEST

Description The test (Rorschach, 1921) uses 10 symmetrical inkblots, each on a separate card, half monochromatic, the others with colour. Subjects have to describe the cards, and response latencies and orientation of the cards are recorded. Then subjects have to elaborate these descriptions and answer questions about them.

Scoring Originally there were two systems for scoring the Rorschach, those of Beck (1944) and Klopfer and Kelley (1942), both time-consuming and requiring considerable training and practice. That they yield different interpretations of the Rorschach protocols gives little cause for confidence. Nor are these the only schemes. Recently Exner (1986) has tried to put the scoring on to an empirical basis, but almost all the scoring requires subjective judgement.

Examples of variables These are taken from Exner: *form*, where the response depends only on form, said to be related to introspection; *shading texture*, where dimensionality depends on shading, said to be related to negative self-appraisal and *chromatic colour*, claimed to indicate affect.

Although, below, I shall discuss the problems common to projective tests, which include low reliability and validity, it is so obvious that the nature of the responses and their scoring categories will invite low reliability because they are subjective that I must mention the Holtzman Inkblot Test (HIT) (Holtzman *et al.*, 1968). The HIT was developed as an objectively scorable set of inkblots: two parallel forms each of 45 inkblots which can be scored with a high reliability.

THEMATIC APPERCEPTION TEST

Description The Thematic Apperception Test (TAT) (Murray, 1938; Morgan and Murray, 1936), consists of 31 stimuli each on a card. One of these cards is blank. Subjects are required to say what the individuals in the pictures are feeling and thinking and to explain their actions. The TAT pictures, which portray somewhat ambiguous figures in ambiguous situations, are explicitly designed to stimulate the imagination and elicit fantasy, although Murray (1938) regarded the pictures as unstructured rather than ambiguous. Cards 12 and 13 are typical: a young woman sits, staring into space, chin in hand (12); four men rest on grass (13).

Variables Originally the TAT was designed to measure Murray's (1938) theory of personality involving needs and presses as described in *Explorations in Personality*. There were 19 needs and their corresponding presses, including the well-known need achievement. In addition, emotions and emotional trends can be assessed.

However, as Swartz (1978) argued, many users of the TAT do not score the test as it was originally intended. Rather they use it to test their own dynamic theories of personality, and Murray (1971) claimed that any intuitive person, even without training, could make valid inferences from the TAT (which, incidentally, is well suited to psychoanalytic interpretation).

Thematic Apperception Test variants There have been a number of variants of the TAT, including:

1   The Children's Apperception Test (CAT) (Bellak and Bellak, 1949). The CAT is a TAT for children in two forms, one with animal cards, the other with humans.
2   The Blacky Pictures (Blum, 1949). This is a test designed to test psycho-analytic, developmental hypotheses. It shows a family of dogs, including the puppy Blacky, in situations relevant to psychoanalytic theory.
3   The Test PN (Corman, 1969). This is a French development of the Blacky Pictures which uses pigs rather than dogs and is claimed by its author to be superior to the original.
4   The Object-Relations Technique (ORT) (Phillipson, 1955). The ORT attempts to assess with TAT-like pictures but deliberately more ambiguous, the modern psychoanalytic concepts of object-relations theory (Klein, 1948, Fairbairn, 1952).

Finally, to finish this brief description of some projective tests I shall discuss a test which requires subjects to draw: the House–Tree–Person test.

HOUSE–TREE–PERSON TEST

Description In the House–Tree–Person (HTP) test (Buck, 1948, 1970), subjects are requested to draw a house, a tree and a person. There are two phases in the HTP: in the first, the subject completes the drawings in pencil and answers questions about them. In the second there is a similar procedure but with coloured drawings.

Variables Although a measure of intelligence is obtainable from the HTP, it is primarily a personality test. The manual to the test (Buck, 1970) lists no variables but rather gives detailed accounts of how to interpret the drawings. A few examples will illustrate the flavour of this test, which certainly fits Eysenck's (1959) description (p. 144). Thus the house is considered to be a self-portrait. Emphasis on eaves implies an over-defensive and suspicious attitude, although the rationale for such an interpretation is never given. If curtains are drawn closed in the windows of the house, this is also regarded as defensive, as is the absence of a garden path, and so on.

These descriptions of some well-known projective tests are intended only to allow readers to follow the arguments about their nature and defects which I present below. For more details of the tests and their conventional scoring systems, readers are referred to the respective test manuals or to Semeneoff (1971), or Kline (1995).

Projective tests as scientific measures

In the light of the normal criteria for assessing the value of psychological tests in term of reliability and validity (see Chapter 2), there is general agreement that projective tests cannot stand scrutiny. The case was put most succinctly by Vernon (1963):

- *Poor reliability.* Scored blind there is poor agreement between scorers. Even the sex of the subject may not be correctly recognised.
- *Poor validity.* Most projective tests have little evidence for their validity. What there is, as Eysenck (1959) argued, is often weak. Support for a hypothesis does not constitute proof, as has been fully discussed in Chapter 1. Karon (1981), in her scrutiny of the TAT tries to counter the studies showing low validity by arguing that only in the hands of skilled testers does it work properly.
- *Testing the deepest layers of personality.* As Vernon (1963) pointed out, it is highly unlikely that projective tests do, in fact, measure some profound aspects of personality which other methods fail to tap since it has been found that the scores are influenced by contextual variables of many kinds. These include the race of the tester; the sex of the tester; the manner of administering the test; and the views of subjects concerning what the test measures.
- *The rationale of scoring systems.* Eysenck (1959) pointed out that there is no rationale, for example, in scoring the Rorschach. Thus it is claimed that this test can measure, *inter alia*, motivations, abilities, temperaments, attitudes. This is a far cry from all other scientific measures and the principles of psychometrics.

Of course, some projective tests, as has been seen, have some sort of rationale, the Blacky Pictures and the Test PN being based on psychoanalytic theory – although as far as Eysenck was concerned this would be worse than no theory.

Against this depressing background of inadequacy it must be asked why projective tests continue to be used at all. There are a number of reasons for this which I shall mention briefly:

- They are unique and rich sources of data. As our earlier descriptions of projective tests indicate, they yield data of a kind to be obtained from no other source. In principle, therefore, they ought to be valuable.
- Some results have been impressive. There is some evidence that in skilled hands, these tests can be useful. Carstairs (1957) studied the Rajput in India. His interpretations of their protocols yielded, it appeared, interesting insights into the psychology of their systems of belief. It would seem madness to jettison such data (see above). However, it must be stressed these interpretations were subjective and not quantified.
- Some objective scoring systems have been developed for projective tests, and these certainly improve their reliability. For example, Holley (1973) described G analysis for the Rorschach test. This involved a content analysis of the Rorschach protocols and a subsequent G analysis of these data. G analysis is essentially a special form of Q factor analysis in which people, rather than tests, are correlated. It uses the G index, a coefficient of correlation which avoids difficulty factors (Holley and Guilford, 1964). However, although this method did discriminate between schizophrenics and depressives and was shown to be applicable to the TAT (Hampson and Kline, 1977) and to the HTP (Hampson and Kline, 1977; Kline and Svasti-Xuto, 1981), I shall not discuss it further here, since the content analysis on which G analysis depends clearly possesses no unit of measurement, even if it is reliable. This same objection applies to the other objective scoring systems for projective tests, described by Murstein (1963) and Zubin et al. (1965).

Conclusions concerning projective tests

Although it is the conventional wisdom (Eysenck, 1959) to dismiss projective tests as worthless for the scientific study of personality, I have described them briefly together with some methods of analysis because this viewpoint is really not true. Some objective and reliable scoring schemes remove an important source of error from these tests. Furthermore, as I argued previously (Kline, 1995), it is clearly the case that the data from these tests are unusual and rich compared with the responses to the items of personality questionnaires which I shall discuss in the third section of this chapter. Thus it would be folly to abandon them completely as methods to study personality, a viewpoint shared by Semeneoff (1971).

However, from the viewpoint of the criticisms of Michell (1990, 1997), it is self-evident that projective tests could never meet the criteria of scientific measurement, as defined in the natural sciences. There is no true zero and no unit of measurement. For the purposes of developing truly scientific measures, the aim of this book, it is certain that projective tests will play no part.

Objective tests

The objective tests which I shall discuss in this section are of the kind listed by Cattell and Warburton (1967) and defined, as mentioned previously, as tests which can be objectively scored and whose purport is hidden from subjects. Cattell (e.g. 1957) referred to the scores obtained from these tests as T data in contradistinction to Q data from questionnaires and L data based upon actual observations of behaviour. Cattell and colleagues have the most extensive experience of any psychologists in the use of objective tests and it is, therefore, to their work which I shall mainly refer. Cronbach (1984) refers to this approach to testing as performance testing.

Rationale of objective tests

The definition of objective tests makes it clear that there could be enormous numbers of them. All that is required is a task with three characteristics: it is impossible to guess what it measures; it can be objectively scored; and it yields variance. As should be obvious from this book, psychometrics is the study of variance, human variation, so that a task which yields no variance is unsuitable as a test (although, incidentally, any such might be of some interest psychologically).

Since there must be an infinity of such possible tasks it is obviously necessary to devise some rationale for their construction. For example, I could devise an objective test: the computer test. Subjects are instructed to copy a short sequence of letters, digits and symbols on the computer. The following scores could be obtained: overall speed; latency of response to each item in the list; difference in average times for letters, digits and symbols; errors; pressure on the keys; corrections; response when forced to copy a symbol not on the keyboard. To eliminate typing ability as a variable a non-standard keyboard could be used. In addition, distractors could be introduced at certain points in the list and response times compared with and without distractors.

This example makes clear the problem with almost all objective tests: that of validity. It is not obvious what scores derived from this test would measure. If they turned out to be highly correlated with typing ability, it would be useless as a personality test. Similarly, it could be that the variance was simply specific to this test, again making it worthless. Thus having been invented, objective tests require proof of validity. Furthermore, since the invention of objective tests seems limited only by the ingenuity and patience of the test constructor, a rationale is essential.

In the Cattell and Warburton (1967) compendium of objective personality and motivation tests, listing 688 tests from which more than 2,300 variables are derived, few, at that time, showed much evidence either of reliability or validity, and unfortunately this defect still obtains. However, an extensive taxonomy of tests and a rationale were set out, and I shall summarise the main points.

A taxonomy of tests

A consideration of objective tests (actually all tests) makes it clear that there are three sources of variation: the test instructions; the test materials; and the scoring of the responses. For example, the test instructions may require subjects to be inventive, as in a projective test such as the Rorschach, or selective, as in a test with forced-choice items. Cattell and Warburton (1967) list 13 such instructional and test material variations (the two separate categories being run together since, as is obvious, they interact). Three of these are particularly important for objective tests:

1   Immediate meaning versus referent meaning. In some tests there is no meaning beyond the test. Reaction times are a good example. In others, however, the items refer to opinions, for example, and thus involve external referents. It is in these cases where we find typical test distortions due to inevitable subjectivity.
2   Itemised versus global presentation. Some tests consist of sets of items, others only a single task.
3   Psychological decisions. Tests differ in the types of decision required to respond to them. Some require cognition, others judgement of feelings and yet others judgements of familiarity or recognition.

Objective tests are often constructed such that they have immediate meaning, and require judgements of feelings and familiarity. Many are single tasks.

Response-scoring parameters

There are six sources of variation in the compendium in respect of how tests are scored. One of these is particularly relevant to objective tests – the objective versus self-evaluative – and I shall discuss it briefly. Some objective tests resemble personality inventories consisting of lists of items. However, there is a crucial difference between the way they are scored. Take the item adapted from T8 in the compendium: 'If a chemist takes 20 mins to make up a prescription how good is the performance?' Subjects are required to rate it from very good to very poor.

If this were an item in an inventory 'Attitudes to treatment' in one of the numerous studies so beloved in health psychology into the social psychology of disease, the responses to this item would be absolutely believed. Sixty-five per cent, it would be announced, believed that that their pharmacist took too long to complete prescriptions. This would be attributed to right-wing propensities in government, or even racism. However, in objective tests the scoring is quite different. From a list of similar items, all with different content but demanding ratings from very good to very poor, the number of poor and very poor responses for each individual is counted. This is a measure of critical evaluation. It is objective and impossible to guess its meaning. It is hard, therefore, to fake. It is interesting and informative to the understanding of objective tests to note the scores that can be obtained from this opinionnaire:

- number of critical responses;
- faster speed of judgement;
- greater variability in judgement;
- number of moderate responses; and
- better memory for items included in the test. It should be noted that in objective test batteries it is not uncommon to have a recall test of items in an inventory, perhaps 5 or 10 minutes after it was presented.

Finally, one other objective test-relevant response should be noted: the physiological. In some objective tests these are employed, a good example being the startle response to a pistol shot.

This taxonomy of tests is useful to a test constructor in that it indicates all possible forms which a test may take. However, it says nothing about content, and Cattell and Warburton (1967) are forced to admit that much depends upon rather vague intuitions and ideas such as clinical experience, observations in everyday life, folklore, proverbs and literary sources. Finally, there is a further problem involving objective tests, and this concerns the influence of ability. Any test which involves knowledge or requires rapid performance or the following of complex instructions may be distorted by ability factors. However, such tests can be eliminated at the stage of validation by factoring them together with personality and ability tests.

Examples of objective tests

Hundleby (1973) listed a number of objective tests which did load personality factors. The following tests loaded an anxiety factor:

- greater number of admissions of minor wrongdoings;
- greater acquiescence in answering questionnaires;
- higher score on a check-list of annoyances; and
- little confidence that a good performance could be reached in a wide range of novel scores.

It is to be noted that all these variables were obtained from objectively scored questionnaires. The following tests loaded an assertiveness factor:

- preference for socially acceptable rather than socially unacceptable book titles;
- faster tapping speed;

- faster tempo of arm and leg circling;
- faster speed of reading when asked to read at normal rate;
- higher speed at reading poetry and copying stick figures; and
- greater preference for sophisticated or highbrow activities.

This last set of tests illustrates the problem of constructing and identifying factor-pure objective tests of personality or motivation. It is highly unlikely that this factor is not distorted by ability since speed of reading is related to intelligence, as was pointed out in the previous chapter.

In fact there are two published objective tests, one of personality, the Objective Analytic Battery (OAB) (Cattell and Schuerger, 1978), the other of motivation, the Motivation Analysis Test (MAT) (Cattell et al., 1970b).

The OAB is claimed to measure 10 factors: ego standards; independence; evasiveness; exuberance; emotional balance; realism; self-assurance; exvia (Cattell's name for extraversion); anxiety; and discouragement. On account of the somewhat equivocal evidence for validity in the test manual, Kline and Cooper (1984b) carried out a factor analytic study of this test, locating the factors in a rotated simple-structure solution relative to the main personality and ability factors. The results were disappointing. Not only did the OAB items fail to form 10 factors, what factors there were were mixtures of ability and personality. The anxiety and extraversion factors failed to line up with these factors as measured by the EPQ (Eysenck and Eysenck, 1975) or Cattell's 16 Personality Factor (16PF) test. It is impossible to argue, from this study, that the OAB is valid.

The MAT is claimed to measure 10 factors, some relating to ergs (basic drives) and some to sentiments (culturally moulded drives). These are respectively: mating, assertiveness, fear, narcissism (defined as comfort seeking) and pugnacity; and self-sentiment, superego or conscience, career, sweetheart and parental home. Within these factors are two components, unintegrated and integrated, corresponding approximately to the unconscious and conscious aspects of these drives (Cattell and Child, 1975).

However, Cooper and Kline (1982) carried out a study similar to our previous investigation (Kline and Cooper, 1984b) of the OAB, in which a simple-structure rotation of the MAT and 16PF tests was computed. The 10 MAT factors failed to emerge, and item analysis of the separate MAT scales revealed that most of them did not form scales at all. On psychometric grounds the MAT cannot be a valid test.

Conclusions concerning objective tests

It can be seen from this discussion of the rationale of objective tests that they are highly interesting measures. However, in the compendium (Cattell and Warburton, 1967), it is quite clear that the vast majority of such tests had no evidence for validity. This is because the necessary research had not been done, rather than because they had been shown to be invalid. However, this defect has not really been seriously addressed in the interim period. Our own studies of the published batteries, the OAB and the MAT, which followed the methods advocated by Cattell (1978) as closely as was possible, cast considerable doubt on their validity – and these are considered to be the best objective tests.

Yet the paradox remains that the genuinely scientific tests of personality – ratio scales with units of measurement, equal intervals and true zeros – will be, by definition, objective tests. We want to use measures which involve time or distance, because these involve units of measurement. There are such in the Cattell and Warburton compendium; for example, the slow line drawing test. Here subjects have to draw a line as slowly as possible. The shorter the line, the slower the drawing. Yet this measure is unlikely to be a good test simply because it has a rather weak theoretical basis. Thus, for example, although the BIP (discussed in Chapter 7) did not turn out as well as had been hoped, this test had a clear theoretical basis, namely that intelligence was based upon the speed of processing bits of information. Whether calculated as bits per second or speed, this was a scientific scale. The theoretical basis of drawing speed as a measure of personality is such that even if this test correlated positively with some other personality scales it would be difficult to use it as a measure of personality.

Thus what is required for the development of good scientific measures of personality is a clear theoretical account of the nature of temperament and motivation which would provide a basis for test development. How this might be done is considered in the next chapter, but it must be concluded here that objective personality tests will not stand scrutiny in this capacity simply because they are atheoretical.

Personality questionnaires

The third category of personality tests comprises personality questionnaires or inventories. These consist of sets of questions or items to which subjects have to reply, essentially, 'Yes'/'No' or 'True/False' as the item applies to them. These personality tests are much the most widely used tests of personality for a number of reasons which are set out below.

- *High reliability.* These tests can be made highly reliable, in comparison to projective and objective tests. As was pointed out in Chapter 2, reliability is partly dependent on the number of items. Construct 20 items per scale and a usable reliability (>0.7) is normally obtained.
- *Ease of administration.* These tests are usually administered to groups and require no great skill in test administration. It is, therefore, easy to build up large normative samples and collect sufficient data for reliable factor analysis.
- *Utility in applied psychology.* All this has made personality questionnaires attractive to applied psychologists, and a considerable collection of data on clinical, educational and occupational groups has been obtained.
- *Utility in theoretical psychology.* The fact that personality questionnaires are

reliable and large samples can be tested has made them ideal for factor analysis and the development of a theoretical factor structure analogous exactly to the factor structure of abilities which was discussed in Chapters 6 and 7.

Background to the current work on the structure of personality

To understand the current consensus concerning the structure of personality it is necessarily briefly to outline how personality questionnaires came to be used as the basis for this structure. When this has been done I shall discuss some of the problems involved in this work. Only then, in Chapter 9, will we be in a position to evaluate the most modern research.

The pioneers in the factor analysis of personality questionnaires, Guilford (1959) and Cattell (1957), realised that the success of factor analysis in elucidating the structure of abilities could be repeated in the more complex field of personality by applying factor analysis to personality questionnaires. Cattell, indeed, developed an enormous programme of research to this end, which is still continuing, and he formulated a number of principles which it is worth examining because, in many cases, failure to adhere to them has led to worthless findings.

- In elucidating the structure of a field it is necessary to ensure that the whole field has been sampled, otherwise factors may simply be missed. Cattell attempted to do this by searching the dictionary for all trait terms and ensuring that all these were embraced in his original items. This was the origin of the semantic personality sphere (Cattell, 1957).
- It is essential to ensure that the scales have a validity beyond the fact that the items load a factor. This is the problem of bloated specifics, and it will recur in our discussions of personality factors.
- It is also essential, as Cronbach (1957) argued, to link psychometric factors either in the sphere of ability or that of personality into the constructs of experimental psychology. It is particularly valuable to explore their genetic and their physiological bases as this, at a stroke, if any are found, ensures that the factors cannot be bloated specifics, and gives them psychological meaning. It is almost self-evident that any factors claimed to be basic to personality should be observable in the higher apes and mammals since we share so large a proportion of DNA with them.

All these principles are important if factor analysis is to be useful in elucidating the structure of personality. These principles, it should be noted, are in addition to the necessary principles underlying technically sound factor analyses which must be observed for meaningful results. These have been discussed in Chapter 3.

Unfortunately, as has been argued by Cattell (1981), Cattell and Kline (1977) and Kline (1993), much research in the field of personality has failed to adhere to either the technical or the logical principles which have been mentioned above and is of little substantive value. Furthermore, there are problems with personality questionnaires themselves which are so severe that they must be discussed before we examine the factors which are claimed to account for their variance.

Differences between personality test items and ability test items

I believe that differences between personality test items and ability test items are the key issue to many of the problems and misunderstandings concerning the structure of personality. The scores on a typical intelligence test represent the number of items in the test which individuals got right. Our study of the items in intelligence tests indicated that these were problems involving reasoning, often in the form of analogies or working out common categories among objects. Such items are chosen by test constructors as a sample of typical reasoning problems at different levels of difficulty. If a subject gets an item right it is clear that that subject can solve that problem, reason at that level of difficulty (excluding guessing, for the sake of the argument). Thus performance on an IQ test reflects a level of reasoning ability. Without such reasoning ability the subject could not have obtained a score. All this is unarguable. The only possible doubt about the validity of IQ tests concerns the generality of the reasoning tapped by the items. That it is not test specific is supported by the correlations with other, external criteria. However, even if the items require reasoning that is specific to IQ tests, there is no doubt that the items, to be answered correctly, do require such reasoning.

Now consider some typical items from personality tests:

- I enjoy going to the pictures. Yes/No.
- In new situations I sometimes feel afraid. Yes/No.
- If I had to choose, I would prefer going round a bank to going to a classical opera. Yes/No.

These three items are not taken from any published test since it destroys the validity of a test to broadcast the items, but they are entirely typical of personality test items of even the best tests. Immediately the difference, as compared with ability tests, is obvious. To answer 'Yes' to the second item, for example, does not inevitably mean that the subject feels afraid in new situations, for the following reasons:

- The subject may be lying.
- The subject may be mistaken, perhaps wrongly believing at that time that they feel afraid. The subject may have little insight.
- The subject may interpret 'feeling afraid' in a way different from the test

constructor, who perhaps regarded 'afraid' as evidenced by sweating, horrible feelings in the gut and near panic, whereas the subject thought that being afraid was a far less severe condition.

- The subject may interpret 'new situation' differently from the test constructor. They might regard 'new' as meaning something totally different, such as finding oneself on the moon or having to operate on a patient without training, whereas the constructor had envisaged 'new' as going to a new restaurant with people one did not know.

- The interpretation of 'sometimes' obviously raises all the problems of interpretation which have been discussed with reference to the other words in this item.

- It is obvious that the other items are similarly problematic.

In brief, self-reports of behaviour cannot be equated with the actual behaviour. This is a major difficulty with personality questionnaires and must call into question the meaning of factors which are extracted from them.

The leading personality test constructors are not unaware of this difficulty and psychometrics has attempted to deal with it, but not wholly successfully except in a few cases. Cattell (1957) and Eysenck (1967) argued that when a subject endorses the item 'In new situations I sometimes feel afraid' we do not take this to be either true or false. This response of putting 'true' to this item is regarded as a behaviour. If it can be shown to predict neuroticism or to load an identified factor of neuroticism or anxiety then it can be included in an anxiety scale. Cattell actually calls the data obtained from questionnaires Q and Q' data: Q data are data from items which are simply introspections; Q' data are data from items which have been shown to be valid as behaviour. This argument, of course, overcomes at once all the problems which I discussed above. However, in truth, this is rarely done. Most test constructors are content to demonstrate that items load a factor. Only a few go further and try to identify the factor against external criteria. Furthermore, the manuals to many tests exemplify the meaning of the factor by reference to the items loading on it. This is nonsensical unless it is assumed that the items reflect behaviour.

For example, McCrae (1996) attempts to explain the nature of openness by listing items from the Californian Psychological Inventory (Gough, 1957) which correlate with the scale. This is meaningful only if the items are taken at their face value. Thus the fact that the items 'Women should not be allowed to drink in cocktail bars' and 'A large number of people are guilty of bad sexual conduct' correlate with the Openness scale is held to demonstrate its validity and add to our knowledge of the variable. Apart from the fact that it assumes the truth of the responses to these items, it also reveals a depressing lack of statistical common sense since these correlations are 0.17 and 0.12 in the case of the former item and 0.21 and 0.16 in the case of the latter. At best, only 4 per cent of the variance has been explained.

It should be pointed out that it follows from the treatment of personality test items as Q' data that item writing is rendered difficult. If responses are regarded as behaviour rather than veridical truth, it is somewhat pointless to go to great length to write accurate items. Indeed, this was the point of objective tests, which we have discussed above.

Some readers may think that my objections to personality questionnaire items are somewhat absurd, exaggerated, academic, logically possible but unlikely seriously to affect findings. However, this naïve view of personality questionnaires is not tenable for a variety of reasons.

Perhaps the most telling of the arguments is the most general. Introspection, as the history of psychology shows, is simply not reliable as a source of information. One does not have to accept the whole panoply of psychoanalysis to accept that there are unconscious determinants of our behaviour and that these can never be revealed by introspection or by answering simple questions, as in personality inventories. Freud (1923) described many defence mechanisms in his paper 'The ego and the id'. These are unconscious mechanisms for keeping out of consciousness painful or repressed feelings or ideas. Not only is there some experimental evidence supporting the notion of defences from the percept-genetic research of Kragh and Smith (1970), but these concepts, under different names such as 'coping mechanisms', have been extensively studied by Horowitz (1989) and Vaillant (1977). There is little doubt that such mechanisms play a part in our self-perception, thus ensuring, as a consequence, that simple questionnaire items can never yield much more than simple factual information. Actually this is why, despite projective tests' psychometric imperfections, some psychologists have continued to use them. Indeed, even cognitive psychology, using the principles of information processing, has found a place for defence mechanisms, although eschewing such a Freudian term (Marcel, 1983). In summary, it is simply contrary to any reputable account of human psychology to imagine that much could be learned from simple questions. If it could, there would be no problems in understanding human behaviour and there would be no subject called psychology because there would be no need for it.

As was suggested earlier in this section, psychologists, beguiled by the successes of factor analysis in the field of abilities, have sought to use the technique with personality tests. When this is done, just as with ability tests factors emerge. However, since, as I have argued, these factors are not *per se* personality factors, because the items are not samples of behaviour but self-reports, it is necessary to consider the nature of factors in personality questionnaires and how these factors may be validated.

Nature of the factors in personality questionnaires and their identification

There are a few simple principles for identifying questionnaire factors which are set out below.

1   Construct validation is necessary, and is best done by locating the factor within a proper theoretical framework. The most notable exponent of this approach is Eysenck (1967), who has demonstrated the nature of the personality factors neuroticism, extraversion and psychoticism by linking them theoretically and experimentally to conditioning, by establishing their physiological basis and their heritability. In addition, he has established their wider behavioural manifestations in clinical studies of neurosis and psychosis, criminality and smoking (see Modgil and Modgil (1986) for a brief summary of much of this work).

2   Cattell also attempted the same feat. He based his theoretical account as closely as possible on the factors revealed by his enormous programme of research from the 1940s onwards, although he was not ignorant of the major psychological theories. He, like Eysenck, always sought external validation for the factors and considered them to be identified with L factors based upon actual observations of subjects (Cattell, 1957). In addition the factors were related to educational, clinical and occupational criteria and their heritabilities were estimated. Cattell considered that any scientific account of personality must be based upon quantified variables and that factor analysis was the appropriate method to discover and measure them. Cattell (1981) set out just such a theoretical account. His approach is essentially that adopted in this book, except that I am attempting to improve the measurement of the variables.

3   If there are benchmark measures of variables it is possible to identify factors by locating them in factor space bounded by these measures. As I have argued elsewhere (Kline, 1995), this is possible in the cases of intelligence (both fluid and crystallised) and extraversion and neuroticism or anxiety.

Only factors identified by these methods should be regarded as valid. In fact, as will be discussed in the next chapter, there are remarkably few personality factors which have been properly identified.

Nunnally (1978) described the many ways it was possible to fool oneself with factor analysis, and this is regularly evident in journal articles, despite his warnings. Cattell (1978) argued that much factor analytic work was simply wrong, and nowhere is this more the case than in the field of the construction of personality tests. It is a simple matter to write personality test items, to subject them to factor analysis and to produce a scale in which the items all load a common factor. Many test constructors then identify the factor from the items loading on it and a new variable is discovered. This is unsatisfactory for three reasons.

• Response sets can give rise to factors. Two response sets, acquiescence, the tendency to agree with an item regardless of content, and social desirability, the tendency to respond to an item because it is socially desirable so to do, are particularly influential, as Cronbach (1946) showed. Jackson (1997) claimed that social desirability was the first component among many personality test items, although I have never found this in my own research. Nevertheless, neither of these response sets can be ignored.

- There is a problem of tautologous factors. It is quite possible to create a factor by writing items which are more or less paraphrases of each other: 'I like going to parties'; 'I enjoy a good party with plenty of noise'; 'I like a quiet night in best of all' (scored negatively); 'I like going out with a group of friends'; and so on. Such items correlate positively and form a factor. If they did not, it would mean that the subject was entirely inconsistent. These factors are known as bloated specifics. Many tests appear to be of this kind, especially brief but reliable three- or four-item tests, as in studies of locus of control (Lefcourt, 1991). Such factors might be regarded as semantic factors since the factor loadings indicate that the items mean much the same thing.

Rating scales

A brief mention must be made of rating scales. These consist of adjectives and subjects have to rate themselves on a five-point scale indicating the extent to which each adjective is a good description of their behaviour. Essentially, therefore, they are little different from personality questionnaires. Analysis of such rating scales yields similar factors to those in questionnaires, and a common use for such scales is to demonstrate that, in different cultures, with different languages, the same structure emerges (see, for example, the work of De Raad and Szirmack, 1994). Goldberg (e.g. 1982) is perhaps the best-known worker in this field. Such factors must reflect semantics as well as behaviour, and their agreement with personality questionnaire factors supports the doubts concerning the meaning and validity of these latter.

Conclusions

From all these arguments it is clear that the results from personality tests have to be treated with extreme caution. As has been demonstrated, projective tests are not in accord with the principles of scientific measurement and those objective tests which have been studied are not apparently valid. However, it is likely that objective tests derived from personality theory could provide the scientific tests which are the goal of this book.

Personality inventories are the current basis for the psychometrics of personality. However, as has been argued, although they are amenable to factor analysis and can be made highly reliable, personality test factors are crucially different from ability factors because their items are not samples of the behaviour to be studied but self-reports. These are unlikely to be accurate and valid for many reasons, and thus personality factors need to be identified by theoretical and external criteria. Personality factors identified by item loadings are not acceptable.

Finally, it must be pointed out that even if any personality factors have been validated, these do not meet the criteria of scientific measurement set out by

Michell (1997) for the reasons already advanced in previous chapters. However, if these are well-established variables with useful predictive power it is clearly the task of psychometrics to measure them properly.

In Chapter 9, therefore, I shall set out the best-validated personality and motivation factors and suggest how they might be measured scientifically.

9

PERSONALITY STRUCTURE AND SCIENTIFIC MEASUREMENT

As was made clear in Chapter 8, any personality structure determined by the factor analysis of personality questionnaires is different in kind from the structure of abilities. This is because of the nature of the items in personality questionnaires, which are not, *per se*, examples of the behaviour to which the items refer. The identification of such factors, therefore, is necessarily only inferential and subjective, and powerful evidence of validity is required other than identification of factors by the items loading on them.

Despite all these problems, however, there is a surprising agreement among the factor analysts of personality concerning the major second-order factor structure although it has to be said that two of the leading older workers in this field, Eysenck and Cattell, have refused to adhere to the consensus. Each has preferred his original solutions. As I have indicated in the previous chapter, I also believe that the currently popular solution, the big five, or the five-factor model, is far from satisfactory.

Before I set out the various factor structures, it must be pointed out that none of these factors has the same impressive evidence for its psychological importance as is the case for the intelligence factors. These are such that they have to be accommodated into any coherent theory of cognitive functioning, whether based on psychometric analysis, cognitive experimental psychology or neural networks. Although there is some good evidence supporting two of the personality factors, extraversion and anxiety, this is still far less than that for the ability factors. The evidence for the other personality factors is not compelling.

The Eysenck factors

Eysenck was involved in the study of personality from the 1940s until his death in 1997. Of all those who have used factor analysis to structure the complexities of personality, Eysenck was the most favourably disposed to other experimental methods of investigation. He took seriously the advice of Cronbach (1957) to blend psychometric and experimental psychology. He attempted to tie in his personality questionnaire factors to psychological theory and to biological and genetic mechanisms. Whatever his factors are, they are not simply collections of items which form factors.

Eysenck (e.g. 1967, 1992) postulated three personality factors as accounting for much of the variance in personality:

- *E – Extraversion.* The extravert is noisy, sociable, outgoing, a lover of excitement and stimulation. The introvert, on the other hand, is quiet, inward-looking, reflective, even withdrawn.
- *N – Neuroticism.* The high scorer on N is anxious (actually, this factor is labelled 'anxiety' by other researchers), a worrier, somewhat unstable, given to swings of mood, excitable. The low scorer is stolid and phlegmatic. It should be noted that this factor is a trait factor. Trait anxiety must be distinguished from state anxiety. This latter is the anxiety almost all normal individuals feel at certain impending events: a visit to the dentist, examinations, interviews and ultimately death.
- *P – Psychoticism.* The high scorer, almost always male and often criminal, is characterised by a lack of empathy. This makes him cruel, unfeeling, aggressive, unreliable and unconscientious. Further, high scorers enjoy danger and violence and strange or novel sensations.

These factors are measured by the EPQ (Eysenck and Eysenck, 1975). Although there is a newer version of this test, the EPQ-R, the huge research basis for these factors rests on the older test. Of course, the psychological meaning of the factors in both tests should be the same. Extraversion is conceived of as the behavioural, personality manifestation of the arousability of the central nervous system, specifically the ascending reticular system. Neuroticism, on the other hand, is related to the lability of the autonomic nervous system and this accounts for the characteristic symptoms of state anxiety: sweating, tremors, sick feelings and, *in extremis*, fainting. P, psychoticism, is related to the levels of androgen. This accounts for its higher level in males and its relation to criminality. As might be expected, the population variance, in the West, in these three factors has a considerable genetic determination, and the important environmental determinants are within rather than between families: that is, specific to individuals within each family rather than shared. This is highly important in the light of many social-psychological claims concerning the origins of individual differences in personality, as Eysenck (1992) delights to point out. This is a brief summary of an enormous amount of research into the nature of the variables.

Finally, it should be noted that factor analysis of the EPQ clearly demonstrates that these three factors are easily replicated, although the present author finds that extraversion and neuroticism are not orthogonal but modestly and negatively intercorrelated (e.g. Draycott and Kline, 1995). Indeed, Kline and Barrett (1983) found that the factor loadings of the EPQ E and N items were virtually perfect, all loading only their factors, such that the EPQ could and should be used as a marker variable for these questionnaire factors. The P factor items were less good, although they easily reached the criteria for good test construction (see Kline, 1993).

Conclusions

In brief, it would be difficult not to include these three factors, E, N and P, in any list of reliable, replicable and validated personality questionnaire factors. Nevertheless, as has been pointed out, these factors are second-order, broad variables, which provides an obvious source of difficulty. Given the complexity of human personality it is not unreasonable to argue that three factors are simply too few plausibly to account for all its variation. More factors are required.

In our discussions of factor analysis throughout this book, it should be clear that such an objection is difficult for factor analysis to answer objectively. The number of factors is always a function of the variables which are in the analysis. Somehow, to provide a convincing argument that x was the correct number of factors it would be necessary to demonstrate that all variables had been sampled. Even if this had been done, in the field of personality, as was pointed out in Chapter 8, much also depends on item writing. It is all too easy to construct bloated specifics, collection of items which are essentially paraphrases.

Cattell's factors

This discussion naturally leads on to a consideration and brief description of the work of Cattell (e.g. 1957, 1981). As was the case with Eysenck, Cattell developed an enormous programme of research which attempted to establish the most important personality factors and embrace them in a theory of personality which would be scientific because all variables would be identified factors and thus measurable. This was intended to set it aside from all other personality theories, which involve concepts and notions difficult or impossible to measure. Cattellian personality theory (Cattell, 1981) is, by the conventional standards of psychometrics, quantified.

Cattell was well aware that exploratory factor analysis depended on proper sampling of subjects and variables. To achieve the latter he sampled the dictionary of trait terms, reduced it by omitting synonyms, and factored ratings of all these terms in order to ascertain the most important factors, work fully described by Cattell and Kline (1977). These so called L factors formed the basis of his questionnaire factors, thus ensuring that these also sampled the whole population of personality variables. This work resulted in one of the best-known personality questionnaires, the Cattell 16 Personality Factor test (Cattell et al., 1970a).

These factors have been extensively studied by Cattell and his colleagues. In the technical handbook to the test can be found the scores of large numbers of different occupations and clinical groups, the scores of different national groups, and regression equations for success in many of the occupations for which there are norms. In addition to this there are heritabilities for all the factors, and developmental studies from the age of 4 up to old age. These factors are far more than mere collections of items.

As an approach to the factor analytic study of personality this huge programmatic effort by Cattell is a superb example of the genre. Cattell, indeed, is one of the major psychometrists. However, there are some problems with this work which unfortunately prevent it from being the definitive factor analytic account of personality. These can be briefly set out but I have fully discussed them elsewhere (Kline, 1979, 1994b).

- The reliabilities of the 16PF test are far lower than is desirable for accurate measurement.
- The parallel form reliabilities of the test are also low. This means that the different forms are not equivalent and this makes comparison of results difficult.
- Most factor analyses of the 16PF test fail to recover the 16 factors. Cattell has always claimed that technical deficiencies in the factor analyses, particularly the failure to reach simple structure, were the reasons for this. However, Kline and Barrett (1983) followed Cattell's methods and reached simple structure. Only eight factors emerged, and these were composites of the scales.
- Kline and Barrett (1983) and Kline (1993, 1995) concluded from a detailed study of the origins of the 16PF test that the failure to reach a 16-factor simple structure was due to the fact that Cattell (e.g. 1957, 1973) had claimed to have found 16 factors when in fact the loadings were far lower than is normally acceptable, i.e. 0.3. In brief, there never were 16 factors in these questionnaires. Much of the difficulty arose from the fact that Cattell's early work was carried out before the age of powerful computing and short-cut methods had to be employed. Howarth (1976) makes this same point. However, while this now seems to be generally accepted by all except those working with Cattell, this group still claims that 16 factors are the best account of the variance in personality questionnaires.
- One of the defences adopted by Cattell and colleagues concerns the fact that failure to find 16 factors occurred in studies in which the item correlations were factored (Boyle et al., 1995). As has been argued in Chapter 2, items are unreliable, and this, according to Boyle et al. (1995), creates the problem. Rather it is necessary to factor clusters of items or item parcels, as they are called by Cattell (1973). However, this was done by Kline and Barrett (1983), who followed precisely the procedures outlined by Cattell for creating item parcels. The 16 factors failed to emerge. This argument will not do, as will not the claim that 16 factors account for more of the variance than the five-factor model (Mershon and Gorsuch, 1988). As we have seen from our discussions of factor analysis, this is virtually bound to be the case. In my view these counter-arguments fail.
- Although Kline and Barrett (1983) failed to extract the 16 factors, at the

second order the test seemed to make sense. Extraversion and anxiety were clear and correlated highly with their counterparts in the EPQ. Furthermore, there were two other second-order factors which could be identified: tough-mindedness and conventionality. These four are similar to those in the five-factor model. Noller *et al.* (1987), Boyle (1989) (who factored the EPI, the Comrey and the 16PF scales) and Amelang and Borkenau (1982) claimed that the reliable variance in the 16PF was in fact that of the big five factors.

However, Boyle *et al.* (1995) make some excellent points in their discussion of the second orders in the Cattell 16PF which I shall summarise here and in the next section, on the five-factor model, to which they are also relevant. Krug and Johns (1986) carried out a technically sound factor analysis of the 16PF using more than 17,000 subjects with the results cross-validated on males and females in the sample. Five factors were clearly identified: extraversion, anxiety, tough poise, independence and control. There are several points to be noticed here. The first is that these factors, derived from so large a sample and cross-validated, are indubitably reliable. Second, although they resemble the factors in the five-factor model they are not the same. Finally, although they are statistically reliable, there is a difficulty in that given the dubious nature of the original 16 factors in the 16PF the identification of these factors must be accepted with some caution.

In brief, despite the brilliance of the 16PF it seems unlikely that these factors can be the definitive account of the variance in personality questionnaires.

The five-factor model

Recently, consensus has arisen, excluding Cattell and Eysenck, as has been obvious, that five factors best account for the variance in personality questionnaires. I too cannot accept this claim, for reasons that will become clear in this section.

The factors in the model

Costa and McCrae (1992b) use the NEO Personality Inventory (revised) to measure these factors: extraversion, anxiety, agreeableness, conscientiousness and openness. There are no problems with the first two factors; virtually all researchers regard these as two major personality questionnaire factors. The difficulties lie in the three other factors.

As I have pointed out elsewhere (Kline, 1993), the consensus concerning the five-factor model arises from the fact that it has been claimed that these five factors can be found in the Gough Adjective Check List (Piedmont *et al.*, 1991), the MMPI (Costa *et al.*, 1985), the EPI (McCrae and Costa, 1985), the PRF (Costa and McCrae, 1988) and the Myers–Briggs (McCrae and Costa, 1989). Many well-known researchers seem to accept that these factors account for the variance in personality questionnaires (e.g. Pervin, 1990; Digman, 1990; Goldberg, 1992).

However, this consensus ignores some important points which run counter to it and, in my view, render it untenable. Boyle *et al.* (1995) summarise many of these arguments. The first argument concerns the correlations often found between C, O and A. As Eysenck points out, these factors are not independent. This was certainly the case in a study of the five-factor model by Draycott and Kline (1995), with the NEO and the EPQ. Factors P, C, A and O all loaded the same canonical variate, confirming the lack of independence and their relationship to P. Furthermore, Eysenck points out that the provenance of these three factors is dubious. Costa and McCrae are unable to relate these factors to any kind of coherent theory or biological mechanism. Actually King and Figueredo (1997) attempted to remedy this deficiency in a study of 100 chimpanzees whose behaviour was rated using trait adjectives from the five-factor model together with those for dominance. They claimed to find the big five factors along with dominance, which is accepted as being important in chimpanzee groups. However, examination of the factors is disappointing. Openness was defined by two variables, inventive and inquisitive, which are far from an adequate description of this factor. Furthermore, two variables are not enough to define a factor (Cattell, 1978). Emotionality was also weak, having three defining variables: stable, emotional and unemotional. This study cannot be used as biological support for the five-factor model.

Another serious objection to the big five, as Boyle *et al.* (1995) argue and demonstrate, is that the big five solutions do not approximate simple structure, as judged from the hyperplane count. Costa and McCrae (1992a) attempt to counter this point by arguing that simple structure is not as important as was once thought and that many personality traits are multifactorial. This is to ignore the work on plasmodes by Cattell (1978) and earlier by Thurstone (1947). There is a rationale to simple structure: that it is replicable; that it tends to find causal, fundamental structures; and that it fits the scientific method (Occam's razor). Once factors are selected because they fit a predetermined theory, the power of factor analysis is abandoned. There is an infinity of solutions and there must be a rational selection among them. For all these reasons I believe that the five-factor model should not be regarded as the best solution to the problem of factor structure in personality questionnaires. Block (1995) has recently endorsed all these arguments. It is pertinent to note here that a confirmatory factor analysis of the Revised NEO failed to find five factors (Parker *et al.* 1993).

Conclusions

The five-factor solution is certainly not acceptable. The correlations between agreeableness and conscientiousness and the fact that openness is related to intelligence, although clearly not a measure of intelligence (McCrae, 1996), ensure that this is not an optimal solution. The mere fact that factors can be obtained, as was shown in Chapter 8, does not confer psychological meaning in the field of personality questionnaires. There can be no doubt that the five-factor model does not represent simple structure.

Eysenck (1992) noted the deplorable absence of theorising in respect of the big five factors. This is so, yet in reality these results can be more meaningfully interpreted. In our study of factors among personality questionnaires (Kline and Barrett, 1983) it was shown that in many studies there was frequently a factor of obsessional traits, although it was often given different names. Thus Rokeach (1960) called it the dogmatic personality, Freud (1908) the anal character; Kline (1971) developed a personality questionnaire for it, Ai3Q. All these were similar to the authoritarian personality (Adorno *et al.*, 1950) and the obsessional personality (Sandler and Hazari, 1960). Kline and Cooper (1984c) carried out a factor analytic study of these scales and demonstrated that they did, indeed, load a clear second-order factor obsessional personality. It seems possible that these other variables are different manifestations of this basic factor. Thus the political form of obsession-ality is the authoritarian personality. In religious attitudes it is manifested as dogmatism and in personal habits as the anal character. Psychoticism would appear to be a more clinical form of the factor. This would satisfactorily account for A and C of the big five, and to some extent O also since the authoritarian and dogmatic personalities are clearly low O, as described by McCrae (1996).

Thus I would argue that from questionnaires three reliable second-orders have been found: extraversion, anxiety or neuroticism and the obsessional factor. Eysenck's P is clearly important in this factor and it is possible that psychoticism is its most fundamental aspect. More work is required on this point.

Measuring these factors

There can be no doubt that if we want to measure these factors by questionnaire, as regards extraversion and anxiety the EPQ is an outstanding test. Barrett and Kline (1980), on a large random sample from the UK, showed a virtually perfect factor structure and item analysis for these scales. Since, as has been argued, there is considerable construct validation for the factors, these are undoubtedly bench-mark measures. For the third factor there is less agreement, but Eysenck's P, Cattell's G, superego from the 16PF and Ai3Q all load this factor. However, all these tests are questionnaires. The scores are aggregates of items, and although there is some evidence that the tests measure the constructs they are supposed to measure, they are far from the criteria for scientific measurement discussed by Michell (1997). The question therefore to be answered is this. How can scientific measures of these variables, which factor analysis suggests are important in personality, be constructed?

Scientific measures of personality

What is required, it will be remembered, are equal-interval ratio scales with a unit of measurement. This rules out personality questionnaires. Objective tests, as defined by Cattell (1957), overcome the difficulty with questionnaire items but still provide no meaningful unit of measurement, at least in most cases.

It is instructive to consider the BIP measure of intelligence, discussed in Chapter 7. This was considered as a possible scientific measure because it did provide a unit of measurement, the number of bits of information. Unfortunately, it was unclear to what extent this measure was related to intelligence. It was possible to develop such a measure because the Erlangen school had a clear theoretical account of intelligence; for the purposes of this argument it is irrelevant whether that theory was correct or not. What is required, therefore, is a similarly clear theoretical account of personality.

Such accounts are hard to find in the field of personality and are restricted to the theories of Eysenck (e.g. 1967) and their modification by Gray (1982), who is mainly concerned with anxiety. Until theories are developed, scientific measurement will be impossible. In Chapter 10 I shall discuss in more detail how such scientific tests might be developed and here I shall give a few simple examples. According to Eysenck (1967), extraverts are harder to condition than introverts and, having been conditioned, their responses extinguish more quickly. If this is so then it makes sense to attempt to develop a standard conditioning test. The scores obtained are the number of trials to learning and the number of unreinforced presentations before extinction. These fulfil the criteria of proper scientific measurement.

As regards anxiety, this is supposed to reflect the lability of the autonomic nervous system. Eysenck (1967) has attempted what he calls objective measures of this phenomenon and an example is the measurement of sweating in standard conditions of heat and humidity to standard stimuli. Measures of psychogalvanic response (PGR), which reflect this, have been used for many years in lie detectors, as have measures of heart rate. All these measures fulfil the standards of scientific testing and with intensive development could be useful. Broadhurst (1959), it should be noted, attempted to measure anxiety in rats through the measurement of faecal deposits. In brief, good theories can lead to proper measurement. The whole problem of the scientific measurement of both ability and personality will be discussed in Chapter 10.

Motivation: structure and measurement

The psychometric study of motivation (dynamic factors) has been far less successful than that of temperament and personality. Indeed, the factor analysis of this field is virtually the province of Cattell and his colleagues (Cattell, 1973, 1985; Cattell and Child, 1975; Boyle, 1991). Because motivational factors have far less construct validity than personality and ability factors I shall deal with them here only briefly. It is by no means certain that any of these factors would form even a basis for comparison in the development of a genuinely scientific measure of motivation.

States, moods and drives

Motivational, dynamic factors account for why we do what we do, in contrast to the temperamental factors of personality, which are concerned with how we carry out our actions. In thinking about dynamics it is customary, at least in everyday language, to talk of moods, states and drives, and this convention has been followed in psychometric work.

Distinction between states and traits

The distinction between traits and states has been most clearly stated by Cattell (e.g. Cattell, 1973; Cattell and Kline, 1977). Traits are stable over time; that is, their variance on repeated measurement is small. Most of the personality variables which we have discussed are traits, as are the ability factors. We would be amazed if any individual appeared highly intelligent on one occasion and stupid on another. The same applies, but perhaps to a lesser extent, to personality variables such as extraversion. Generally individuals are largely extraverted or introverted.

States, on the other hand, are transient. Anxiety is a perfect example. If we are awaiting the results of a medical test, we are inevitably anxious. This is state anxiety. If it is a good outcome then our anxiety quickly dissipates. If it is bad, it does so but more slowly. Individuals are able to accept, to a large degree, even the worst prognoses.

This example clarifies the distinction between states and traits. Trait anxiety, one of the most important temperamental factors, is stable and enduring. It is our general level of anxiety. State anxiety is transient and fluctuates according to our experiences. In the measurement of anxiety it is important to distinguish between state and trait anxiety, and this can be done by means of the State–Trait Anxiety Inventory (Spielberger et al., 1986).

This transience and variability, of course, is true of all states. Some states are short, possibly of only a few seconds' duration. Others are longer, such as depression, which may, in some unfortunate individuals, be so prolonged as to be essentially a trait.

Distinction between states and moods

Although there is a vernacular distinction between states and moods, in the factor analytic work of Cattell these are regarded as identical. And the discussion above, on the distinction between states and traits, makes it obvious why this should be so. While it is conventional to call anxiety or fatigue a state, it is usual to call transient states such as anger, elation or irritability moods. Yet there is no real difference between these and states. Thus moods and states are regarded as identical and defined as variables which fluctuate over time, according to experiences and, in many cases, inner feelings.

Importance of states and moods

The aim of psychometrics is, *inter alia*, to predict behaviour. Perfect prediction implies, in most case, full understanding, and where it does not, it is likely quickly to lead to it. Thus it is clear that the measurement of moods and states is essential. Nowhere is this more evident than in sport. Anxiety frequently cripples performance, as does fatigue or anger. The tennis player angry at a line call may well lose the next game. It is the control of such moods and states that is the mark of the champion, sometimes being more important than outright ability. Thus in any proper understanding of behaviour, assessment of moods and states is essential.

However, before I discuss the measurement of moods and states, it is necessary to discuss another aspect of the dynamics of human behaviour: drives. Just as moods and states are important in understanding and predicting behaviour so are drives. Some people appear to have a high drive to succeed, often called the need for achievement (McClelland, 1961). Others are happy to do as little as possible. Clearly, status on such a variable has a powerful influence on behaviour. In brief, human motives are important.

Human drives and motives

The psychometric, factor analytic study of drives, as has been stated, has been largely neglected except by Cattell. This is because there are severe problems, both psychometric and conceptual, in the study of motivation.

- *Conceptual problems*. Factor analysis, to be an effective exploratory procedure, relies on proper sampling of the salient variables. However, in the field of motivation this is particularly difficult because there is little agreement among theorists as to what these variables are (see Kline, 1993, and Cattell and Kline, 1977, for a full discussion of this point). A few examples will illustrate the problem. Thus Freud (1940) generally argues that sex and aggression are the main human drives and that the task of civilisation is to control these. In the later works of psychoanalysis the notion of eros and thanatos, the life and death instincts, comes to the fore (Fenichel, 1945). Murray (1938) postulates 22 human drives – needs, and their accompanying presses in the environment – to account for human motivation. McDougall (1932) listed 15 propensities, which are certainly drives, and Adler, to take a last example, 1, the upward striving for superiority. It is not clear where an empirical factor analyst would start.
- *More profound conceptual problems*. Skinner (1953), along with all behaviourists and many experimental psychologists, regards the term 'motivation' as redundant, reflecting a naïve tendency to reification which is antithetical to science. Aggressive behaviour is observed and we cite aggression as the cause. The evidence, however, for this aggression is this same aggressive behaviour. All instincts, drives and motives can, on this analysis, be seen to

171

be redundant. On this account we must seek only what reinforces the observed behaviour. All such abstract terms are vacuous. Although there is force in this argument, some abstract concepts are not simply circular and thus redundant. We see an apple falling and argue that its fall is due to gravity. However, this concept explains a whole range of other phenomena which are by no means so obvious. The same is true of intelligence, a notion which simple-minded psychologists have attempted to attack on these same grounds. We have to be careful about the postulation of drives but they are not *per se* meaningless. Finally, it should be noted that through classical conditioning, according to Dollard and Miller (1950), almost any stimulus can act as a drive. Once again the factor analyst is left in confusion.

- *Implications of animal psychology.* Although extrapolation from other species is a dangerous trap, it is the case that motivation in human beings is unlikely to be entirely different from that in lower organisms, to take the anthropocentric view. From ethology we might look for sign stimuli and releasers (e.g. Lorenz, 1966), and sociobiology (Wilson, 1978) sees all behaviour as stemming from the desire to perpetuate one's genes, a truly unitary and presumably higher-order factor, which may not be so different from the postulations of psychoanalysis. However, none of this provides immediate or obvious guides for factor analysis

- *Psychometric problems.* In addition to the difficulties of sampling the field of variables there are other psychometric problems in the study of motivation. These concern the distinction, which has already been discussed, between states and traits, the latter being stable over time, the former fluctuating and variable. These problems are discussed below

- *Time and R factor analysis.* Since states are distinguished from traits by their transience, any factor analysis designed to elicit states must involve time. If it does not, as Cattell (1973) has argued, resulting factors could be traits. This simple point has been virtually ignored, unfortunately, by all factorists other than Cattell and colleagues. Normal, R, factor analysis, which involves the factor analysis of correlations on one occasion, cannot, logically, discriminate states from traits. This renders dubious much work in the field on moods and states such as that of Howarth (1980) or Nowlis and Green (1957). These workers use the present tense in state items and the terms 'generally' or 'usually' for traits, thus hoping to discriminate the factors in this way. However, Watson (1988) showed that varying the time scales in six different ways had little effect on the results, thus casting doubt on this device. Such items may be only face valid. For these reasons such work has to be treated with considerable caution. Cattell (1978) discusses different types of factor analysis which can be used in the elucidation of states.

- *P technique.* In this a subject is tested many times on a battery of tests. These correlations are then factored. The set of factors is unique to each individual and accounts for the changes over time. They are, therefore, and must be, state factors. However, this technique has been rarely used because subjects

172

who are willing to undergo so much testing are difficult to find. This, of course, affects the sampling. Not only are there few subjects but these are unlikely to be representative. Furthermore, constant retesting is likely to affect the validity of the tests. Another difficulty is that the time interval between testing, for some states, would have to be so short as to be impracticable.

- *dR technique.* In this subjects are tested on two occasions and the differences in scores are factor analysed. Such factors again must be states. As Cattell (Cattell, 1973; Cattell and Kline, 1977) has argued, the advantage of this method lies in the fact that big samples can be used, although this is counterbalanced by the unreliability of difference scores due to the unreliability of tests (Cronbach, 1984). However, if samples are split and only replicated factors interpreted, this problem can be overcome.

- *Chain P technique.* This is a compromise intended to combine the advantages of P and dR technique. In it, data can be arranged such that occasions and subjects can be effectively multiplied together, 50 subjects on 5 occasions being equivalent to 250 occasions.

- *Conclusions.* P technique is the most reliable despite its problems, and dR technique with replicated factors can be valuable. R technique must be treated with caution until the factors can be shown to be genuinely state factors.

Results: state and motivational factors

Because of all the problems of sampling drives, the need for repeated measurements for P and dR technique and the short-term nature of many moods and states, which defies proper measurement, the factors emerging from these researches will be listed but only briefly discussed. These factors have far less evidence for validity than ability or trait factors.

Boyle *et al.* (1995), who are essentially describing the work of Cattell, set out the various factors, but ignored problems with the actual tests used to elucidate the factors. This weakens the force of their otherwise excellent review and these tests must be examined.

The Eight-State Questionnaire

The only evidence for the validity of the Eight-State Questionnaire (Curran and Cattell, 1976) cited in the manual is factor loadings of the scales with the pure factors. However, this notion of concept validity is always dubious since the meaning of pure factors is unclear. Boyle and Katz (1991) found that two factors accounted for the variance in this test: extraversion/arousal and a negative state factor. This finding is similar to the claims made by Watson and Tellegen (1985), who have suggested that two factors account for mood variance: positive and negative affect. Until this Eight-State Questionnaire is validated, any factors derived from its use must be treated with caution and subjected to their own validation.

Barton and Cattell (1981) have developed the Central State–Trait Kit, which measures both traits and states. The items, despite Cattell's pleas for P analysis, rely on 'How you usually are' to measure traits and 'How you are now' to measure states. Since this test measures or attempts to measure the second-order factor structure of traits, described by Cattell, and their corresponding states, it is a test which may appear limited since this structure may not be the best account, as has been argued. Again there is little evidence for the validity of these scales and the test has to be regarded as experimental.

Because the tests of both states and moods used by Cattell are of unknown validity it is necessary to be highly cautious concerning the status of his mood factors. They are clearly not such as to form an obvious baseline in attempting to construct new, scientific measures of states with clear units of measurement.

The Motivational Analysis Test

The Motivational Analysis Test (MAT) (Cattell *et al.*, 1970b) is used by Cattell and his colleagues to measure motivational variables, drives, which they call ergs, and sentiments, ergs being basic, biological drives in contrast to the sentiments, which are culturally moulded. Within each of the 10 drives measured by the MAT are two components, the integrated and the unintegrated, which correspond roughly to the conscious and unconscious aspects of motivation (Cattell and Child, 1975).

The MAT is highly interesting on two counts. First, it is an objective test and thus, in principle at least, is not likely to be plagued by the problems which afflict questionnaires. Furthermore, it recognises that motivation is not entirely conscious, unlike standard interest tests which ask simple questions as if psycho-analysis had never existed. Boyle *et al.* (1995) report that there are six second-order factors accounting for the variance in this test, although they make no real effort to interpret them.

However, a study by Cooper and Kline (1982) casts considerable doubt on the validity of this test. The MAT and the 16PF were subjected to a Direct Oblimin simple-structure factor analysis. Eight factors emerged from this study but none fitted any postulated structure or made sense if the scales were valid. An item analysis of the scales also showed that the items did not fit the scales. This test requires considerable revision and development before it could yield substantive, replicable factors which were indubitably drives.

Change and trait-change factors

Cattell (1973) and Cattell and Kline (1977) set out the factors claimed by Cattell and his colleagues in some detail. However, in view of all the problems and difficulties, I shall list them below with little comment. Before I do this, one point needs to be noted.

In dR analyses of the second-order trait factors, factors emerged which corresponded to the traits. These were labelled trait-change factors, and were, as Cattell (1973) claimed, a new concept. While some of these, such as anxiety, were clearly moods or states, some of them seemed to make little sense if conceived in that way, but represented the growth and decline of traits and were not at all motivational. Thus in the list of state factors set out below, only those trait-change factors which Cattell (1973) argued were motivational are included.

Well-substantiated state factors, according to Cattell (1973) are anxiety; exvia (extraversion); alertness; independence; general depression; psychoticism; stress; repression; fatigue; arousal; regression; depression (guilt); and a further depression factor. However, as has been indicated, the tests from which these factors are derived do not seem sufficiently validated for us to regard this list as anything but tentative, suggestive rather than definitive.

Other mood factors

Watson and Tellegen (1985), in a study of mood factors, claimed that two factors accounted for much of the variance in most mood scales: positive affect and negative affect. Cooper and McConville (1989), in a study of the Eight-State Questionnaire and the Tellegen scales, demonstrated that this positive factor was essentially the state exvia factor and the negative factor was anxiety. This was similar to the work of Boyle and Katz (1991) in their factor analytic study of the Eight-State Questionnaire. Meyer and Shack (1989) factored the Tellegen scales with the revised form of the EPQ, the EPQ-R. They claimed that positive affect was simply extraversion, whether measured as state or trait, while negative affect was anxiety. Finally, it should be noted that Cooper and McConville (1990), in a study of mood variability, showed that some subjects tended to be variable on all scales while, conversely, others hardly varied on any of them. Of course, these results could be explained by the fact that there are common factors underlying the scales and these may indeed be positive and negative affect, or even the ubiquitous extraversion and anxiety.

CONCLUSIONS

It can be concluded that in the search for scientific measures of mood, despite the problems of the scales, positive and negative affect would be the best starting-point, even if, ultimately, it may prove impossible to discriminate these from extraversion and anxiety.

Motivational factors

Cattell's *Human Motivation and the Dynamic Calculus* (1985) contains the most complete account of his work on motivation. The factors are derived from objective tests and the 10 clearest of these are measured by the MAT, which also assesses strength of motivation (but see p. 174).

The main ergs are food seeking; mating; gregariousness; parental pity; exploration; escape to security; self-assertion; narcissistic sex; pugnacity and acquisitiveness.

The main sentiments are career; home–parental; mechanical; religious; self-sentiment; sports and games; sweetheart–spouse; superego. Sweney *et al.* (1986) and Gorsuch (1986) summarise much of the evidence in support of these factors, but it is clear that far more is required before they could be regarded as substantive rather than experimental. Sweney and Cattell (1980) developed the Vocational Interest Measure (VIM), an objective test battery measuring sentiments likely to be of use in vocational psychology. However, as yet there are insufficient data relevant to the validity of the test and the factors cited above.

Strength-of-interest factors

Strength-of-interest factors are highly interesting since they take into account the complexity of interests and the fact that much motivation is unconscious and not easily open to introspection. It is, of course, this very complexity which renders of little scientific worth attitude and interest questionnaires with simple, direct items. However, it has to be said that although these factors have been proposed for more than twenty years there is still little research into their validity. These factors are alpha, the component related to the satisfaction of conscious desires; beta, realised interest, the component implicated in answering standard attitude or interest questionnaires; gamma, the moral component of interest, that which is implicated in the middle-class pretence of high aesthetic interest; delta, the physiological factor, the autonomic response to the thrill of excitement; epsilon, a conflict factor which Cattell relates to repression; plus two further unidentified factors, zeta and eta.

CONCLUSIONS

These objective test factors of motivational structure and strength of attitudes are valuable contributions from factor analysis because they do not reduce the field to psychological inanity, as do standard attitude tests. As a guide for the development of scientific tests these strength-of-interest tests are not valueless, although they could not be used as a test of any new measure as could the g factors. Nevertheless, factor delta, the physiological factor, is relevant for scientific test construction because if the physiological correlates of strength of interest were identified, some physiological measures with units of measurement might be developed.

Earlier in this chapter, in the case of the temperamental factors which had been well supported, some initial possibilities of scientific measurement were briefly discussed. In the next chapter we shall set out and discuss in detail how such scientific measures might be produced. This will involve some general principles which apply to all such measures and some more specific examples and instances relevant to the ability, personality and motivation factors, which, despite the imperfections of psychometric measurement, clearly have some substantial psychological significance and meaning.

10

THE NEW PSYCHOMETRICS

Principles and theory

So far in this book I have demonstrated that conventional psychometrics has isolated a number of ability and personality factors which have sound evidence for their validity and psychological meaning and significance. In the field of abilities two factors stand out with great clarity: fluid and crystallised intelligence. There is a genuine and well-founded consensus about this claim among psychologists who understand factor analysis. In the field of personality, on the other hand, the factors are not so clearly delineated because the items of personality questionnaires are referential and not themselves exemplars of the behaviour under investigation. Furthermore, the current consensus, the five-factor model, was shown in Chapter 9 to be mistaken. Rather, three factors appear to have clear psychological significance: extraversion, anxiety and obsessionality, this latter on the argument that psychoticism is part of this factor.

It was the hope of psychometrics (e.g. Cattell, 1981; Kline, 1980) that well-defined factors could provide the basis of a quantified psychology, since it is clear that simple-structure factor analysis can reveal important fundamental variables within the matrix to which it is applied. Yet after more than ninety years of factor analytic endeavour, no such theoretical structure has emerged, despite the gargantuan efforts of Cattell (1981) in *Personality and Learning Theory*. This huge and mathematically complex publication has not made an impact beyond his colleagues, and in any case, as has been shown in this book, some of his findings have been difficult to confirm.

I have argued that despite the mathematical rigour of psychometrics, so rigorous that in fact many psychologists have been forced or have preferred to ignore the work, psychometric measurement is far different from measurement in the natural sciences, as Michell (1990, 1997) has demonstrated. I have argued that if psychometrics is to progress, it is necessary to improve its measurement techniques so that they conform to those in the natural sciences, essentially having clear units of measurement and real zeros, the former being the critical element. The tacit assumption of psychometrics has been the arguments of Stevens, who claimed that measurement was no more than a method of assigning numbers to variables. However, the problem here, as Michell (1997) has pointed out, is not only that the resulting measurement is quite different from that in the natural sciences (despite the development of conjoint measurement) but that its philosophical assumptions are antithetical to those of science. Thus Stevens' arguments are based on the assumptions of operationalism: that a variable is defined by its methods of measurement. Yet the endeavours of science depend on the notion of there being an objective truth which it is the aim of science to find.

This is not a sterile academic issue. In the first chapter I attempted to show that the current emphasis, particularly in the more or less innumerate social sciences, which unfortunately now include many parts of psychology, on relativism is a mistake. On the basis of the careful analyses of Searle (1995), I argue that it still makes sense to think of some kind of external reality and thus to hold to a correspondence theory of truth, which is the basis of the scientific method. Quantification, too, is an essential of the scientific method, in subjects in which the variables can be quantified. However, it is incoherent to use a system of quantification which denies external reality, as does that of Stevens and psychological measurement in general. This, however, is not to assume that the scientific method, *per se*, is bound to yield important knowledge. I have been careful to show that the scientific method appears to be the best method so far discovered to reveal knowledge of the world but that there is no a priori necessity that it should do so. Its justification, in the natural sciences, is that it works.

Of course, none of these objections would be powerful if psychometrics had made the superlative advances in understanding and knowledge which are the province of the natural sciences. Despite the claims of Eysenck (e.g. 1986) that clinical psychology should be the application of scientific principles discovered in the laboratory, this is far from the case, as is also true in other applications of psychometrics in educational and clinical psychology. There are no clear theories or indisputable findings which can be reliably used, in contrast to the chemistry and physics of engineering or the biology and biochemistry of medicine. However, this is not to say that psychometrics has failed. It has not. The survey and examination of psychometric methods and of what has been found in psychometrics up to the present date, in the second part of this book, actually demonstrated two important points. First, it revealed that the majority of factors isolated by factor analysts, especially in the field of personality and motivation, were little more than artefacts of the method. It is simple to create tautologous factors or bloated specifics. These are not worthy of investigation.

However, it did reveal, as has been argued, a small number of factors of psychological significance and some power in applied psychology. It is the task of the new psychometrics to measure these accurately and with precision, as has been done in the natural sciences. If this is achieved, psychometrics can advance. The point is that these few psychologically significant factors are, at present, imperfectly measured. Results are confounded with error even though the main observations are probably correct.

The new psychometrics: principles of measurement

As has been made clear, the new psychometrics is aimed at providing measures that are the equal of those in the natural sciences and which, therefore, allow mathematical analysis. In the relevant chapters on ability and personality I have already made a few tentative suggestions of what such measures might be, which turned out to be easier in the case of abilities than it was for personality.

It is now necessary to examine and establish some principles on which new measures might be built and then instantiate these with some new tests. I shall begin this with a brief scrutiny of the BIP (Lehrl and Fischer, 1988), which was discussed in Chapter 7, because it illustrates the principles and the difficulties of the new psychometrics.

The BIP

The BIP, or basic period of information processing, is defined as the shortest possible time for a person to process one bit of information. However, to measure this requires a theory of information processing, and, as we have discussed, the Erlangen school utilised the theoretical approach of Frank (1969). I shall not reiterate here the evidence for and against the BIP as a measure of intelligence. That is not the point. What the fact of the BIP illustrates is the necessity for a properly articulated theory of intelligence, or any other variable, if a genuinely scientific measure is to be constructed.

As the advocates of a more experimental approach to intelligence than the factor analytic have argued, e.g. Hunt (1976), the problem with defining intelligence as reasoning ability is that the term is too descriptive and broad, and fails to indicate what is involved in such reasoning. This is what theories of intelligence which go beyond the descriptive must try to do, and the BIP is part of a quite explicit theory – namely that intelligence and thus intelligence test scores, if their error is excluded, depend on the rate of information processing. Thus measurement of intelligence in these terms means measurement of this processing speed. The BIP has a unit of measurement, the time taken to process one bit of information, and is clearly an equal-interval scale.

The fact that, as it now appears, the BIP is unlikely to be an efficient measure of intelligence, at least as measured by intelligence tests, does not affect the argument. This is a genuinely scientific measure, although it may be that its theoretical underpinning, the Frank model of information processing, is not correct. However, a different, better model could be used to improve measurement.

Importance of the theoretical model

It is clear from the example of the BIP and the arguments above that the construction of scientific measures to replace psychometric tests requires good theorising. Without this it is impossible to know where to begin. This is in complete contrast to traditional psychometrics, where the aim was atheoretical and empirical: to explore the field and by factor analysis pick out the important variables.

Nearly one hundred years ago this was undoubtedly the correct strategy for psychometrics. As we have seen, it has yielded a relatively small number of important variables in the field of personality and ability, variables which must be studied experimentally, as the leading psychometrists, Cronbach, Eysenck and Cattell, have advocated. Factor analysis is the beginning, not the end, of research. This is where the new psychometrics must take over from the old. From the experimental studies of personality and ability factors proper, theoretical accounts of the factors must be developed. From these, scientific measures can be constructed.

Other possible scientific measures of intelligence

In Chapter 7 I examined in some detail other possible approaches to the scientific measurement of intelligence, derived from attempts by cognitive psychologists to understand the processes of intelligence. These again demonstrate the principle of the necessity for a good theory before such measures can be developed. Elementary cognitive tasks (ECTs) demonstrate this point convincingly. As Carroll (1993) makes clear, there are very large numbers of ECTs that have been claimed to measure some basic cognitive process which might be implicated in intelligence or in any other of the larger ability factors. In general, however, it was disappointing to find that these ECTs tended to load up on one factor, presumably of cognitive speed, although they purported to be measuring independent processes. Until cognitive psychology can develop a good theory of intelligence, which, as Mulhern (1997) points out, it does not have, it is unlikely that ECTs will provide a useful basis for scientific measures of psychology. Indeed, as he argues, many of the ECTs to be found in the literature are little more than intuitive accounts of what intelligence might be like. Thus it is hardly surprising that, on analysis, they are not powerful in elucidating its nature. It should be pointed out at this juncture that it is perfectly possible that intelligence is an aggregate of such processes, which therefore on their own might not correlate highly with intelligence test scores. How such scientific ECT measures did combine to measure intelligence, if they were to, would, of course, constitute an impressive theory of intelligence.

Nevertheless, as they stand ECTs are not likely to form a basis for scientific measures of intelligence until a good cognitive account of intelligence is assembled. Even then care will have to be taken that such measures are not confounded with cognitive speed.

Reaction times (which are, of course, a special class of ECT), including inspection time, have been used as an attempt to measure intelligence on the grounds that (and note the theory, without which the attempt would have been implausible) intelligence may be a function of the speed or efficiency of neural processing.

Both these measures – RT and IT – are scientific in the sense of Michell (1997). However, apart from the fact that the actual correlations of both these variables with intelligence are too low to enable the theoretical basis to be tenable, there are so many other competing explanations for account for the correlations that, had they been higher, these measures could not have been regarded as of proven validity. Rabbitt (1985) has claimed that there are high-level processes, involving monitoring, in reaction-time tasks, and it is these which could provoke the correlation with g, and similar claims have been made in relation to inspection time (Anderson, 1992; Deary and Stough, 1996). However, despite these imperfections, reaction time and inspection time illustrate the necessity for a good theory of intelligence if scientific measures are to be constructed.

Conclusions

This discussion makes it clear that the way forward for the new psychometrics is experimental and biological. If a clear, precise theory of intelligence can be developed, it should be possible to develop scientific measures of the variable. I mention here the biology of intelligence because Jensen has argued (most recently, 1997) that g is so basic a construct that it is essentially biological. Thus it may be that measurement will be physiological rather than psychological.

Psychophysiological measures of intelligence

It should be obvious that a good understanding of any psychological phenomenon would be incomplete if it did not include its neurological basis. It has been argued by some psychologists that to attempt to embrace physiology is to take one step along the sinful road of reductionism. Yet this is not so. It would be absurd to claim a knowledge of vision without understanding the functions of the eye and the visual system. The same applies to intelligence, and over the years there has been a considerable research effort into the physiology of intelligence. It would be beyond the confines of this chapter to describe this work in any detail, but a brief summary will be sufficient, especially of those aspects which might provide us with some scientific measures of intelligence. Fortunately the review by Jensen (1997) is a useful basis for this purpose.

The first point to note is that despite the genetic identity of the brains of monozygotic twins, it is possible that owing to different early experiences and random internal and external events there is effectively different functional wiring in their brains. Given this possibility, of which much has been made by Edelman (1987) – whose work, however, is highly controversial – the high correlations for intelligence between identical twins are even more remarkable.

There is another important point made by Jensen (1997), which has also been stressed in this book, namely the continuity between human and mammalian capacities. Thus according to Finlay and Darlington (1995) there is an average between-species ($N = 131$) correlation, for the ten main brain structures, of 0.96.

This means that the main difference between mammalian brains is one of size. From this Jensen argues that variation in brain structures and their relative sizes in normal human beings must be virtually zero.

It is also highly unlikely, Jensen continues the argument, that the operational processes of the brain differ from individual to individual, exactly as is the case with other less complex organs. From all this Jensen claims that individual differences in personality and ability do not result from differences in the operating processes of the brain (for there are none) but from other aspects of cerebral physiology which modify the efficiency of information processing. On such a basis Jensen argues that the study of the neuropsychology of intelligence falls into two separate parts: the brain structures and neural processes which enable intelligent behaviour, and the physical conditions which give rise to individual differences in intelligence. It is these latter which are relevant to the search for scientific measures of intelligence.

Jensen's approach to this problem is very much his own and involves two technical points which must be explicated before summarising his findings.

The method of correlated vectors

The method of correlated vectors is employed by Jensen to ensure that the correlation of some physical variable is with g, rather than a mixture of other abilities, as can arise in working with tests of ability. The g loadings from a battery of tests are obtained. Since these are the values to be correlated, a minimum of 10 tests is required, and the more the better. These g loadings form the g vector. The correlations of these tests with a physical variable are then obtained. This is the P vector. The correlation between these two vectors reflects the correlation of the physical variable with g provided that the effects of differences in the reliabilities of the tests in the battery are partialled out. This is easily done from a vector of the test reliabilities.

Meaning of the correlation between vectors

This correlation between the g vector and the physical vector does not indicate the size of the relationship between individual differences in g and the physical variable. It shows with considerable reliability the existence of a relationship. The size of this correlation must be computed from individuals' g factor scores and their status on the physical variable.

Intrinsic (functional) or incidental correlations

Intrinsic correlations are within families. This is determined by investigating whether the correlations occur between siblings, rather than only between families, between the means of siblings across different families.

The within-families correlation is calculated with the differences between siblings' scores on a psychometric tests and the differences between siblings on the physical variable. The correlation indicates the extent of the covariance among siblings. The cause of this intrinsic correlation can be genetic or environmental or both. If it is genetic, in full or in part, it demonstrates pleiotropy, where phenotypically different traits are influenced by the same genes. However, if the correlation exists only between families, it is incidental and represents no functional connection between the variables.

The between-families correlation is computed from the sum of siblings' scores on the psychometric test and the sum of scores on the physical test. This correlation, on its own, usually indicates genetic heterogeneity. Through cross-assortative mating the genes for the traits have become associated within families, although there is no functional connection (shown by the absence of the within correlation). Eye colour and height exemplify this phenomenon. Normal correlations between individuals can be decomposed into these two components. As Jensen argues, it makes sense before examining the correlations between physical variables and psychological traits to first investigate whether or not they are intrinsic. Only where the correlations between physical variables and psychological traits are intrinsic is further research into the relationship worthwhile.

There is a further point which makes the investigation of the physiological basis of g valuable. As Jensen (1997) argues, research generally indicates a high heritability for IQ scores, and g seems to be responsible for this heritability when the method of correlated vectors is used (Pedersen *et al.*, 1992). This implies that g is the most strongly linked of all abilities to a physical substrate and thus not only the most fruitful area of investigation for the study of the psychophysiology of intelligence and cognitive ability but also an ideal basis for the development of a scientific, physical measure of intelligence.

Physical variables showing intrinsic correlations with g

It is clear from the arguments already adduced that it is those physical variables which yield an intrinsic correlation with g that are likely to be useful as a basis for the scientific measurement of intelligence. Jensen (1997) lists the following variables: myopia; brain and head size; glucose metabolic rate; reaction time; average evoked potential; and nerve conduction velocity.

Some comments are required concerning the relationship of these findings to the scientific measurement of intelligence. First, it should be obvious that myopia offers little opportunity for such measurement. The correlation with IQ is only about 0.25 and it is an example of pleiotropy. I shall say no more about it.

Head size and brain size are more interesting. Jensen (1994), using the method of correlated vectors, showed that the magnitude of a subtest's g loading predicted the correlation of that test with head size. Head size correlates about 0.5 with brain size so that it is a poor substitute for the latter, although it has been so used. More accurate assessments are possible from magnetic resonance imaging, and a meta-analysis of 10 such studies yields a correlation of brain size and IQ of 0.36.

Rushton and Ankney (1996) in their survey estimate the correlation between brain size and cognitive ability to be as high as 0.44. As Jensen (1997) points out, the reasons for this correlation are not known, although there are several possibilities. However what is clear is that brain size cannot be used as a measure of intelligence. The correlation is too small.

The glucose metabolic rate (GMR) is perhaps more promising as a possible scientific measure, although all results need further replication on larger samples. GMR is measured by positron emission tomography (PET) scans, in which the fate of radioactive glucose is scanned in different parts of the brain as individuals solve problems. The rationale of this test is simple in that glucose is the main fuel of brain metabolism. Haier (1993), who has done much of this work, has a good account of his research programme which Jensen (1997) succinctly summarises. Within individuals GMR increases with task difficulty. However, high-IQ subjects have a lower GMR than low-IQ subjects while solving the same problem, although there are complex interaction effects between ability levels and the difficulty of the problems to be solved (Larson et al., 1995). High-IQ subjects show greater localisation of GMR, which is diffuse in low-IQ subjects. The effect of practice in problem solving results in a lesser GMR. Finally, the method of correlated vectors applied to the WAIS shows a high correlation between a test's g loading and its correlation with GMR. From this it could be argued that GMR reflects brain efficiency. This interpretation is supported by the finding that in a sample of subjects suffering from mental retardation or from Down's syndrome the GMR was higher than normal (Haier et al., 1995).

The measurement of GMR looks a promising candidate for development as a scientific measure of intelligence. Thus, first we would expect to improve the accuracy of its measurement. Then the average GMR to a set of standard problems might provide a powerful scientific measure. This example again shows the necessity to have a good theory of intelligence, this one being that intelligence is equated with the metabolic efficiency of the brain. Were this to turn out true, or even if it could be shown to be a large factor in intelligence, there would appear to be good opportunities for the pharmacological improvement of human ability.

Simple reaction time and ECTs as measures of intelligence have already been fully discussed and I shall say no more about them except to reiterate that it is unlikely that they would be useful as measures of intelligence. However, as Jensen (1997) argues, the fact that average reaction times and their variances do correlate at all with IQ must be fully accounted for in any adequate account of intelligence.

The study of the relation of average evoked potential, AEP (or ERP – event-related potential) and EEGs to intelligence is a problem area partly because of the disparity of results. Thus Hendrickson and Hendrickson (1980) claimed that a string measure of EEG correlated highly with IQ, and they provided a biochemical theory of intelligence to go alongside it. Yet this has proved impossible to replicate, as discussed by Barrett and Eysenck (1992) and Deary and Caryl (1993). These authors, who surveyed with great care virtually all studies, were forced to conclude that there was a remarkable inconsistency in the findings. It was often possible to obtain a moderate correlation between some EEG or AEP measure and intelligence only for this to fail to replicate on further examination. This makes it difficult to attribute much weight to more recent but positive findings. Thus, for example, Anokhin and Vogel (1996) found a correlation of 0.304 between Raven's Matrices and frontal-peak alpha frequency in males of well above average intelligence. Bates and Eysenck (1993) with 76 subjects showed that attention reverses the normal relationship found between string length and intelligence. Bates et al. (1995) with 21 subjects found that string length changed differentially with attention among high- and low-IQ subjects. Furthermore, differences in string length between the high and low conditions of attention accounted for 53 per cent of the variance in IQ scores. However, given the small sample sizes and the difficulties of replication, great caution needs to be shown concerning the implications of these studies. Robinson (e.g. 1993) has also produced some remarkable results with EEG and intelligence and personality, also providing a complex theory of his own. However, all his findings seem to be based upon one study, which, given the difficulties of replication in this area, is a problem. Certainly Barrett and Eysenck (1992) were not able to replicate some of his results.

If EEG measures do reflect brain activity it is not surprising that some correlations are found with psychological variables. Indeed, it would be amazing if there were not. Until, however, there is a much better theoretical account of precisely what brain activity is involved in intelligence (solving problems) and until EEG measurement becomes far more precise, it is unlikely that scientific measures will be derived from EEG.

It should be noted that this is the view of Stelmack and Houlihan (1995) too. In their review of ERP studies and their relationship to intelligence and personality, they argue that ERPs are an incomplete reflection of the electrical activity of the brain. They agree with Brody (1992), who claimed that the hope of using ERP as a reliable, culture-free biological index of intelligence is vain. However, these authors do report studies in which faster P300 latencies are associated with higher intelligence. Caryl and Harper (1996) studied ERPs and elementary cognitive tasks: visual inspection time and pitch discrimination. They found that the P300 amplitude was lower but latency was greater in difficult as compared with easier trials. In a similar study of auditory and visual inspection time Caryl et al. (1995) argued that although the ERPs to both tasks were similar, they revealed that different aspects of the stimulus processing mechanism were critical, a finding which, given the different sensory modes, is not surprising. However, as Stelmack and Houlihan (1995) argue, even with P300 there is complication from the influence of N, neuroticism. Such findings do not imply that a good test of intelligence could be derived from P300 measurement. Despite all these difficulties it is interesting that whatever correlations there are in this field, according to Jensen (1997), they are (through the method of correlated vectors) attributable to g.

Finally, we come to nerve conduction velocity (NCV). Since reaction time studies and work with ECTs all suggest that speed is a factor in individual differences in mental ability, it is reasonable to hypothesise, as Jensen (1997) does, that NCV might account for some proportion at least of variance in g. However, there are contradictions in the findings. When NCV was measured in the median nerve in the arm, two studies showed positive correlations with IQ (Vernon and Mori, 1992; Wickett and Vernon, 1994) and two showed correlations approaching zero (Reed and Jensen, 1991; Rijsdik et al., 1995). Jensen (1997) is unable to find any obvious cause for these discrepancies. Reed and Jensen (1992) measured NCV in the visual tract between the retina and the visual cortex in almost 150 male students. This correlated 0.27 with fluid ability. Although this is significant, it accounts for only just over 7 per cent of the variance. NCV measures, as they stand, would not do as scientific measures of intelligence.

One other issue examined by Jensen concerns the work of Miller (1994), who hypothesises that differences in mental ability could arise from differences in the degree of myelination in the axons of the brain. Such a theory could account for many of the correlations with the physical variables discussed above; that is, those with intrinsic correlations with g. At the present this is a hypothesis which seems to account for many of the findings, although caution must be shown since the variability among the results is so considerable. Clearly this theory needs detailed physiological support. If it were to prove correct, a measure of myelination might provide us with a good scientific measure of intelligence. If there were a perfect correlation the term 'intelligent' would be somewhat redundant. This, however would be an excellent result of good physiology. Perhaps, as Freud (1940) suggested in the case of psychoanalysis, ultimately the notion of g will become redundant as biochemistry and neurology advance. Spearman (1927) certainly thought that this would be so.

Conclusions

From all these arguments concerning biological measures of intelligence, it is clear that at present there is none which could be used. In the future, with the development of psychophysiology, this could change. Measures of the speed of nerve conduction and axon myelinisation might prove useful. Measures derived from brain electrical activity, unless there are spectacular advances in methods and precision of measurement, are not good candidates as scientific measures of intelligence. There is more hope for PET scans of the uptake of glucose, although far more research in this area, with large samples of individuals, is required. Thus, in summary, there are rational grounds for the hope that, in the not too distant future, biological, scientific measures of intelligence may be developed. Much will depend not only on research but on good theorising about the nature of intelligence.

Scientific measures of personality: extraversion and neuroticism (anxiety)

It is clear, I hope, from our discussion of possible scientific measures of intelligence that although, at present, it cannot be claimed that any such have been developed, the outlook is far from hopeless. This is because, as I have argued, there are relatively clear theories of what intelligence might be, theories which provide sound opportunities for scientific measurement. How different is the case for personality.

As has also been made clear, there are many different definitions of personality – as many, indeed, as there are theorists. Furthermore, the vast majority of these, interesting as they might appear, are far from scientific. Thus many are stated so vaguely that precise hypotheses are impossible and the variables used are immune to measurement. Nor is this true only of older clinically based theories. For example, constructivist personality theory (Hampson, 1992), claiming that personality is really in the eye of the beholder, while admitting there is, perhaps, something biological to behold, defies measurement, both psychometric and scientific. It exemplifies the retreat from science of the social sciences.

Psychometric personality theory, especially that of Eysenck (1967) and Cattell (1981), particularly the latter, does not fall into this error. These are both examples of trait theory but ones where the traits are clearly stated and investigators are provided with clear measuring instruments. In both cases the traits have been defined through factor analysis. Since, as has been argued throughout this book, factor analytic psychometrics, although falling short of scientific measurement, appears to have discovered, and measured with some precision, important variables, it is these, in the field of personality, which deserve scrutiny and an attempt to develop genuinely scientific measures.

Thus in this section of the chapter I shall consider how such scientific measures of neuroticism or anxiety and extraversion might be developed. These factors have been selected for three reasons. First, these are the two factors accounting for the most variance in all studies and they are the most pervasive of factors. Second, there is some theorising about their nature which provides a basis for the development of scientific measures. The final reason is related to this point, namely that most other factors seem atheoretical, thus presenting an insoluble puzzle as to how they could be better measured.

Scientific measures of neuroticism

In this section I shall discuss (and inevitably at this stage, this will involve some speculation) the scientific measurement of Eysenck's N factor, which was shown in Chapter 8 to be essentially identical with Cattell's trait anxiety and the anxiety factor in the system preferred by Costa and McCrae.

According to Eysenck's (1967) formulation, N is related to the lability of the autonomic nervous system. Those high on the trait are thought of as easily aroused, whereas the low scorer has a system requiring far more stimulation before it responds. This theoretical account does allow some possible scientific tests for N, as will be discussed below. Before this, mention should be made of the work of Gray (1981), which is essentially similar. However, in this the two factors of extraversion and anxiety are rotated through 45 degrees. This results in two different dimensions:

- anxiety, a dimension of neurotic introversion, at one pole, and stable extraversion at the other;
- impulsivity, a dimension of neurotic extraversion, at one pole, and stable introversion at the other.

Despite these theoretical differences between Gray and Eysenck it is clear that both theories involve these same two variables.

A biological account, which is necessary for any scientific theory of personality given the genetic similarity between primates and human beings, in suggesting scientific measures of N, is not simply a case of reductionism. Thus it is not envisaged that there is some biological variable which has a perfect correlation with N and can, therefore, be used as a perfect substitute, although this would be wonderful were it the case. Rather it is seen as more likely in principle that a number of biological, scientific measures might be produced, each related to N, and some function of which, perhaps including scientific measures of the environment, might then measure the variable. This same argument applies, of course, to the measures of intelligence discussed in the previous section.

For my discussion of possible scientific measures of N I am indebted to a brilliant survey of this field by Fahrenberg (1992) which summarises the highly confusing and sometimes contradictory research on the psychophysiology of neuroticism and anxiety. It must be realised that the purpose of Fahrenberg's work was quite different from mine and he makes no mention of scientific measurement. His work raises a problem which makes it unlikely that any scientific measure of N could be based on the notion of autonomic lability. Indeed, it goes further than this: it challenges the viability of the underlying physiology. This problem is response fractionation. This is defined by Haynes and Wilson (1979) as the lack of agreement between different physiological measures of apparently the same construct. It is particularly the case, Fahrenberg argues, with physiological concepts such as activation, arousal, anxiety and stress. Indeed, this was noted by Lacey (1967), who stressed the fact that for different individuals different physiological indices of arousal might be pertinent. Such fractionation and response specificity render it highly unlikely that any such physiological indices, although they have real units of measurement, would ever be satisfactory as measures of N, or indeed E since the same principles apply. Such response specificity means also that it is unlikely that a function of various different measures could be produced. Thus Fahrenberg (1992) concluded his section on response fractionation with the following points, all gloomy for the development of scientific measures of N and E. It must be noted that these conclusions are based upon a large number of investigations.

- Response fractionation is a general phenomenon in psychophysiological activation processes. As has been argued, this means that the problem will arise in the study of extraversion, to be discussed in the next section. This is because extraversion is seen in Eysenck's theory as related to arousal of the central nervous system.

- Although an individual's score on one activation variable may reflect the functioning of some response system, there is no evidence that their score on another variable related to that system will be correlated with it. This particular finding is clearly a problem for the development of scientific measures, especially if the work of Lacey (1967), showing that there were individual differences in which part of the system was activated, is taken into account.

- It is impossible, as the above implies, to predict an individual's state on one activation variable from her score on another variable.

- This holds for different marker variables for different autonomic subsystems.

- It holds also for the non-significant or zero correlations between self-report and physiological measures.

Before we draw conclusions about the development of scientific physiological measures of N a few more points deserve note. First, it is dubious whether the concept of arousal has any meaning at all. On account of fractionation there is simply no evidence for a unidimensional arousal or activation. This applies not only to neuroticism and anxiety but also to the putative physiological indices of extraversion (Stelmack, 1990). Given this, Fahrenberg argues, single measurements of heart rate, EEG or electrodermal activity are simply not coherent with the physiological findings,

With all these difficulties, a detailed review of the research findings is out of place for the purposes of this chapter and readers are referred to Fahrenberg (1992). Nevertheless, some results are of interest, although they confirm what is already implicit. In a study of state anxiety by van Heck (1988) – different from trait anxiety, as was shown in Chapter 8, but still important for purposes of scientific measurement – zero correlations were found between a large number of physiological indices. Physiologically, at least, anxiety is not unitary.

Myrtek (1984) investigated correlations between a large number of measures of autonomic lability, as defined by Eysenck (1967). No evidence of a general factor could be obtained. Thus again, terms such as autonomic lability and physiological reactivity are not tenable on physiological grounds. Hence fractionation not only renders measurement difficult, but also destroys its theoretical basis as far as N is concerned. Since this is the case it is not surprising that Myrtek (1984) showed that none of these physiological indices correlated either singly or together with his measure of N (the EML scale of the Freiburg Personality Inventory (Fahrenberg and Selg, 1970)).

Conclusions

These are obvious and may be brief:

- No physiological index has been found which is reliably correlated with N and which could, therefore, be used, alone or with other tests, to measure N.
- Fractionation makes it unlikely that any physiological measures now in use could be used, although it is possible that some kind of function could be developed.
- The concept of autonomic lability seems to have no physiological support.
- This means that the physiological basis of N needs to be put on to a better and more reliable foundation.
- Only when this is done will it be possible to develop physiological measures of the variable.
- This is not to ignore fractionation. However, the definition of this concept implies a correlation between variables which is not found. Better physiology may show that such expectations of correlation were false, in which case the concept of fractionation would disappear.

Scientific measures of extraversion

Eysenck (1967) has claimed that extraversion is linked to the arousal level of the central nervous system, particularly the ascending reticular system. Extraverts are chronically under-aroused, and hence stimulus hungry. Introverts, on the other hand, are highly aroused, hence their liking for quiet and solitude. As was the case with N, this type of theorising should allow the development of scientific, physiological measures of extraversion.

However, as has been argued above, problems of response specificity and fractionation will be relevant here, just as was the case with extraversion. Thus what we shall be seeking from the research literature (and what we failed to find for N) are physiological measures which correlate highly with E and thus might be used as measures for this factor on their own or in some function with other variables.

The search for such variables in a literature which is even more confusing and contradictory than that connected with neuroticism has been aided by an excellent summary of the research by Stelmack and Green (1992), who, like Fahrenberg, adopt a rigorous methodological approach. Various physiological indices have been investigated in relation to extraversion, most of them based upon the concept of arousal.

Skin conductance level (SCL) has been measured after stimulation in both extraverts and introverts selected on the Eysenck scales. Generally, under low or neutral conditions of stimulation differences between personality groups are seldom found (e.g. Coles *et al.*, 1971), although there is some evidence of higher SCLs for introverts in challenging conditions (Fowles *et al.*, 1977). A few studies show that spontaneous fluctuations of SCL are higher in introverts than extraverts, although one must question the meaning of 'spontaneous'. Introverts are more likely to be thinking about themselves than are extraverts, which might account for such differences, since they occur only in a few studies. Generally, Stelmack and Green conclude that there is little evidence from studies of SCL that introverts are more highly aroused. SCL will certainly not do as part of a scientific measure of E.

It is possible to measure skin conductance response (SCR) to stimulation, and there have been many studies of this sort testing the claims that extraversion is related to arousal. Stelmack and Green (1992) point out that there have been considerable differences in results among these studies, partly because they were so varied in their experimental methods: in stimuli, in intensity of stimuli, in subject selection and in recording of results. Nevertheless, Stelmack and Green make some generalisations which appear to hold up: low-intensity stimuli show no differences between introverts and extraverts (Coles *et al.*, 1971, exemplifies this finding); with more intense visual and auditory stimuli there is a greater SCR for introverts than extraverts (e.g. Mangan and O'Gorman, 1969), a result which is reversed with high-intensity auditory stimuli (<90 dB). While the former finding is compatible with the claim that introverts are more aroused, the latter is not, although Stelmack and Green (1992) suggest that the findings indicate that individuals seek an optimal arousal level.

However, I do not want to discuss these results in more detail since it is clear that the reversal of the results with more intense stimuli rules out the use of SCR as a scientific measure of E. So too do the fluctuations in findings with experimental conditions and selection of subjects. In addition, Smith *et al.* (1984) showed that levels of SCL and SCR could be affected by caffeine intake but in different ways for extraverts and introverts. All this, although interesting theoretically, makes the use of either SCR or SCL dubious for the scientific measurement of E.

Stelmack and Green (1992) examine the evidence concerning the relationship between extraversion and physiological indices such as cardiovascular activity, systolic blood pressure and biochemical activity. The results are quite inconclusive and none is such that there is any present or near future possibility that any of these physiological indices could form part of any scientific measure of extraversion.

However, with EEG the position is different. There have been many studies relating EEG activity to extraversion and these still continue. Unfortunately, up till 1983, at least, the research was riddled with methodological problems such that, according to Gale (1983), all results have to be treated with extreme caution. Nevertheless, as Stelmack and Green argue, perhaps a cautious generalisation about the results can be made: for introverts there seems to be a higher level of cortical activity (arousal) in conditions between the semi-somnolent and the stressful. In sleep, however, no differences between extraverts and introverts have been observed.

Whereas EEGs are recordings of spontaneous cortical activity, ERPs are indices of cortical activity which arises from stimulation, or in cognitive processing, e.g.

remembering or attending to items. The relation of extraversion to ERPs to auditory arousal has been studied. There is some support for the claim that introverts are more aroused than extraverts (despite problems with the concept which have already been noted). Nevertheless, the results are not clear-cut since, as Stelmack *et al.* (1977) demonstrated, tonal frequency affects the results, as do other features of the experimental conditions. All this means that auditory ERPs are unlikely, even with development, to prove useful as scientific measures of extraversion. Similarly, attempts to show differences in the ERPs of introverts and extraverts in different attentional sets have not been sufficiently conclusive for this form of ERP to be used as a measure of introversion–extraversion.

There is one other interesting set of findings, relevant to the scientific measurement of extraversion, which is discussed by Stelmack and Green (1992). This concerns studies of extraversion and auditory brainstem evoked responses (BERs). The first two waves of BER are derived from the auditory nerve and the cochlear nucleus. The fifth wave is determined by the inferior colliculus. Furthermore, these auditory BERs are invariant in different stages of sleep and arousal and even coma (Campbell and Bartoli, 1986; Achor and Starr, 1980).

The relevance of all this to the notion of arousal is clear. If differences between extraverts and introverts in auditory BER can be shown, then it is clear that these differences are independent of arousal, thus casting doubt on Eysenck's (1967) physiological basis for extraversion and for Gray's modification of this to the limbic structures. Differences in axonal or synaptic transmission in the peripheral nervous system would have to be invoked instead. This is important, since BER differences between extraverts and introverts have been found by Andress and Church (1981), Stelmack and Wilson (1982) and Szelenberger (1983), although Stelmack and Green (1992) report that some studies have failed to replicate these results.

Conclusions

It is evident that as yet there is no physiological index which could be used as a scientific measure of extraversion. In the previous section it was noted that the term 'arousal' had little physiological meaning, given response specificity and fractionation. Furthermore, since BERs indicate that peripheral structures may be involved in what differences have been found between extraverts and introverts, it is clear that the physiological basis of extraversion–introversion requires further investigation. As yet, as I have argued, the findings are too complex and inconsistent for any putative indices of arousal (dubious as the concept is) to be useful as scientific measures of extraversion.

Other possible scientific measures of extraversion and anxiety

For extraversion and neuroticism I have carefully examined possible physiological measures that could be derived from underlying theory, particularly that of Eysenck. However, as we have seen, the findings are not promising. The theory appears to be defective or too broad and insufficiently precise. In this section I shall examine what other measures might be developed.

In Chapter 9 it was pointed out that part of the theory underlying extraversion implicates classical conditioning. It is claimed (Eysenck, 1967) that extraverts are harder to condition than introverts and, having been conditioned, they extinguish more quickly. As was suggested in that chapter, in principle it might be possible to develop a standard conditioning procedure in which trials to learning and extinction formed the measure. However, the problem here, as was pointed out many years ago by Vernon (1963), and which has not been resolved, is the question concerning the unitary nature of conditionability. If there is no single factor of conditionability it makes no sense to argue that there are differences in conditionability between extraverts and introverts. Even if there were some significant differences, it would be necessary to show that other factors did not affect conditionability before it could be used as a reliable indicator of status on extraversion. This is an area worthy of investigation.

In Chapter 8 another possible source of scientific personality tests was suggested: the compendium of objective tests by Cattell and Warburton (1967). The problem here was that the tests had little evidence for validity and that those considered by Cattell to be the best, those in the Objective Analytic battery, were shown not to be valid (Kline and Cooper, 1984b). However, the most serious problem with these tests has been highlighted in the present chapter. Here it has become perfectly obvious that the development of scientific measures of personality is dependent on good theorising. Thus, for example, the BIP measure of intelligence had a precise theoretical account of information processing as a basis. That it is imperfect means only that this particular theoretical account of intelligence is imperfect. Since the compendium of objective tests is essentially atheoretical it is unlikely that it will prove useful for the development of scientific measures of personality or motivation.

The hypothesis that attributes are quantitative

Michell (1997) attacked current psychological measurement on two grounds: that psychological measures are not scientific, and that there is doubt as to whether the attributes purportedly measured are quantitative. The first has been the focus of this book. I shall now deal briefly with the second, which has been mentioned at various points throughout this book, before concluding.

As Michell argued, it is by no means necessary that attributes are quantitative – and, of course, if they are not, attempts to measure them are futile. Whether an attribute is quantitative is an empirical question and it should be established before measurement is attempted.

Holder (1901) set out five conditions which have to be fulfilled before an attribute may be said to be quantitative. It is usually difficult to demonstrate these characteristics directly, although in the case of the fundamental measurement of length (other than in astronomical or particle magnitudes) this can be done. Here the concatenation of rods can demonstrate that length has a quantitative structure. However, as was discussed in Chapter 2, the development by Luce and Tukey (1964) of conjoint measurement theory does allow the quantitative structure to be tested without concatenation. Rasch scales exemplify conjoint measurement and it is possible to apply the methodology to other psychometric scales, as was done with letter series by Stankov and Cregan (1993) and, in a more complex methodology, by Michell (1994b) to attitudes to nuclear war and homosexuality. However, as has been argued, conjoint measurement still fails to provide, compared with extensive measures, clear units of measurement. That these are essential seems clear from the paper by Coombs (1950), where his ordered metric without a unit of measurement was clearly unsatisfactory for psychometric measurement.

I have argued that the variables to be measured in the new scientific psychometrics are those which have been shown in factor analysis to be replicable and meaningful: the two g factors and three personality factors. In these cases, given their psychological nature, it makes sense to assume that they are quantitative and to hold this hypothesis until it is refuted. This is because their high heritabilities suggest that they are variables whose variance is determined by a combination of genes and environmental factors. Such variables tend to be quantitative and normally distributed.

In measurement theory the importance of establishing that the attribute is quantitative cannot be exaggerated. Indeed, without this, no real measurement is possible. This is succinctly expressed as the representation problem (e.g. Coombs et al., 1970). Measurement represents a numerical model of an empirical relational system, in the world (e.g. weights). The features of the numerical model, therefore, must accurately reflect the real world. Thus the numerical assignment of numbers by some rule cannot be measurement; the numbers must reflect the relations of the objects measured. That is why it is essential that the attribute be shown to be quantitative in structure. Psychometric tests fail to overcome the representational problem. It is assumed that there is a mapping of measurement on to the real world. This, of course, leads to difficulties over the meaning of intelligence and personality tests. Because it is unclear what the scales represent, so their meaning must be unclear – although, as has been discussed, they have been made meaningful from their empirical relationships with other tests and external criteria. All evidence of this kind is the heart of psychometrics. Rasch scales do have a measurement model, but the model manifestly does not fit the real world and its instantiation in scales is dubious (see Chapter 4). However, with the type of scientific measures of ability and personality suggested in this chapter one may hope that these problems can be overcome.

Final conclusions: the new psychometrics

In this final section of the book I shall set out what I believe are the conclusions which may be drawn from the arguments I have presented concerning the need for scientific measurement of psychometric variables and the attempts to provide such measurement.

It is perfectly clear that the psychometric tests developed over the past ninety years through the application of psychometrics have revealed a small number of factors of ability and personality which make good psychological sense and which allow, especially in the case of abilities, good prediction in the applied field. Studies of their psychological nature by the leading psychometricians, such as Eysenck and Cattell, have materially added to psychological knowledge regarding the development of these factors and the contributions of heredity and environment. Furthermore, studies of the methods of factor analysis have made it quite clear why there are so many poor tests and why there is considerable disagreement in the fields of personality and motivation. Many factor analyses are technically flawed, and in the fields of personality and attitudes the nature of the test items is such that factor identification is inferential at best and all factors require external identification. Many tests used in social psychology and health psychology and many lesser personality tests are no more than collections of semantically similar items and are scientifically valueless.

Yet these few good psychometric factors, meaningful and with predictive power – fluid and crystallised intelligence, fluency, visualisation, cognitive speed, extraversion, anxiety and tough-mindedness – are not scientific measures in the sense of Michell (1997). These psychometric tests, reliable and valid as they are, have no units of measurement, are not equal-interval scales, are not additive, have no true zeros and are quite unlike the measures of the natural sciences. Furthermore, it is merely assumed that these attributes are quantitative.

The original purpose of psychometrics was to provide the precise quantification necessary for science. As we can see, it has failed to do this, although it has provided us with promising results. From the arguments developed in this book it can be concluded that it is pointless to attempt to develop further psychometric tests of the traditional kind. For the future, psychometrics must concentrate on the development of scientific, fundamental measures. In this chapter I have surveyed various current possibilities in the field of personality and ability. From this it was clear that there is a profound difference between the new and the traditional psychometrics. The traditional approach is to sample as widely as possible and to explore the field using factor analysis and, more lately, to confirm findings with confirmatory analyses. Traditional psychometrics is atheoretical. It uses factors to form the theories. The new psychometrics, based on fundamental measurement, is quite the opposite. As we saw, the development of fundamental scientific measures depends on theory. Without theory the new psychometrics is impossible.

In this final chapter it is true that I have been unable to set out a clear and unequivocally valid new measure of any of the major factors in personality and ability. Perhaps the BIP is the nearest approach to any yet developed, and this is based on an explicit theory. However, it would be strange if one individual, in the course of writing a book, were able to do what has not been done by armies of researchers over ninety years.

What I hope I have been able to achieve is to demonstrate that the days of traditional psychometrics are over. It is pointless to produce yet another questionnaire with a new set of items loading yet another factor. This is not the way of scientific quantification. Now the efforts of researchers must be devoted to the new psychometrics – the development of fundamental scales of measurement – and this switches the emphasis to psychological thinking and theorising and away from number crunching *per se*. The new psychometrics is for psychologists. These must be trained and prepared to theorise and yet be statistically sophisticated.

It is my hope that once scientific fundamental measures have been developed, psychology will proceed, as has occurred in the natural sciences, to build up a body of knowledge that is not only agreed but genuinely applicable. Thus clinical psychology might genuinely devise treatments that were the application of science, for example. In addition to this, of course, with fundamental measurement mathematical analyses of the variables would be justified and better theories could be developed. The new psychometrics could make psychology genuinely scientific.

Of course, as is obvious, the development of such measures will be difficult. It may be that the task of the new psychometrics is impossible; that fundamental measures will never be constructed. If this is the case, then the truth must be faced that perhaps psychology can never be a science, that the subject matter is not suited to the scientific method. In fields of this kind powerful thinking and speculation will be more effective than poor measurement. In these circumstances, what is now psychology will be divided up: the scientific aspects will be taken up by physiologists and biochemists, the speculative aspects will fall again to philosophy. The remains, atheoretical response counting, the province of clerks, can go without regret and fittingly to the social sciences.

REFERENCES

Achor, J.L. and Starr, A. (1980). Auditory brainstem response in the cat. 1. Intracranial and extracranial recordings. *Electroencephalography and Clinical Neurophysiology*, 48, 154–173.

Adorno, T.W., Frenkel-Brunswick, E., Levinson, D.J. and Sandford, R.N. (1950). The *Authoritarian Personality*. New York, Harper and Row.

AGARD Aerospace Medical Panel Working Group 12 (1989). *Human Performance Assessment Methods* (AGARDograph No. 308). Neuilly-sur-Seine, France.

Amelang, M. and Borkenau, P. (1982). On the factor structure and external validity of some questionnaire scales measuring extraversion and neuroticism. *Zeitschrift für differentiale diagnostische Psychologie*, 3, 119–146.

Anderson, M. (1992). *Intelligence and Development*. Oxford, Blackwell.

Andress, D.L. and Church, M.W. (1981). Differences in auditory brainstem evoked responses between introverts and extraverts as a function of stimulus intensity. *Psychophysiology*, 18, 156.

Anokhin, A. and Vogel, F. (1996). EEG alpha rhythm frequency and intelligence in normal adults. *Intelligence*, 23, 1–14.

Anstey, E. (1966). *Psychological Tests*. London, Nelson.

Appley, M.H. and Trumbull, R. (eds) (1967). *Psychological Stress: Issues in Research*. New York, Appleton-Century-Crofts.

Arrindel, W.J. and van de Ende, J. (1985). An empirical test of the utility of the observation to variables ratio in factor and components analysis. *Applied Psychological Measurement*, 9, 165–178.

Baddley, A. (1986). *Working Memory*. Oxford, Clarendon Press.

Bannister, D. (1970). Science through the looking glass. In Bannister, D. (ed.) *Perspectives in Personal Construct Theory*. London, Academic Press.

Barrett, P. and Eysenck, H.J. (1992). Brain electrical potentials and intelligence. In Gale, A. and Eysenck, M.W. (eds) (1992).

Barrett, P. and Kline, P. (1980). Personality factors in the Eysenck Personality Questionnaire. *Personality and Individual Differences*, 1, 317–333.

Barrett, P. and Kline, P. (1981a). A comparison between Rasch analysis and factor analysis of items in the EPQ. *Journal of Personality and Group Behaviour*, 1, 1–21.

Barrett, P. and Kline, P. (1981b). The observation to variable ratio in factor analysis. *Journal of Personality and Group Behaviour*, 1, 23–33.

Barrett, P. and Kline, P. (1982). Factor extraction: an examination of three methods. *Journal of Personality and Group Behaviour*, 2, 94–98.

REFERENCES

Barrett, P., Eysenck, H.J. and Luching, S. (1989). Reaction time and intelligence: a replicated study. *Intelligence*, 10, 9–40.

Barton, K. and Cattell, R.B. (1981). *The Central State–Trait Kit (CTS): Experimental Version.* Champaign, IPAT.

Bates, T. and Eysenck, H.W. (1993). String length attention and intelligence: focused attention reverses the string length–IQ relationship. *Personality and Individual Differences*, 15, 363–371.

Bates, T., Stough, C., Mangan, G. and Pellet, D. (1995). Intelligence and complexity of the averaged evoked potential. *Intelligence*, 20, 27–39.

Beck, A.T. (1962). Reliability of psychiatric diagnoses: a critique of systematic studies. *Archives of General Psychiatry*, 4, 561–571.

Beck, S.J. (1944). *Rorschach's Test.* Vol. 1: *Basic Processes.* New York, Grune and Stratton.

Bellak, L. and Bellak, S. (1949). *The Children's Apperception Test.* New York, CPS.

Birnbaum, A. (1968). Some latent trait models and their use in inferring an examinee's ability. In Lord, F.M. and Novick, M.R. (eds) (1968).

Block, J. (1995). A contrarian view of the five factor approach to personality description. *Psychological Bulletin*, 117, 187–225.

Blum, G.S. (1949). A study of the psychoanalytic theory of psychosexual development. *Genetic Psychology Monograph*, 39, 3–99.

Bouchard, T.J. (1993). Personal communication.

Boyle, G.J. (1989). Re-examination of the personality type factors in the Cattell, Comrey and Eysenck scales: were the factor solutions by Noller et al. optimal? *Personality and Individual Differences*, 10, 1289–1299.

Boyle, G.J. (1991). Item analysis of the subscales in the Eight-State Questionnaire (8SQ): exploratory and confirmatory factor analyses. *Multivariate Clinical Research*, 10, 37–65.

Boyle, G.J. and Katz, I. (1991). Multidimensional scaling of the Eight State Questionnaire and the Differential Emotions scale. *Personality and Individual Differences*, 12, 565–574.

Boyle, G.J., Stankov, L. and Cattell, R.B. (1995). Measurement and statistical models in the study of personality and intelligence. In Saklofske, D.H. and Zeidner, M. (eds) (1995).

Brand, C.R. and Deary, I.J. (1982). Intelligence and inspection time. In Eysenck, H.J. (ed.) (1982).

Bridgman, P.W. (1927). *The Logic of Modern Physics.* New York, Macmillan.

Broadhurst, P.L. (1959). Application of biometrical genetics to behaviour in rats. *Nature*, 184, 1517–1518.

Brody, N. (1992). *Intelligence.* San Diego, Academic Press.

Brody, N. and Crowley, M.J. (1995). Environmental (and genetic) influences on personality and intelligence. In Saklofske, D.H. and Zeidner, M. (eds) (1995).

Buck, J.N. (1948). Manual for the HTP. *Monograph Supplement 5, Journal of Clinical Psychology.*

Buck, J.N. (1970). *The House–Tree–Person Technique: Revised Manual.* Los Angeles, Western Psychological Services.

Buros, O.K. (ed.) (1959). *5th Mental Measurement Yearbook.* Highland Park, Gryphon Press.

Buros, O.K. (ed.) (1978). *The 8th Mental Measurement Yearbook.* Highland Park, Gryphon Press.

Burt, C.S. (1966). The genetic determination of differences in intelligence: a study of monozygotic twins reared together and apart. *British Journal of Psychology*, 57, 137–153.

Butchvarov, P. (1995). Metaphysical realism. In *The Cambridge Dictionary of Philosophy.* Cambridge, Cambridge University Press.

Campbell, K.B. and Bartoli, E.A. (1986). Human auditory potentials during natural sleep: the early components. *Electroencephalography and Clinical Neurophysiology*, 65, 142–149.

Carroll, J.B. (1980). Individual difference relations in psychometric and experimental cognitive tasks. Lab Report No. 163, University of North Carolina.

Carroll, J.B. (1993). *Human Cognitive Abilities*. Cambridge, Cambridge University Press.

Carstairs, G.M. (1957). *The Twice-Born: A Study of a Community of High Caste Hindus*. London, Hogarth Press.

Caryl, P.G. and Harper, A. (1996). Event related potentials in elementary cognitive tasks reflect task difficulty and task threshold. *Intelligence*, 22, 1–22.

Caryl, P.G., Golding, S.J.J. and Hall, B.J.D. (1995). Event related potentials, visual and auditory inspection time and pitch discrimination. *Intelligence*, 21, 297–326.

Cattell, R.B. (1957). *Personality and Motivation Structure and Measurement*. Yonkers, World Book Company.

Cattell, R.B. (ed.) (1966a). *The Handbook of Experimental Multivariate Psychology*. New York, Rand-McNally.

Cattell, R.B. (1966b). The Scree test for the number of factors. *Multivariate Behavioural Research*, 1, 140–161.

Cattell, R.B. (1971). *Abilities: Their Structure, Growth and Action*. New York, Houghton Mifflin.

Cattell, R.B. (1973). *Personality and Mood by Questionnaire*. San Francisco, Jossey-Bass.

Cattell, R.B. (1978). *The Scientific Use of Factor Analysis*. New York, Plenum.

Cattell, R.B. (1981). *Personality and Learning Theory*. New York, Springer.

Cattell, R.B. (1982). *The Inheritance of Personality and Ability*. London, Academic Press.

Cattell, R.B. (1985). *Human Motivation and the Dynamic Calculus*. New York, Praeger.

Cattell, R.B. and Butcher, H.J. (1968). *The Prediction of Academic Achievement and Creativity*. Indianapolis, Bobbs-Merrill.

Cattell, R.B. and Cattell, A.K.S. (1959). *The Culture-Fair Test*. Champaign, IPAT.

Cattell, R.B. and Child, D. (1975). *Motivation and Dynamic Structure*. London, Holt, Rinehart and Winston.

Cattell, R.B. and Johnson, R.C. (eds) (1986). *Functional Psychological Testing*. New York, Brunner Mazel.

Cattell, R.B. and Kline, P. (1977). *The Scientific Analysis of Personality and Motivation*. New York, Academic Press.

Cattell, R.B. and Schuerger, J. (1976). *The O-A (Objective-Analytic) Test Battery*. Champaign, IPAT.

Cattell, R.B. and Schuerger, J. (1978). *Personality Theory in Action: Handbook for the Objective-Analytic (O-A) Test Kit*. Champaign, IPAT.

Cattell, R.B. and Warburton, F.W. (1967). *Objective Personality and Motivation Tests*. Urbana, University of Illinois Press.

Cattell, R.B., Eber, H.W. and Tatsuoka, M.M. (1970a). *The 16–Factor Personality Questionnaire*. Champaign, IPAT.

Cattell, R.B., Horn, J.L. and Sweney, A.B. (1970b). *Motivation Analysis Test*. Champaign, IPAT.

Chapman, A.J. and Jones, D.M. (eds) (1980). *Models of Man*. Leicester: British Psychological Society.

Chopin, B.H. (1976). Recent developments in item banking. In de Gruijter, D.N.M. and van der Kamp, L.J.T. (eds) (1976).

Cliff, N. (1992). Abstract measurement theory and the revolution that never happened. *Psychological Science*, 3, 186–190.

REFERENCES

Coles, M.G.H., Gale, A.M. and Kline, P. (1971). Personality and habituation of the orienting reaction: tonic and response measures of electrodermal activity. *Psychophysiology*, 8, 54–63,

Coombs, C.H. (1950). Psychological scaling without a unit of measurement. *Psychological Review*, 57, 145–158.

Coombs, C.H., Dawe, R.M and Tversky, A. (1970). *Mathematical Psychology*. Englewood Cliffs, Prentice-Hall.

Cooper, C. and Kline, P. (1982). The internal structure of the Motivation Analysis Test. *British Journal of Educational Psychology*, 52, 228–223.

Cooper, C. and McConville, C. (1989). The factorial equivalence of the state-extraversion positive affect and state-anxiety negative affect. *Personality and Individual Differences*, 10, 919–920.

Cooper, C. and McConville, C. (1990). Interpreting mood scores: clinical implications of individual differences in mood variability. *British Journal of Medical Psychology*, 63, 215–225.

Cooper, C. and Varma, V. (eds) (1997). *Processes in Individual Differences*. London, Routledge.

Cooper, C., Kline, P. and Maclaurin-Jones, C. (1986). Inspection time and primary abilities. *British Journal of Educational Psychology*, 56, 304–308.

Corman, L. (1969). *Le Test P.N. Manuel*. Paris, Presses Universitaires de France.

Costa, P.T and McCrae, R.R. (1988). From catalogue to classification: Murray's needs and the five factor model. *Journal of Personality and Social Psychology*, 55, 258–265.

Costa, P.T. and McCrae, R.R. (1992a). Four ways five factors are basic. *Personality and Individual Differences*, 13, 653–665.

Costa, P.T. and McCrae, R.R. (1992b). *Revised NEO Personality Inventory (NEO PI-R)*. Odessa, FL., Psychological Assessment Resources.

Costa, P.T. and McCrae, R.R. (1997). Six approaches to the explication of facet-level traits: examples from conscientiousness. *European Journal of Personality*. In press.

Costa, P.T., Zondeman, A.B., Williams, R.B. and McCrae, R.R. (1985). Content and comprehensiveness in the MMPI: an item factor analysis in a normal adult sample. *Journal of Personality and Social Psychology*, 48, 925–933.

Cronbach, L.J. (1946). Response sets and test validity. *Educational and Psychological Measurement*, 6, 475–494.

Cronbach, L.J. (1951). Coefficient alpha and the internal structure of tests. *Psychometrica*, 16, 297–334.

Cronbach, L.J. (1957). The two disciplines of scientific psychology. *American Psychologist*, 12, 671–684.

Cronbach, L.J. (1984). *Essentials of Psychological Testing*. New York, Harper and Row.

Cronbach, L.J. and Meehl, P.E. (1955). Construct validity in psychological tests. *Psychological Bulletin*, 52, 281–302.

Curran, J.P. and Cattell, R.B. (1976). *Manual for the Eight-State Questionnaire*. Champaign, IPAT.

Dahlstrom, W.G. and Welsh, G.S. (1960). *An MMPI Handbook*. London, Oxford University Press.

Davidson, D. (1984). *Inquiries into Truth and Interpretation*. Oxford, Clarendon Press.

de Gruijter, D.N.M. (1986). The use of item statistics in the calibration of an item bank. *Applied Psychological Measurement*, 10, 231–238.

de Gruijter, D.N.M. and van der Kamp, L.J.T. (eds) (1976). *Advances in Educational and Psychological Measurement*. Chichester, Wiley.

De Raad, B. and Szirmack, Z. (1994). The search for the big five in a non-Indo-European language. *European Review of Applied Psychology*, 44, 17–24.

Deary, I. and Caryl, P. (1993). Intelligence, EEG and evoked potentials. In Vernon, P.A. (ed.) (1993).

Deary, I.J. and Stough, C. (1996). Intelligence and inspection time: achievements, prospects and problems. *American Psychologist*, 51, 599–608.

Deary, I.J., Egan, V., Gibson, D.J., Austin, E.J., Brand, C. and Kellagahan, T. (1996). Intelligence and the differentiation hypothesis. *Intelligence*, 23, 105–132.

Digman, J.N. (1990). Personality structure: emergence of the five factor model. *Annual Review of Psychology*, 41, 417–440.

Dollard, J. and Miller, N.E. (1950). *Personality and Psychotherapy*. New York, McGraw-Hill.

Draycott, S.G. (1996). Investigations into psychometric measures and their prediction of human performance. PhD thesis, University of Exeter.

Draycott, S.G. and Kline, P. (1994a). Further investigations into the nature of the BIP: a factor analysis of the BIP with primary abilities. *Personality and Individual Differences*, 17, 201–209.

Draycott, S.G. and Kline, P. (1994b). Speed and ability: a research note. *Personality and Individual Differences*, 17, 763–768.

Draycott, S.G. and Kline, P. (1995). The big three or the big five – the EPQ-R versus the NEO-PI: a research note, replication and elaboration. *Personality and Individual Differences*, 18, 801–804.

Draycott, S. and Kline, P. (1996). Validation of the AGARD STRES battery of performance tests. *Human Factors*, 38, 347–371.

Dunlap, W.P., Kennedy, R.S., Harbeson, M.M. and Fowlkes, J.E. (1989). Problems with individual difference measures based on some componential cognitive paradigms. *Applied Psychological Measurement*, 13, 9–17.

Edelman, G.M. (1987). *Neural Darwinism: The Theory of Neuronal Group Selection*. New York, Basic Books.

Edwards, A.L. (1957). *The Social Desirability Variable In Personality Research*. New York, Dryden.

Ekstrom, R.B., French, J.W. and Harman, H.H. (1976). *Manual for Kit of Factor-Referenced Cognitive Tests*. Princeton, Educational Testing Service.

Eliot, J. and Smith, I.M. (1983). *An International Directory of Spatial Tests*. Windsor, National Foundation for Educational Research.

Ellis, B (1966). *Basic Concepts of Measurement*. Cambridge, Cambridge University Press.

Embretson, S.E. (1995). Role of working memory capacity and general control processes in intelligence. *Intelligence*, 20, 169–190.

Embretson, S.E. (1996). The new rules of measurement. *Psychological Assessment*, 8, 341–349.

Ericsson, K.A. (1988). Analysis of memory performance in terms of memory skill. Chapter 5 in Sternberg, R.J. (ed.) (1988).

Exner, J. (1986). *The Rorschach: A Comprehensive System* (2nd edition). New York, Wiley.

Eysenck, H.J. (1953). *Uses and Abuses of Psychology*. Harmondsworth, Penguin.

Eysenck, H.J. (1959). The Rorschach. In Buros, O.K. (ed.) (1959).

Eysenck, H.J. (1967). *The Biological Basis of Personality*. Springfield, C.C. Thomas.

Eysenck, H.J. (ed.) (1979). *The Structure and Measurement of Intelligence*. New York, Springer.

Eysenck, H.J. (ed.) (1981). *A Model for Personality*. Berlin, Springer.

Eysenck, H.J. (ed.) (1982). *A Model for Intelligence*. New York, Springer.

Eysenck, H.J. (1986). Concluding chapter. In Modgil, S. and Modgil, C. (eds) (1986).

REFERENCES

Eysenck, H.J. (1992). Four ways five factors are not basic. *Personality and Individual Differences*, 13, 667–673.

Eysenck, H.J. and Eysenck, S.B.G. (1975). *The Eysenck Personality Questionnaire*. Sevenoaks, Hodder and Stoughton.

Eysenck, H.J. and Eysenck, S.B.G. (1991). *Manual for the EPQ-R*. Sevenoaks, Hodder and Stoughton.

Fabrigar, L.R., Vissar, P.S. and Browne, M.W. (1997). Conceptual and psychological issues in testing the circumplex structure of data in personality and social psychology. *Personality and Social Psychology Review*, 1, 184–203.

Fahrenberg, J. (1992). Psychophysiology of neuroticism and anxiety. In Gale, A. and Eysenck, M.W. (eds) (1992).

Fahrenberg, J. and Selg, H. (1970). *The Freiburg Personality Inventory (FPI)*. Göttingen, Hogrefe.

Fairbairn, W.R.D. (1952). *Psychoanalytic Studies of Personality*. London, Tavistock.

Fenichel, O. (1945). *The Psychoanalytic Theory of Neurosis*. New York, Norton.

Ferguson, G.A. (1949). On the theory of test development. *Psychometrika*, 14, 61–68.

Ferguson Committee (1940). Final report of the committee appointed to consider and report upon the possibility of quantitative estimates of sensory events. *Report of the British Association for the Advancement of Science*, 2, 331–349.

Finlay, B.L. and Darlington, R.B. (1995). Linked regularities in the development and evolution of mammalian brains. *Science*, 286, 1578–1584.

Fleishman, E.A. and Quaintance, M.K. (1984). *Taxonomies of Human Performance: The Description of Human Tasks*. Orlando, Academic Press.

Fowles, D.C., Roberts, R. and Nagel, K. (1977). The influence of introversion/extraversion on the skin conductance response to stress and stimulus intensity. *Journal of Research in Personality*, 11, 129–146.

Frank, H. (1959). Informationästhetik-Grundlagenproblem und erste Anwendung auf die Mime pure. Dissertation, Technical University of Stuttgart.

Frank, H. (1969). *Kybernetische Grundlagen der Pädagogik*. Bd 2. 2nd Agis edn., Baden-Baden.

Freud, S. (1908). Character and anal erotism. In *Standard Edition*, Vol. 9.

Freud, S. (1911). Psychoanalytical notes on an autobiographical account of a case of paranoia (dementia paranoides). *Standard Edition*, 12, 3.

Freud, S. (1923). The ego and the id. *Standard Edition*, 19.

Freud, S. (1940). An outline of psychoanalysis. In *Standard Edition*, Vol. 23.

Freud, S. (1966). *The Standard Edition of the Complete Psychological Works of Sigmund Freud*. London, Hogarth Press and the Institute of Psycho-Analysis.

Friedman, A., Webb, J.T. and Lewak, R. (1989). *Psychological Assessment with the MMPI*. Hillsdale, Erlbaum.

Fulker, D.W. (1979). Nature and nurture: heredity. In Eysenck, H.J. (ed.) (1979).

Furnham, A. (1995). *Personality at Work*. London, Routledge.

Gale, A. and Eysenck, M.W. (eds) (1992). *Handbook of Individual Differences: Biological Perspectives*. Chichester, Wiley.

Gale, A.M. (1983). Electroencephalographic studies of extraversion–introversion: what's the next step? *Personality and Individual Differences*, 4, 371–380.

Gardner, H. (1983). *Frames of Mind: The Theory of Multiple Intelligence*. New York, Basic Books.

Ghiselli, E.E. (1966). *The Validity of Occupational Aptitude Tests*. New York, Wiley.

Goldberg, L.R. (1982). From ace to zombie: some explorations in the language of personality. In Spielberger, C.D. and Butcher, J.N. (eds) (1982).

Goldberg, L.R. (1992). The development of markers for the big five factor structure. *Psychological Assessment*, 4, 26–42.

Gorsuch, R.L. (1974). *Factor Analysis*. Philadelphia, Saunders.

Gorsuch, R.L. (1986). Measuring attitude, interests, sentiments and values. In Cattell, R.B. and Johnson, R.C. (eds) (1986).

Gottfredson, L.S. (1986). Societal consequences of the g factor in employment. *Journal of Vocational Behaviour*, 29, 379–410.

Gottfredson, L.S. (1997a). Editorial. *Intelligence*, 24, 1–12.

Gottfredson, L.S. (1997b). Why g matters: the complexity of everyday life. *Intelligence*, 24, 79–132.

Gough, H.G. (1957). *The Californian Psychological Inventory*. Palo Alto, Consulting Psychologists Press.

Gray, J. (1982). *The Neuropsychology of Anxiety: An Enquiry into the Functions of the Septo-Hippocampal System*. London, Oxford University Press.

Gray, J.A. (1981). A critique of Eysenck's theory of personality. In Eysenck, H.J. (1981).

Gruenbaum, A. (1984). *The Foundations of Psychoanalysis: A Philosophical Critique*. Berkeley, University of California Press.

Guilford, J.P. (1956). *Psychometric methods*. New York, McGraw-Hill.

Guilford, J.P. (1959). *Personality*. New York, McGraw-Hill.

Guilford, J.P. (1967). *The Nature of Human Intelligence*. New York, McGraw-Hill.

Guilford, J.P. and Hoepfner, R. (1971). *The Analysis of Intelligence*. New York, McGraw-Hill.

Guttman, L. (1954). Some necessary conditions for common factor analysis. *Psychometrika*, 19, 149–161.

Guttman, L. (1955). A generalised simplex for factor analysis. *Psychometrika*, 20, 173–192.

Guttman, L. (1966). Order analysis of correlation matrices. In Cattell, R.B. (ed.) (1966a).

Guttman, L. (1992). The irrelevance of factor analysis for the study of group differences. *Multivariate Behavioral Research*, 27, 175–204.

Haier, R.J. (1993). Cerebral glucose metabolism and intelligence. In Vernon, P.A. (ed.) (1993).

Haier, R.J. *et al.* (1995). Brain size and cerebral glucose metabolic rate in non-specific mental retardation and Down's syndrome. *Intelligence*, 20, 191–210.

Hakstian, A.R. (1971). A comparative evaluation of several prominent factor transformation methods. *Psychometrika*, 36, 175–193.

Hakstian, A.R. and Cattell, R.B. (1974). The checking of primary ability structure on a broader basis of performance. *British Journal of Educational Psychology*, 44, 140–154.

Hakstian, A.R. and Cattell, R.B. (1976). *Manual for the Comprehensive Ability Battery*. Champaign, IPAT.

Hakstian, A.R. and Cattell, R.B. (1978). Higher stratum ability structure on a basis of twenty primary abilities. *Journal of Educational Psychology*, 70, 657–659.

Hambleton, R.K. and Jones, R.W. (1993). *Comparison of Classical Test Theory and Item Response Theory and their Applications to Test Development*. Washington, DC, National Council on Measurement in Education.

Hambleton, R.K., Swaminatham, H. and Rogers, H.J. (1991). *Fundamentals of Item Response Theory*. Newbury Park, Sage.

Hampson, S. (1997). The social psychology of personality. In Cooper, C. and Varma, V. (eds) (1997).

REFERENCES

Hampson, S. and Kline, P. (1977). Personality dimensions differentiating certain groups of abnormal offenders from non-offenders. *British Journal of Criminology*, 17, 310–331.

Hampson, S.E. (1992). The emergence of personality: a broader context for biological perspectives. In Gale, A. and Eysenck, M.W. (eds) (1992).

Harman, H.H. (1976). *Modern Factor Analysis*. Chicago, University of Chicago Press.

Hathaway, S.R. and McKinley, J.C. (1951). *The Minnesota Multiphasic Personality Inventory Manual (Revised)*. New York, Psychological Corporation (revised 1967).

Haynes, S.N. and Wilson, C.L. (1979). *Behavioural Assessment*. San Francisco, Jossey-Bass.

Heim, A. (1975). *Psychological Testing*. London, Oxford University Press.

Heim, A.W., Watts, K.P. and Simmonds, V. (1970). *AH4, AH5 and AH6 Tests*. Windsor, National Foundation for Educational Research.

Hempel, C. (1945). Studies in the logic of confirmation. *Mind*, 54, 21–42.

Hendrickson, A.E. and Hendrickson, D.E. (1980). The biological basis of individual differences in intelligence. *Personality and Individual Differences*, 1, 3–33.

Hick, W. (1952). On the rate of gain of information. *Quarterly Journal of Experimental Psychology*, 4, 11–26.

Holder, O. (1901). Quantitative axioms and measurement. Cited by Michell, J. (1997).

Holley, J.W. (1973). Rorschach analysis. In Kline, P. (ed.) (1973).

Holley, J.W. and Guilford, J.P. (1964). A note on the G index of agreement. *Educational and Psychological Measurement*, 24, 749–753.

Holtzman, W.H., Thorpe, J.S., Swartz, J.D. and Herron, E.W. (1968). *Inkblot Perception and Personality: Holtzman Inkblot Technique*. Austin, University of Texas Press.

Horn, J. and Knapp, J.R. (1973). On the subjective character of the empirical base of Guilford's structure of intellect model. *Psychological Bulletin*, 80, 33–43.

Horowitz, M.J. (1989). *Introduction to Psychodynamics*. London, Routledge.

Howarth, E. (1976). Were Cattell's personality sphere factors correctly identified in the first instance? *British Journal of Psychology*, 67, 213–230.

Howarth, E. (1980) *Technical Background and User Information for State and Trait Inventories*. Edmonton, Alberta, University of Alberta Press.

Hundleby, J.D. (1973). The measurement of personality by objective tests. In Kline, P. (ed.) (1973).

Hunt, E. and Pellegrino, J. (1985). Using interactive computing to expand intelligence testing: a critique and prospectus. *Intelligence*, 9, 207–236.

Hunt, E.B. (1976). Varieties of cognitive power. In Resnik, R.B. (ed.) (1976).

Jackson, D.N. (1984). *Multidimensional Aptitude Battery, Manual*. Port Huron, Research Psychologists Press.

Jackson, D.N. (1997). *The Measurement of Motivation for Academic Achievement*. Paper at the Spearman Conference, University of Plymouth, July 1997.

Jennrich, C.I. and Sampson, C.F. (1966). Rotation for simple loadings. *Psychometrika*, 31, 313–323.

Jensen, A.R. (1980). *Bias in Mental Testing*. Glencoe, Free Press.

Jensen, A.R. (1982). Reaction time and psychometric g. In Eysenck, H.J. (ed.) (1982).

Jensen, A.R. (1987a). Individual differences on the Hick paradigm. In Vernon, P.A. (ed.) (1987).

Jensen, A.R. (1987b). The g beyond factor analysis. In Royce, R.R. *et al.* (eds) (1987).

Jensen, A.R. (1994). Psychometric g related to differences in head size. *Personality and Individual Differences*, 17, 597–606.

Jensen, A.R. (1997). The neurophysiology of g. In Cooper, C. and Varma V. (eds) (1997).

Johnson, J.H., Null, C., Butcher, J.N. and Johnson, K.N. (1984). Replicated item level factor analyses of the full MMPI. *Journal of Personality and Social Psychology*, 47, 105–114.

Joreskog, K.G. and Sorbom, D. (1984). *LISREL VI: Users' Guide* (3rd edition). Mooresville, Scientific Software.

Kaiser, H.F. (1958). The Varimax criterion for analytic rotation in factor analysis. *Psychometrika*, 23, 187–200.

Kamin, L.J. (1974). *The Science and Politics of IQ.* Harmondsworth, Penguin Books.

Karon, B.P. (1981). The Thematic Apperception Test. In Rabin, A.I. (ed.) (1981).

King, J.E. and Figueredo, A.J. (1997). Five factor model plus dominance in chimpanzee personality. *Journal of Research in Personality*, 31, 251–271.

Klein, M. (1948). *Contributions to Psychoanalysis, 1912–1945*. London, Hogarth Press and Institute of Psycho-Analysis.

Kline, P. (1971). *Ai3Q.* Windsor, National Foundation for Educational Research.

Kline, P. (ed.) (1973). *New Approaches in Psychological Measurement*. Chichester, Wiley.

Kline, P. (1979). *Psychometrics and Psychology*. London, Academic Press.

Kline, P. (1980). The psychometric model. In Chapman, A.J. and Jones, D.M. (eds) (1980).

Kline, P. (1981). *Fact and Fantasy in Freudian Theory*. Routledge, London.

Kline, P. (1991a). *Intelligence: The Psychometric View*. London, Routledge.

Kline, P. (1991b). Sternberg's components: non-contingent concepts. *Personality and Individual Differences*, 12, 873–876.

Kline, P. (1993). *The Handbook of Psychological Testing*. London, Routledge.

Kline, P. (1994a). *An Easy Guide to Factor Analysis*. London, Routledge.

Kline, P. (1994b). *Personality: The Psychometric View*. London, Routledge.

Kline, P. (1995). *The Handbook of Psychological Testing*. London, Routledge.

Kline, P. (1997). Comments on quantitative science and the definition of measurement in psychology. *British Journal of Psychology*, 88, 385–387.

Kline, P. (1999). *The Handbook of Psychological Testing* (2nd edition). London: Routledge.

Kline, P. and Barrett, P. (1983). The factors in personality questionnaires among normal subjects. *Advances in Behaviour Research and Therapy*, 5, 1414–1202.

Kline, P. and Cooper, C. (1984a). The factor structure of the Comprehensive Ability Battery. *British Journal of Educational Psychology*, 54, 106–110.

Kline, P. and Cooper, C. (1984b). A construct validation of the Objective-Analytic Test Battery (OATB). *Personality and Individual Differences*, 5, 328–337.

Kline, P. and Cooper, C. (1984c). A factorial analysis of the authoritarian character. *British Journal of Psychology*, 75, 171–176.

Kline, P. and Svasti-Xuto, B. (1981). The HTP in Thailand with four and five-year old children. *British Journal of Projective Psychogy*, 26, 1–11.

Kline, P., Draycott, S.G. and McAndrew, V.M. (1994). Reconstructing intelligence: a factor analytic study of the BIP. *Personalty and Individual Differences*, 16, 529–536.

Klopfer, B. and Kelley, D.M. (1942). *The Rorschach Technique*. Tarrytown-on-Hudson, World Book Co.

Kragh, U. and Smith, G.S. (1970). *Percept-Genetic Analysis*. Lund, Gleerups.

Krantz, D.H., Luce, R.D., Suppes, P. and Tversky, A. (1971). *Foundations of Measurement*. Vol. 1. New York, Academic Press.

Kranzler, J.H. (1990). The nature of intelligence: a unitary process or a number of independent processes? Unpublished doctoral dissertation, University of California at Berkeley.

Krug, S.E. and Johns, E.F. (1986). A large-scale cross-validation of second-order personality structure defined by the 16PF. *Psychological Reports*, 59, 683–693.

Krzanowski, W. J. (1988). *Principles of Multivariate Analysis*. Oxford, Clarendon Press.

Kyllonen, P.C. (1985). *Dimensions of Information Processing Speed*. Brooks Air Force Base, Texas, Air Force Systems Command.

Kyllonen, P.C. and Christal, R.E. (1990). Reasoning ability is (little more than) working memory capacity. *Intelligence*, 14, 389–433.

Lacey, J.I. (1967). Somatic response patterning and stress: some revision of activation theory. In Appley, M.H. and Trumbull, R. (eds) (1967).

Laming, D. (1997). A critique of a measurement-theoretic critique: commentary on Michell, 'Quantitative science and the definition of measurement in psychology'. *British Journal of Psychology*, 88, 389–391.

Larson, G.E., Haier, R.J., LaCasse, L. and Hazen, K. (1995). Evaluation of a mental effort hypothesis for correlations between cortical metabolism and intelligence. *Intelligence*, 21, 267–278.

Lefcourt, H.M. (1991). Locus of control. In Robinson, J.P. *et al.* (eds) (1991).

Lehrl, S. and Fischer, B. (1988). The basic parameters of human information processing: their role in the determination of intelligence. *Personality and Individual Differences*, 9, 883–896.

Lehrl, S. and Fischer, B. (1990). A basic information psychological parameter (BIP) for the reconstruction of the concepts of intelligence. *European Journal of Personality*, 4, 259–286.

Levy, P. (1973). On the relation of test theory and psychology. In Kline, P. (ed.) (1973).

Likert, R.A. (1932). A technique for the measurement of attitudes. *Archives of Psychology*, 140, 44–53.

Loehlin, J.C. (1987). *Latent Variable Models*. Hillsdale, Erlbaum.

Longstreth, L.E. (1984). Jensen's reaction-time investigations of intelligence: a critique. *Intelligence*, 8, 139–160.

Lord, F.M. (1974). *Individualised Testing and Item Characteristic Curve Theory*. Princeton, Educational Testing Service.

Lord, F.M. (1980). *Applications of Item Response Theory to Practical Testing Problems*. Hillsdale, Erlbaum.

Lord, F.M. and Novick, M.R. (eds) (1968). *Statistical Theories of Mental Test Scores*. New York, Addison Wesley.

Lorenz, K.Z. (1966). *On Aggression*. London, Methuen.

Luce, R.D. and Tukey, J.W. (1964). Simultaneous conjoint measurement: a new type of fundamental measurement. *Journal of Mathematical Psychology*, 1, 1–27.

McClelland, D.C. (1961). *The Achieving Society*. Princeton, Van Nostrand.

McCrae, R.R. (1996). Social consequences of experiential openness. *Psychological Bulletin*, 120, 323–337.

McCrae, R.R. and Costa, P.T. (1985). Comparison of EPI and psychoticism scales with measures of the five factor theory of personality. *Personality and Individual Differences*, 6, 587–597.

McCrae, R.R. and Costa, P.T. (1989). Reinterpreting the Myers–Briggs Type Indicator from the perspective of the five factor model of personality. *Journal of Personality*, 57, 17–40.

McDougall, W. (1932). *Energies of Men*. London, Methuen.

Mackintosh, N.J. (1986). The biology of intelligence? *British Journal of Psychology*, 77, 1–18.

Mangan, G.L. and O'Gorman, J.G. (1969). Initial amplitude and rate of habituation of orienting reaction in relation to extraversion and neuroticism. *Journal of Experimental Research in Personality*, 3, 275–282.

Marcel, A.J. (1983). Conscious and unconscious perception: an approach to the relations between phenomenal experience and perceptual processes. *Cognitive Psychology*, 15, 238–300.

Maturana, H.H. and Varela, F.J. (1980). *Autopoiesis and Cognition, the Realisation of the Living*. Dordrecht, Reidel.

May, J., Kline, P. and Cooper, C. (1987). The construction and validation of a battery of tests to measure flexibility of thinking in army officers. APRE working papers WP15/87.

Medawar, P.B. (1984). *The Limits of Science*. London, Oxford University Press.

Mershon, B. and Gorsuch, R.L. (1988). Number of factors in the personality sphere: does increase in factors increase predictability of real life criteria. *Journal of Personality and Social Psychology*, 55, 675–680.

Meyer, G.J. and Shack, J.R. (1989). Structural convergence of mood and personality: evidence for old and new directions. *Journal of Personality and Social Psychology*, 57, 670–691.

Michell, J. (1990). *An Introduction to the Logic of Psychological Measurement*. Hillsdale, Erlbaum.

Michell, J. (1994a). Numbers as quantitative relations and the traditional theory of measurement. *British Journal for the Philosophy of Science*, 45, 389–406.

Michell, J. (1994b). Measuring dimensions of belief by unidimensional unfolding. *Journal of Mathematical Psychology*, 38, 244–273.

Michell, J. (1997). Quantitative science and the definition of measurement in psychology. *British Journal of Psychology*, 88, 355–383.

Mill, J.S. (1943). *A System of Logic*. London, University of London Press.

Miller, E.M. (1994). Intelligence and brain myelination: a hypothesis. *Personality and Individual Differences*, 17, 803–832.

Miller, L.T. and Vernon, P.A. (1996). Intelligence, reaction time and working memory in 4–6 year-old children. *Intelligence*, 22, 155–190.

Modgil, S. and Modgil, C. (eds) (1986). *Hans Eysenck: Consensus and Controversy*. Lewes, Falmer Press.

Morgan, C.D. and Murray, H.A. (1936). A method of investigating phantasies. *Archives of Neurology and Psychiatry*, 34, 289–306.

Mulhern, G. (1997). Cognitive processes, mental ability and general intelligence. In Cooper, C. and Varma, V. (eds) (1997).

Murray, H.A. (1938). *Explorations in Personality*. New York, Oxford University Press.

Murray, H.A. (1971). *Manual to the Thematic Apperception Test*. Boston, Harvard University Press.

Murstein, B.I. (1963). *Theory and Research in Projective Techniques*. New York, Wiley.

Myrtek, M. (1984). *Constitutional Psychophysiology*. New York, Academic Press.

Neisser, U. (1967). *Cognitive Psychology*. New York, Appleton-Century-Crofts.

Nettelbeck, T. (1982). Inspection time: an index of intelligence. *Quarterly Journal of Experimental Psychology*, 24A, 299–312.

Noller, P., Law, H. and Comrey, A.L. (1987). Cattell, Comrey and Eysenck personality factors compared: more evidence for the five robust factors. *Journal of Personality and Social Psychology*, 53, 775–782.

Nowlis, V. and Green, R.F. (1957). The experimental analysis of mood. Brussels, *Proceedings of the 15th International Congress of Psychology*.

Nunnally, J.O. (1978). *Psychometric Theory*. New York, McGraw-Hill.

Nunnally, J.O. and Bernstein, A. (1994). *Psychometric Theory*. New York, McGraw-Hill.

O'Hear, A. (1989). *An Introduction to the Philosophy of Science*. Oxford, Oxford University Press.

REFERENCES

Parker, J.D.A., Bagby, R.M. and Summerfeldt, L.J. (1993). Confirmatory factor analysis of the Revised NEO Personality Inventory. *Personality and Individual Differences*, 15, 463–466.

Pedersen, N.L., Plomin,R., Nesselroade, J.R. and McClearn, G.E. (1992). A quantitative genetic analysis of cognitive abilities during the second half of the life span. *Psychological Science*, 3, 346–352.

Pedley, R R (1953). *The Comprehensive School*. Harmondsworth, Penguin.

Pervin, L. (ed.) (1990). *Handbook of Personality Theory and Research*. New York, Guilford Press.

Petrill, S. *et al.* (1996). DNA markers associated with general and specific cognitive abilities. *Intelligence*, 23, 191–204.

Phillips, K. and Fulker, D.W. (1989). Quantitative genetic analysis of longitudinal trends in adoption designs with application to IQ in the Colorado Adoption Project. *Behaviour Genetics*, 19, 621–658.

Phillipson, H. (1955). *The Object Relations Technique*. London, Tavistock.

Piedmont, R.L., McCrae, R.R. and Costa, P.T. (1991). Adjective checklist scales and the five factor model. *Journal of Personality and Social Psychology*, 60, 630–637.

Pitcher, G. (ed.) (1964). *Truth*. Englewood Cliffs, Prentice-Hall.

Plomin, R. and Petrill, S. (1997) Genetics and Intelligence: what's new? *Intelligence*, 24, 53–77.

Plomin, R. *et al.* (1994). DNA markers associated with high versus low IQ: the IQ quantitative trait loci (QTL) project. *Behaviour Genetics*, 24, 107–118.

Plomin, R. *et al.* (1995). Allelic associations between 100 DNA markers and high versus low IQ. *Intelligence*, 21, 31–48.

Plomin, S.A. *et al.* (1998). Failure to replicate a QTL association between a DNA marker identified by EST00083 and IQ. *Intelligence*, 25, 179–184.

Popper, K. (1959). *The Logic of Scientific Discovery*. New York, Basic Books.

Posner, M.I. (1978). *Chronometric Explorations of Mind*. Hillsdale, Erlbaum.

Potter, J. and Wetherell, M. (1987). *Discourse and Social Psychology: Beyond Attitudes and Behaviour*. London, Sage.

Rabbitt, P.M.A. (1985). Oh g Dr. Jensen or g-ing up cognitive psychology? *Behavioural and Brain Sciences*, 8, 238–239.

Rabbitt, P.M.A. (1996). Do individual differences in speed reflect 'global' or 'local' differences in mental abilities? *Intelligence*, 22, 69–88.

Rabin, A.I. (ed.) (1981). *Assessment with Projective Techniques*. New York, Springer.

Rasch, G. (1960). *Probabalistic Models for Some Intelligence and Attainment Tests*. Copenhagen, Denmark Institute of Education.

Raven, J.C. (1965a). *Progressive Matrices*. London, H.K. Lewis.

Raven, J.C. (1965b). *Mill-Hill Vocabulary Scale*. London, H.K. Lewis.

Reed, T.E. and Jensen, A.R. (1991). Arm nerve conduction velocity (NCV), brain NCV, reaction times and intelligence. *Intelligence*, 15, 33–47.

Reed, T.E. and Jensen, A.R. (1992). Conduction velocity in a brain nerve pathway of normal adults correlates with intelligence level. *Intelligence*, 16, 259–272.

Reeves, D.L., Winter, K.P., LaCour, S.J., Raynsford, K.M., Vogel, K. and Grisset, J.D. (1991). The UTC-PAB/AGARD STRES battery: user's manual and systems documentation. Pensacole, Naval Aerospace Medical Research Laboratory.

Resnik, R.B. (ed.) (1976). *The Nature of Intelligence*. Hillsdale, Erlbaum.

Rijsdik, F.V., Boomsma, D.L. and Vernon, P.A. (1995). Genetic analysis of peripheral nerve conduction velocity in twins. *Behaviour Genetics*, 25, 341–348.

Roberts, R.D. (1997). The factor structure of reaction (RT) and its relationships to intelligence. Paper at the Second Spearman Conference, July 1997, Plymouth.

Roberts, R.D., Pallier, G. and Stankov, L. (1996). The basic information processing (BIP) unit, mental speed and human cognitive abilities: should the BIP R.I.P.? *Intelligence*, 23, 133–155.

Robinson, D.L. (1993). The EEG and intelligence: an appraisal of methods and theories. *Personality and Individual Differences*, 15, 695–716.

Robinson, J.P., Shaver, P.R. and Wrightsman, L.S. (eds) (1991). *Measures of Personality and Social Psychological Attitudes*. New York, Academic Press.

Rokeach, M. (1960). *The Open and Closed Mind: An Investigation into the Nature of Belief Systems and Personality Systems*. New York, Basic Books.

Romney, D.M. and Bynner, J.M. (1992). *The Structure of Personal Characteristics*. Westport, Praeger.

Rorschach, H. (1921). *Psychodiagnostics*. Berne, Hans Huber.

Rorty, R. (1991). Objectivity, Relativism and Truth. Cambridge, CUP.

Roskam, E.E. (1985). Current issues in item-response theory: beyond psychometrics. In Roskam, E.E. (ed.) (1985).

Roskam, E.E. (ed.) (1985). *Measurement and Personality Assesment*. Amsterdam, Elsevier.

Royce, R.R., Glover, J.A. and Witt, J.C. (eds) (1987). *The Influence of Cognitive Psychology on Testing*. Hillsdale, Erlbaum.

Rushton, J.P. and Ankney, C.D. (1996). Brain size and cognitive ability: correlations with age, sex, social class and race. *Psychonomic Bulletin and Review*, 3, 21–36.

Saklofske, D.H. and Zeidner, M. (eds) (1995). *The International Handbook of Personality and Intelligence*. New York, Plenum.

Sandler, J. and Hazari, A. (1960). The obsessional: on the psychological classification of obsessional character traits and symptoms. *British Journal of Medical Psychology*, 33, 113–132.

Schmidt, F.L. and Hunter, J.E. (1998). The validity and utility of selection methods in personnel psychology: practical and theoretical implications of 85 years of research findings. *Psychological Bulletin*, 124, 261–274.

Scruton, R. (1994). *Modern Philosophy*. London, Sinclair Stevenson.

Searle, J. R. (1995). *The Construction of Social Reality*. London, Penguin.

Semeneoff, B. (1971). *Projective Tests*. Chichester, Wiley.

Skinner, B.F. (1953). *Science and Human Behaviour*. New York, Macmillan.

Skuder, P. *et al.* (1995). A polymorphism in mitochondrial DNA associated with IQ. *Intelligence*, 21, 1–12.

Smedslund, J. (1978). Some psychological themes are not empirical: reply to Bandura. *Scandinavian Journal of Psychology*, 19, 101–102.

Smith, B.D., Wilson, R.J. and Davidson, R.A. (1984). Electrodermal activity and extroversion: caffeine, preparatory signal and stimulus intensity effects. *Personality and Individual Differences*, 5, 59–65.

Spearman, C. (1904). General intelligence: objectively determined and measured. *American Journal of Psychology*, 15, 201–292.

Spearman, C. (1927). *The Abilities of Man*. London, Macmillan.

Spielberger, C.D. and Butcher, J.N. (eds) (1982). *Advances in Personality Assessment*. Vol. 1. Hillsdale, Erlbaum.

Spielberger, C.D., Gorsuch, R.L., Lushene, R.E., Vagg, P.R. and Jacobs, G.A. (1986). *Manual for the State–Trait Anxiety Inventory-Form Y*. Palo Alto, Consulting Psychologists Press.

Stankov, L. and Cregan, A. (1993). Quantitative and qualitative properties of an intelligence test: series completion. *Learning and Individual Differences*, 5, 137–169.

Stankov, L. and Roberts, R.D. (1997). Mental speed is not *the* basic process of intelligence. *Personality and Individual Differences*, 22, 69–84.

Stankov, S., Boyle, G.J. and Cattell, R.B. (1995). Models and paradigms in personality and intelligence research. In Saklofske, D.H. and Zeidner, M. (eds) (1995).

Stelmack, R.M. (1990). Biological bases of extraversion: psychophysiological evidence. *Journal of Personality*, 58, 293–311.

Stelmack, R.M. and Green, R.G. (1992). In Gale, A. and Eysenck, M.W. (1992).

Stelmack, R.M. and Houlihan, R.M. (1995). Event-related potentials, personality, and intelligence: concepts, issues and evidence. In Saklofske, D.H. and Zeidner, M. (1995).

Stelmack, R.M. and Wilson, K.G. (1982). Extraversion and the effects of frequency and intensity on the auditory brainstem evoked response. *Personality and Individual Differences*, 3, 373–380.

Stelmack, R.M., Achorn, E. and Michaud, A. (1977). Extraversion and individual differences in auditory evoked potential. *Psychophysiology*, 14, 368–374.

Sternberg, R.J. (1977). *Intelligence, Information Processing and Analogical Reasoning: The Componential Analysis of Human Abilities*. Hillsdale, Erlbaum.

Sternberg, R.J. (1985). *Beyond IQ: A Theory of Human Intelligence*. Cambridge, Cambridge University Press.

Sternberg, R.J. (1986). Inside intelligence. *American Scientist*, 74, 137–143.

Sternberg, R.J. (ed.) (1988). *Advances in the Psychology of Human Intelligence*. Vol. 4. Hillsdale, Erlbaum.

Sternberg, R.J. and Gardner, M.K. (1983). Unities in inductive reasoning. *Journal of Experimental Psychology: General*, 112, 80–116.

Sternberg, S. (1969). Memory scanning: mental processes revealed by reaction time experiments. *American Scientist*, 57, 421–457.

Stevens, S.S. (1946), On the theory of scales of measurement. *Science*, 103, 667–680.

Stevens, S.S. (1951). Mathematics, measurement and psychophysics. In Stevens, S.S. (ed.) *Handbook of Experimental Psychology*. New York, Wiley.

Strawson, P.F. (1964). Truth. In Pitcher, G. (ed.) (1964).

Swartz, J.D. (1978). The TAT. In Buros, O.K. (ed.) (1978).

Sweney, A.B. and Cattell, R.B. (1986). *Manual for the Vocational Interests Measure*. Champaign, IPAT.

Sweney, A.B., Anton, M.T. and Cattell, R.B. (1986). Evaluating motivation structure, conflict and adjustment. In Cattell, R.B. and Johnson, R.C. (eds) (1986).

Szelenberger, W. (1983). Brainstem auditory evoked potentials and personality. *Biological Psychiatry*, 18, 157–174,

Terman, L.M. and Merrill, M.A. (1960). *Stanford–Binet Intelligence Scale*. New York, Houghton Mifflin.

Terman, L.M. and Oden, M. (1959). *The Gifted Group at Mid-life*. Stanford, California University Press.

Thorndike, E.L. (1919). *An Introduction to the Theory of Mental and Social Measurements*. New York, Teachers College, Columbia.

Thurstone, L.L. (1947). *Multiple Factor Analysis: A Development and Expansion of Factors of the Mind*. Chicago, University of Chicago Press.

Undheim, J.O. (1981). On intelligence II. A neo-Spearman model to replace Cattell's theory of fluid and crystallised intelligence. *Scandinavian Journal of Psychology*, 22, 181–187.

Undheim, J.O. and Gustaffsson, J.E. (1987). The hierarchical organisation of cognitive abilities: restoring general intelligence through the use of linear structural relations (LISREL). *Multivariate Behavioral Research*, 22, 149–171.

Vaillant, G.E. (1977). *Adaptation to Life*. Boston, Little, Brown.

van Heck, G.L. (1988). Modes and models in anxiety. *Anxiety Research*, 1, 199–244.

Velicer, W.F. (1976). Determining the number of components from the number of partial correlations. *Multivariate Behavioural Research*, 12, 3–32.

Vernon, P.A. (ed.) (1987). *Speed of Information Processing and Intelligence*. Norwood, NJ, Ablex.

Vernon, P.A. (ed.) (1993). *Biological Approaches to the Study of Human Intelligence*. Norwood, NJ, Ablex.

Vernon, P.A. and Mori, M. (1992). Intelligence, reaction times and peripheral nerve conduction velocity. *Intelligence*, 16, 273–288.

Vernon, P.E. (1950). *The Measurement of Abilities*. London, London University Press.

Vernon, P.E. (1960). *Intelligence and Attainment Tests*. London, London University Press.

Vernon, P.E. (1961). *The Measurement of Abilities*. London, London University Press.

Vernon, P.E. (1963). *Personality Assessment*. London, Methuen.

Vernon, P.E. and Parry, J.A. (1949). *Personnel Selection in the British Forces*. London, London University Press.

Vickers, D., Pietch, A. and Hemingway, T. (1995). The frequency accrual speed test, FAST: a new measure of mental speed. *Personality and Individual Differences*, 19, 863–879.

Vigil-Colet, A., Perez-Olle, J. and Fernandez, M. (1997). The relationship of basic information processing measures with fluid and crystallised intelligence. *Personality and Individual Differences*, 23, 55–65.

Waller, N.G. and Reise, S.P. (1989). Computerised adaptive personality assessment. *Journal of Personality and Social Psychology*, 57, 1051–1056.

Watson, D. (1988). Vicissitudes of mood measurement: effects of varying descriptions, time-frames, and response formats on measures of positive and negative affect. *Journal of Personality and Social Psychology*, 55, 128–141.

Watson, D. and Tellegen, A. (1985). Towards a consensual structure of mood. *Psychological Bulletin*, 98, 219–235.

Wechsler, D. (1944). *Measurement of Adult Intelligence* (3rd edition). Baltimore, Williams and Wilkins.

Wechsler, D. (1958). *The Measurement and Appraisal of Adult Intelligence* (4th edition). Baltimore, Williams and Wilkins.

Wickett, J.C. and Vernon, P.A. (1994). Peripheral nerve conduction velocity, reaction time and intelligence: an attempt to replicate Vernon and Mori (1992). *Intelligence*, 18, 127–131.

Wilson, E.O. (1978). *On Human Nature*. Boston, Harvard University Press.

Woliver, R.E. and Saeks, S,D. (1986). Intelligence and primary aptitudes: test design and tests available. In Cattell, R.B. and Johnson, R.C. (eds) (1986).

Wood, R. (1978). Trait measurement and item banks. In de Gruijter, D.N.M. and van der Kamp, L.J.T. (eds) (1976).

Wright, B.D. (1985). Additivity in psychological measurement. In Roskam, E.E. (1985).

Zubin, J., Eron, L.D. and Schumer, F. (1965). *An Experimental Approach to Projective Techniques*. London, Wiley.

NAME INDEX

SUBJECT INDEX

A factor 167, 168
ability 92, 94, 95, 142; basic 118; cognitive 99, 104, 185; factor analysis 51, 52, 62, 68; field 38; fluid 187; mental 187; multivariate analyses and test construction 79, 86; musical 120–1; personality measurement 148, 152, 153; personality and motivation 144; personality structure 155, 162, 169, 173; predictive 133; principles and theory of new psychometrics 178, 180, 181, 197; psychophysiological measures of intelligence 183, 184, 185; quantitative attributes 196; retrieval 103; scientific measurement and measurement in natural sciences 35, 42, 43; structure 162; tests 29, 40, 128, 152, 156–8; verbal 56, 85, 104, 105, 106, 109, 110, 139, 140; see also intelligence and ability
academic achievement 38, 86, 111–12, 138, 139
accuracy 22, 26, 28, 34, 133, 134
achievement 94, 115, 171; see also academic achievement
acquiescence 159
acquisitiveness 176
activation 189
additive conjoint measurement 45, 46–7, 49–50, 80, 82–6, 94
additive processing model 129
additivity 47, 49
adjectives 160
AGARD tests 128, 129–34
age 133, 134
agreeableness 57, 58, 61, 166, 167
AH6 test 133, 138, 139
Ai3Q 168
alertness 175
alpha coefficient 33, 34
alpha factor 176
analogies 110, 141
analytic test 72
anger/aggression 170, 171
animal psychology 172
anxiety 23–4, 61, 189, 196; factor analysis 57, 58;

multivariate analyses and test construction 74, 85; personality and ability 157; personality measurement 152, 153; personality questionnaires 159; personality structure 162, 166, 169, 170, 171, 175; scientific measurement and measurement in natural sciences 31, 36, 37, 40; state 163, 170, 190; see also neuroticism
application 116, 141
Applied Psychology Unit (Cambridge) 109
Archimedean condition 47
arithmetical processing see mathematical ability
arousal 173, 175, 189, 191, 192, 193
artificial intelligence 115
arts subjects 133
assertiveness 152–3
associative memory 104
attainment 38
attention 186
attitudes 33, 35, 76, 77, 79, 148, 195
attributes 78, 79, 92, 99; quantitative 49, 51–2, 94, 194–6
auditory: arousal 193; brainstem evoked response 193; inspection time 186; perception 103; stimuli 192
authoritarian personality 38, 168
autonomic lability 189, 190, 191
average evoked potential 184, 185, 186

base units 26
basic ability 118
basic information parameter 116
basic period of information processing 137–40, 143, 154, 169, 180, 194, 197
basic reasoning 106, 114
benchmark tests 28
beta factor 176
beta weights 54, 86
biserial correlation 74
Blacky Pictures 147, 148
bloated specifics 31, 34, 101, 102, 155, 160, 164, 179

217